FRIENDSHIP AND SOCIETY

FRIENDSHIP AND SOCIETY

*An Introduction to Augustine's
Practical Philosophy*

DONALD X. BURT, O.S.A.

WILLIAM B. EERDMANS PUBLISHING COMPANY
GRAND RAPIDS, MICHIGAN / CAMBRIDGE, U.K.

© 1999 Wm. B. Eerdmans Publishing Co.
255 Jefferson Ave. S.E., Grand Rapids, Michigan 49503 /
P.O. Box 163, Cambridge CB3 9PU U.K.

Printed in the United States of America

04 03 02 01 00 99   7 6 5 4 3 2 1

Library of Congress Cataloging-in-Publication Data

Burt, Donald X.
Friendship and society: an introduction to Augustine's
practical philosophy / Donald X. Burt.
p.   cm.
Includes bibliographical references.
ISBN 0-8028-4682-3 (pbk.: alk. paper)
1. Augustine, Saint, Bishop of Hippo.   I. Title.
B655.Z7B854   1999
189′.2 — dc21   99-40410
CIP

Contents

v

CONTENTS

Contents

CONTENTS

Preface

Despair is the residue of great expectations that cannot be realized. It is therefore prudent to specify at the very beginning the purpose of the present volume. It is aimed at introducing the thought of Augustine to the ordinary non-professional English-speaking audience. It assumes no great knowledge of philosophy or previous acquaintance with St. Augustine. Each chapter begins with an attempt to lay out as clearly as possible the problem to be examined, ethics, politics, philosophy of history, etc. It does not contend that the categories used in the explanation were used by St. Augustine, just that the questions raised (for example, "What is good?" "What is the nature of the state?") were addressed by Augustine — though not necessarily in any formal work devoted to such questions. Obviously much will be left out. The sources of Augustine's doctrine and its influence are important topics but beyond the scope of this volume. My main concern is to lay out as accurately as possible my understanding of Augustine's thought on the issues that came to be categorized under the term "practical philosophy." Since this work is intended for an English-speaking audience, the citations and bibliography emphasize the sources available in English. Obviously much more has been written on Augustine and for those who wish to go further a list of broader bibliographies is suggested. If my presentation of Augustine's thought is accurate and understandable to the ordinary educated reader, then the goal of this volume will have been realized.

Introduction

Augustine's life and thought were driven by his search for happiness. He was convinced that if happiness was ever to be achieved, it could only be through possession of some really existing good that would permanently satisfy the basic desires that he shared with the rest of the human race: the desire for life, meaning, and love. He would have agreed with Kant that, as we search for happiness in this present life, we ask three fundamental questions: "What can I know?" "What can I hope for?" "What should I do?"[1] Thus, speculative philosophy (the description of the real world inside and outside each individual) must precede practical philosophy. We must discover what the real world is like, especially ourselves and God, before we can have reasonable hopes. We must at least know ourselves and God before we can determine how we should act now to be true to our human nature and thereby achieve union with God. In a previous book I have examined Augustine's speculative philosophy; the pages that follow will examine his practical philosophy: his philosophy of history, his ethics, his social and political philosophy.[2]

After some introductory thoughts on the "human predicament," the story of the divisive alienation and healing affection that seems to tear us apart and then force us together, Augustine's philosophy of history will be considered. This establishes the context in which humans must work out

1. *Critique of Pure Reason*, A 805, B 833.
2. Donald X. Burt, *Augustine's World: An Introduction to His Speculative Philosophy* (Lanham, MD: University Press of America, 1996).

their pursuit of happiness. There are many questions to be considered here. Where did I come from and where am I going? What are the forces which determine the making of my history and the history of the human race? Is human history going in a definite direction or is it simply moving in circles? Do I have some control over my destiny or is it in the hands of some blind fate? Or, worse still, is it controlled by some malevolent force?

In the field of ethics one considers whether there are some acts that I should do and others that I should not do. It is claimed that "I must do good and avoid evil," but this principle makes sense only if I can give reasonable answers to the questions "Why must I do good?" and "What makes an action good?" Furthermore, even if I can answer these questions I have still not solved the problem of how to make myself a truly good person. Ethics thus must also ask which virtues are the essential building blocks of good character, able to nurture that highest example of the human person: the magnanimous and magnificent human being who is both great-souled and able to do great things.

One's social and political philosophy begins with the fact that we humans are thrown together with others of our kind. How should we deal with them? Should we seek to be united by some bond of friendship? Should we follow the example of John Galt in Ayn Rand's novel *Atlas Shrugged,* treating others with polite selfishness. Or should we take seriously Sartre's dictum — "Hell is other people" — and try to live our lives in splendid isolation, dealing with others only to the extent that it is necessary to preserve our own well-being? The argument of this book is that at the root of Augustine's practical philosophy is the love of friendship. The ideal relationship of human with human, of humans with God and, indeed, of body and soul in each individual is a relationship of friend to friend.

This theme is carried through Augustine's discussion of the family and the state. The questions that arise are numerous. Is the institution of marriage a good thing or (as the Manicheans thought) an instrument for increasing the prevalence of evil in the world? What is the purpose of the family: to simply unite with one's best friend or, indeed, to contribute to the continuation of the race? Where does the authority of the family come from? What is the basis for the claim that someone is in charge, and does such a claim automatically lessen the dignity of those who must obey? Is the married life the "best" way to live a virtuous human life?

Granted that the family is a "natural" society in that it fulfills a natural need, can the same be said of political society? Is the state a necessary evil in our present wounded condition or is there something about it that would make it necessary even in a society of sinless and perfect human beings? What are the powers of the state and are there any limits on them? Where does the authority to rule come from? What are the characteristics of the ideal ruler? Is there a "best form" of government? How should the state react to the fact of violence in human society? How should I?

Augustine's answers to these and many other questions will be examined in the pages that follow. Together they constitute his practical philosophy, his thoughts on how to deal with life as we continue our ever moving journey to that eternal home, "The City of God."

CHAPTER 1

The Human Predicament:
Alienation and Affection

In one of his philosophical treatises Augustine gives a description of the human condition which does much to point out both the wonder of the universe we populate and the reason it is so difficult for us to appreciate its wondrous character. We are, he says, like those who, when confronted with a beautiful mosaic floor, spend all their time focusing their gaze on one tile and, as a result, are unable to grasp the marvelous order of the whole.[1]

Developing his analogy, one might say that most of us are like a troop of ants making their laborious way across the glorious floor of the Sistine Chapel. As we progress along we concentrate all our attention on that one little stone that is before us. We wave our tiny antenna looking for any source of immediate pleasure or immediate pain. We bury our heads in the here and now, never raising our eyes to the whole picture of what in fact this land we are crossing is really like. And as far as raising our eyes to those heavens above where we might see pictured in radiant colors the story of our origins and our destiny — why, that is simply out of the question! The sky is too high, and we have become habituated to looking down at that one little piece of the grand mosaic of time and space which is our own particular rock for the moment. We look at our precious pebble and say: "This is my life!"

It is sad that we live such narrow lives, but we can only get beyond

1. *On Order*, 1.1.

1

our little piece of the mosaic if we are willing to risk going out and seeing the universe beyond our day by day experience. We must move beyond our narrow geography into a philosophy of history if we are ever to get the grand view and to come to understand where we really are.

This was one of the great ventures attempted by Augustine. He endeavored to tell the story not simply of Aurelius Augustine but of humankind itself — indeed, to tell the story of all reality. It must be admitted that this drive to see the whole mosaic was not present in him from the beginning. In his early years he was more concerned about fun and fame than about philosophy. He began to think about the possibility of getting the "grand picture" only after reading Cicero's *Hortensius* in his late teens. Reading this work, he was inspired for the first time to raise his sights from the dust of the moment — the daily satisfaction of his bodily wants, the daily contest to be a "winner" in life, a well-paid, well-respected, and sometimes feared manipulator of words. For the first time in his life he began to dream of grasping the whole picture, what everything was like and how he fitted in. He experienced a longing (though, to be truthful, still only intermittently) for an understanding of his place in that multifaceted mosaic that was the world of Creator and creature.

Even in these first days of his tentative search for wisdom, Augustine came to perceive that he was driven by two great thirsts, thirsts much deeper and maddening than his earthy desires for sex and success. He realized that all of his more pedestrian and somewhat perverse thirsts were driven by his desire for happiness and his desire "to get it all together" — to find, in himself and with the world, the peace of union.

He saw the anxious activity of his mind in separating concepts through analysis and bringing them together again in synthesis as an aspect of his love for union.[2] He became convinced that this search for unity was the way to happiness. The experience of happiness depended on his ability to become "one with God" and the necessary means to this end was to become one with the world, especially one with other human beings. The scriptural passage: "Love God with your whole heart; love your neighbor as yourself!" was more than a mandate. It was a prescription for happiness.

Recognizing happiness as the goal or end of humanity and unity as the means to that end, he came to see that the great tragedy of the human condition was alienation. Every human being is a cracked pot. We want to

2. *Ibid.*, 1.18.48.

be whole but we live fractured lives, afflicted by separations within ourselves, separations between ourselves and other individuals, and separation from that one being who can bring final happiness, the infinite God. The history of humanity as Augustine saw it was a process of separation and "coming together." In the beginning there was God: an absolute unity which yet in the trinity of persons allowed for the possibility of a "love for another." In that world before time there was both infinite unity and infinite love and this was the basis for a happiness which itself was infinite.

The first great mystery in this story is why God would wish to change things. There was no "need" for any other "being" beyond God and for this reason the existence of any created thing could only be described as a purely gratuitous free act. The only pressure upon God to create "humans" or anything else could only be the pressure coming from the Divinity itself to share its goodness and happiness with others. The paradox of creation is that love, the proposed instrument of union, was the cause of the first separation. It was not unlike a parent tossing a baby into the air with the intention and hope of having the infant fall back into love's arms, now laughing with excitement after its brief experience of being on its own. God made humans separate from himself. They were made in his image but they were not God. They were made different but with the power of effecting a new union, a union with the Infinite by a free act of love.

In the first days of their existence humans came close to exercising this power perfectly as they walked together with God in their peaceful paradise. In Eden they were friends with themselves, friends with each other, friends with their God. They had been given the ordered equilibrium of all parts, the balance of appetite, the harmonious correspondence of conduct and conviction that brings internal peace. They had the ordered obedience to God's eternal law that makes for peace between human and God. They had the regulated fellowship that is the root of peace between human and human. In all aspects of their lives they had peace, that "calm that comes from order," and in that peace they were happy.[3]

This idyllic situation was not to last. Those first humans began to look into themselves too much. The object of their love changed from what was outside them to what was inside. They saw their power and their beauty and their shared goodness and became proud, saying to themselves: "Why cannot I stand on my own two feet?" In choosing themselves, the first humans chose isolation. They became alienated from the rest of real-

---

3. *The City of God*, 19.13.1.

ity by a narcissistic concentration on self. In becoming withdrawn they sought a unity that had to be spurious because they were meant for something more. They were like a leg, amputated from its nourishing body, trying desperately to make its own way in the world. They separated themselves and created the first true "crack" in reality, a terrible rupture that can come only from free beings choosing to go their own way.

This gap deepened and spread until humans found themselves aliens in a harsh world. They were separated from themselves, from each other, and from their God, and it seemed that nothing could be done about it. They still had the native power to bring about union: they still could love. But they seemed either to be oblivious of their power or incapable of using it well. They were like drunkards sitting in a car, forgetting how to turn it on or unable to control its wild accelerations and misdirections once started. They needed help but were too intoxicated to know it.

The Incarnation (the coming of God as a human being) was the first step in reunification. Through Christ it was again possible for humans to be in union with the Creator. As in the Trinity, so now between human and God, the bonding force was love: now help was given to paralyzed humans sitting immobile in their little vehicles, not knowing how to start or where to go. A healing grace-filled balm was provided so that disabled humans could overcome their wounds and bridge the separations within themselves and in their external relations.

Through this outside help, as well as their own reawakened freedom, individuals were again able to move toward harmony with all reality. Their progress was not to be perfect nor would it be easy, but progress was at least possible and, perhaps most importantly, allowed for false starts and sudden stalls. The process given to humans was never given to their angelic cousins — a way of making amends when inevitable failures in love occurred. They were told: "You are living in a land of hope, a land not of perfection but of forgiveness, a land where humans will always need (and have the right) to say "I'm sorry!"

For Augustine, alienation is the great tragedy of our human condition. But our great glory in these days after Christ is that we can understand that tragedy and remedy it through love. For Augustine, love is the glue by which the divisions inside and outside each one of us can be corrected. Illumination and grace are the remedies for the "fracturing" that we experience within ourselves; and, once healed, we shall be finally "all together." Our spirit will be friends with our body and we shall love ourselves as we ought.

4

Through that same illumination and grace we are now able to repair the gaps that separate us from each other and from God. Through God's help and our own exercise of free choice we are able to express true *affection,* that vital energy which seeks to unite conscious free beings in the bond of friendship.[4] In heaven the perfection of our love will "glue us to God" just as, even now in our imperfect state, the objects of our love become glued to us, leaving "footprints" in our mind even when they themselves are absent.[5] Indeed, our ultimate union with God will be much more than a cold intellectual examination of "footprints" of past experiences. We will not simply *recall* what our love *was;* we shall *become* what our love *is.*[6] Through our affection we shall reach out and embrace the love object and become one with it in a most perfect union.

In our present condition, we do not experience such perfect union with our loves. We only experience the need to love, a need rooted in our humanity itself. Augustine says that when we consider the prospect of loving, it is never a question of whether we shall love or not. The only question is "What shall I love and how shall I love it?" We are forced to love because we are drawn naturally to desire and to acquire those realities perceived as good.[7] When I say "I love you!" this says nothing to an outsider except that I perceive you as being a good. You are not changed by my desire for you, but I am changed in a radical way. In loving you I am not only drawn towards you, I become like you. Augustine once wrote that "My love is my weight; wherever I go it is my love that draws me there."[8] He might just as well have said: "Whatever I become, it is my love which makes me so." Love lifts us to our place in time and eternity just as earth falls downward towards its proper place and fire rises towards its proper place.[9] Earth and fire cannot make a mistake in their direction but we humans can, and it is on the basis of our correct or incorrect loves that our citizenship in the city of God or in the eternal earthly city will be determined.[10]

The perfection of our love of others in this life and in the next is friendship. It is friendship that can cure alienation among human beings. But it can bring with it a deep sorrow, a sorrow not from the affection itself

4. *The Trinity,* 8.10.

5. *Commentary on Psalm 62,* 17; *The Trinity,* 10.8.

6. *Commentary on the Letter of John to the Parthians,* 2.14.

7. *Commentary on Psalm 31,* 2.5.

8. *Confessions,* 13.9.10; *The City of God,* 14.28.

9. *Confessions,* 13.9.

10. *The City of God,* 14.8.

but from our tendency to pour it out on temporal things as though they were eternal. In this life it is inevitable that every delightful coming is followed by an eventual going, and that each going leaves a wound, a gap, an emptiness, a dis-order which tears at our very being. We shall fall apart someday, and every precious union with a love will someday experience a separation, by death if by no other cause.

The source of this pain of separation is not a misdirected love. It is right, not wrong, for us to wish "not to fall apart." It is right, not wrong, for us to wish that we "be never separated" from our human loves. The problem is not that our love is bad but that it is too intense, too unrealistic. It does bring about a union which can lead to higher things, but we are dissatisfied with it because it is less than we want. We want it to be more perfect than it could ever be and weep when it is not. But at least our love is a good.

A more serious problem occurs when our love is in fact misdirected — when we love things in an "out of order" way, the lesser more than the greater. When this happens, our drive towards love, our desire to desire, brings about a new alienation rather than unity. Our affection becomes a disaffection which separates us from that which we ought to love and need to possess in order to be happy. We are like the adolescent Augustine who was so "in love with love" that he was prepared to be satisfied with any sort of object of love.

The tragedy of the human condition is that the very force which, when rightly used, brings about unity, brings about separation when used wrongly. Affection gone wild leads to disaffection. If all virtues are aspects of good love, all vices are examples of bad love, a love that tears us apart or tears us up or tears us away from those true goods that our very being thirsts to be one with. The result of such misdirected love is chaos rather than order, isolation rather than community.

Each of our disaffecting loves is an aspect of those inherited wounds, ignorance and concupiscence, that are part of the baggage each of us carries into existence. It is easy to see why these wounds cause us to be disaffected. Ignorance separates us from an understanding of what reality is truly like and what we should do about it. It sends us blindly off in wrong directions or so immobilizes us that we cannot go anywhere at all. Concupiscence has a quite different effect. It does not immobilize. Rather it causes a frenetic activity, a chasing after any reality momentarily perceived as good. It drives us either to love true goods in a disorderly fashion or to race after objects which we have made good for ourselves. In a sad paradox, those mad misdirected loves that we call our vices tear us away from the goods that we want to love or should love and need to possess if ever we are to be truly happy.

Augustine recognizes three major categories of this disaffecting love: concupiscence of the flesh, concupiscence of the eyes, pride of life. Those driven by concupiscence of the flesh may be dominated by an eroticism which concentrates only on the pleasures of "their own bodies." Their drive for personal pleasure in the satisfaction of the natural thirst for sex and food and drink makes them concentrate on what is happening inside themselves rather than what is outside. They spend their time "feeling good" rather than reaching out for the good. When this eroticism reaches out to other people it regards them only as objects that bring pleasure. The goal is to be "pleasured" without "getting involved."

This wild desire for temporal pleasures may express itself through an avarice where we become consumed by a passion to possess things.[11] This vice brings about separation for a number of reasons. First of all, we build walls around ourselves by our things. We can never become "one" with them. Indeed, we are in a true sense "subordinate" to them in that they can become more important to us than we are to ourselves. They thus always remain separate from us despite our anxious efforts to clutch them to our hearts. Furthermore they serve as a block to union with other human loves. We may have common property but our property stands in the way of our community. There is always "us" and "them" and "it" — a trinity rather than a unity — perhaps exemplified these days in the pre-nuptial agreements in which human lovers agree who will get "what" of "it" when their partnership dissolves.

The vain curiosity which is part of the "concupiscence of the eyes" is also disaffecting, separating rather than uniting us with true objects of love. It separates by keeping us on the surface of reality. We are like a paint brush glossing over the house of another with no knowledge of or interest in the life within. Preoccupied with rumors and stories about people, we never get to their essence. We are interested more in what they did or what was done to them than in what they are in themselves. We may touch others by such a process but we can never become bound to them.

Inordinate earthly ambition (the "pride of life") has a similar effect. The passion to "get ahead" in this life can be a disaffecting and isolating exercise. We cannot have people "look up to us" or "fear us" or even "respect

11. *Free Choice*, 1.16.

us" for our accomplishments without thereby implying some separation. It is neither physically nor psychologically possible to "look up to" someone without being separate from them.

All of these disordered loves that tear us from our friends and from our God are nothing compared to the havoc caused by the greatest divisive force of all: the satanic sin of pride. This was the fatal sin of the first humans. Awed by their own powers, they decided that there was no need for God, that they could make their way very well on their own. No wonder! Pride by its very nature isolates us from others because it makes us think we are answerable to no one else; indeed, it convinces us that we are better than everyone else. We love passionately but our love is an alienating love because we love no one quite as much as we love ourselves.

Augustine did not believe that the cure for our present human predicament was "to stop loving"; rather, it was simply to learn to "love well." Through such ordered affection one can achieve that peace even here that comes only with the unity of order. For peace and happiness to reign triumphant, such ordered love must begin in the individual and then spread out through all the societies that human beings form. The individual, the family, the state, and the heavenly city are related as concentric circles. The individual is at the center: body and soul, passion and reason, impulse and free choice, divisions in himself/herself that make the life of each person a battle. Without peace within the individual, it is difficult to have peace in the family. Without virtuous individuals and peace-filled families, it is difficult to have peace in the larger society. We must be friends with ourselves and with our families before we can have any hope of being friends with fellow human beings.[12]

When there is peace at the center (in the individual human), there are ripples of love that flow out in ever widening circles embracing more and more in the bond of friendship. On earth this expansion is necessarily imperfect and limited, but it hints at that perfect and infinite friendship of the heavenly city once its membership is fixed beyond time. This uniting love affords a glimpse of what is to come. It is also the way to that blessed state. The peace-makers of this world will finally enjoy the perfect peace of union with God. Then there will no longer be alienation. There will be only love.

Everyday experience demonstrates that this ideal state is not our present condition. We must still fight for that inner peace that comes from

12. *The City of God*, 19.16.

a life lived in accordance with rational ethical principles. We must still seek to develop healthy relationships with others: friends, family, and fellow citizens. In the chapters that follow we shall examine Augustine's thoughts on how we should go about this daunting task. But first we must say something about his philosophy of history, that discipline which sets the scene for the human struggle to achieve peace and happiness in this world and (hopefully) in the next.

CHAPTER 2

Philosophy of History

A. Introduction

It is reasonable to ask why one should begin an examination of practical philosophy with philosophy of history. The answer is that one's philosophy of history sets the context for all activity within that person's individual history. A good context can be the basis for hope; a bad context can cause despair. A bad context may not change moral rules or the rules governing our interaction with others but it can have a serious effect on our willingness to put out the effort to follow those rules. It is difficult to act rationally in a universe which is itself irrational. What is happening in even a rational universe can have a major effect on what we must do here and now, what we need to do for each other. For example, it would not seem to make sense to worry about long range prospects in a world that is likely to end soon. It would be too much to demand that we bring a little light and order into a world that is dark chaos. It is for reasons such as these that Augustine placed his philosophy of history, his "Tale of Two Cities," at the very center of his ethics and his social/political philosophy. Since it is the center, Augustine's philosophy of history is a good place to begin this examination of his practical philosophy.

The proper object of any philosophy of history is the story of the human race, the position of individuals in that story, and the history of the universe in which that story is lived out.[1] As philosophy, it tries to

1. For a good introduction outlining the development and issues in a philosophy

take this phenomenon and make sense of it, to describe its workings in some reasonable fashion. It can go about this task in two very different ways. *Critical* philosophy of history seeks to validate or invalidate the presuppositions of a particular theory. Do the claims of objectivity for our historical knowledge have merit or are such claims confused by the limits on our means of communication? Can we really get the intended meaning of a historical description written at a time and place so different from our own in an idiom which has meaning only to those who have had the historical experience? *Speculative* philosophy of history, while not ignoring such epistemological issues, concentrates on trying to discover some pattern in the history of the human race. It asks whether history is chaotic or whether it develops in accordance with some pattern. If there is a pattern, is it cyclic, constantly repeating itself like a cosmic pin-wheel spinning in time but never truly moving from any "here" to a "there?" Or is the pattern linear, such that our time moves from a defined never-to-be-repeated past towards an equally defined future that is likewise unique and as yet never before experienced? Is the story of the human race something like an arrow traveling straight and true towards a future goal?

It should be noted that a linear philosophy of history does not necessarily imply a beginning or an end. Time may extend back beyond the present universe and may reach far into a future beyond its demise. For example, in the Manichean world-view there is an eternity both before and after the present moment; the conflict between the powers of good and evil always was, is, and will be forever, though perhaps taking different forms.

Finally, a philosophy of history might combine both cyclic and linear approaches. As such, it would admit that we are indeed moving in circles, that history does indeed repeat itself, but would insist that we are moving in a determined direction, perhaps towards a point of extinction or some Nirvana. In this view, the story of human history is something like the Palmer writing exercises some of us endured as children, ceaselessly making spirals across the page until finally we filled up our allotted space and were done. Or, better still, it is like a snowball whirling down a slope, becoming larger and more imposing as it goes along, only to end in the valley below where it ceases to be anything more than a damp memory. If history is in any sense linear, if it is "going somewhere," one must then determine

---

of history, see W. H. Dray, "Philosophy of History," in *The Encyclopedia of Philosophy*, ed. Paul Edwards (New York: Macmillan, 1967), vol. 6, pp. 247-54.

whether this direction is progressive of retrogressive, whether it is moving towards a state that is more perfect or less perfect.

One thing is certain: history is not static. It is constantly moving. But what is the explanation of this motion? Is there a transcendent power that controls its movement or is its movement simply the result of chance? Perhaps history is indeed driven by a force, but is it the blind force like fate which determines that every motion is fixed and unchangeable, rooted in the nature of reality and completely beyond the possibility of modification by any choice on the part of god or human? Is the energy that drives history from within some sort of material principle (for example, the economic forces spoken of by Marx), or is it some sort of spiritual principle like Kant's autonomous reason or Hegel's absolute spirit or Nietzsche's will to power or Sartre's personal freedom or (as we shall see) Augustine's power of love?

Putting the answers to all such questions together, one can then ask whether there is some value in the picture of history presented. Is human existence worthwhile? Does it have any importance, any meaning? If the answer is "No" then perhaps Camus' analogy for life in the myth of Sisyphus is correct: life is absurd and the only important question is whether suicide is the best option.

B. Augustine's Philosophy of History

Augustine derives his philosophy of history from two sources: biblical narratives and his own experience. The most important source is the Bible.[2] He accepts the story of the human race therein described as true history, an account of how we once were, how we are now, and how we someday can be. The facts learned there were supported by his own personal experience of the continuing turmoil and confusion in human life which seemed to prove the assertion of Scripture that something terribly wrong happened to human beings in the distant past: they began to love badly.

Augustine was convinced that human history has been characterized by an opposition between two sorts of love. These different loves drove hu-

2. See John O'Meara, *Charter of Christendom: The Significance of "The City of God"* (New York: Macmillan, 1961). For a helpful bibliography on Augustine's *City of God* see Dorothy F. Donnelly and Mark A. Sherman, *Augustine's "De Civitate Dei": An Annotated Bibliography* (New York: Peter Lang, 1991).

mans into two societies — both of which were in time, yet extended beyond time. He describes them as follows:

> Two cities have been formed by two loves; the earthly city formed by the love of self even to the contempt of God; the heavenly city formed by the love of God even to the contempt of self.[3]

There are many accidental differences to be found among human beings but from God's viewpoint there are essentially only two kinds of people, differentiated by two kinds of love. One love is holy; the other is selfish. One is subject to God; the other attempts to equal him or even surpass him.[4]

The story of this conflict between two loves began before time in that eternity where only God existed, the first and perfect citizen of that city that bore his name. For some reason (and Augustine puzzled over what that reason might be) God decided to create beings necessarily radically different from himself. These obviously did not *have* to exist; indeed they hung precariously in a contingent existence that depended upon the support of divine power. Where God was immutable, they were subject to change and destined by their nature eventually to corrupt and fade away. These fragile beings were pure spirits (angels), composites of spirit and body (human beings), and other beings — some living and some non-living — which were completely material. Each of them reflected in some way the perfection of God (the only pre-existing model for their perfection), the most perfect reflection being the angelic spirits and the souls of humans.

Both angels and humans received the gift of freedom. They were meant someday to be permanent residents in the city of God, but to realize this intention they had to claim citizenship by a free decision whereby they chose to love God more than anything else. The angels received the first challenge to choose God above all and there were some who passed the test and others who failed. One who failed was Lucifer, the brightest star in the

---

3. *The City of God*, 14.28. O'Donnell has suggested that part of Augustine's inspiration in writing *The City of God* came from his experience of the new pilgrim people, the refugees fleeing from the fallen Rome to a foreign land (North Africa) and pining for that distant homeland (James J. O'Donnell, "The Inspiration for Augustine's *De Civitate Dei*," *Augustinian Studies*, vol. 10 [1979], pp. 75-79). See also chapter 3 in his *Augustine* (Boston: G. K. Hall, 1985).

4. *A Literal Commentary on Genesis*, 11.15.

angelic constellation, and others followed him. Their decision was final and forever and it made them the first citizens of the earthly city, that hell where lived the community of those who would be separated everlastingly from their creator.

Like the angels, humans at first walked in innocence with God as their companion, but they too had to confirm that friendship by a free decision. Not yet members of either the city of God or the earthly city, they were faced with the challenge of choosing their citizenship by loving God more than anything else or some non-God more than God. Adam and Eve, of all the humans who would ever exist, were the couple most likely to make the right decision. They were as perfect as they could be as human beings, untarnished by any history of vice, clear of mind and with a will not yet warped by evil tendencies. Moreover, they had *experienced* God, not in his fullness to be sure, but intensely enough to recognize him as a friend. They had felt the happiness that came from "walking and talking" with Infinite Goodness in a pleasant place where there were no past failures to regret, no need to labor for present necessities, and no worry about future tragic possibilities. Apparently the only real temptation they had was the growing conviction that they could make Eden even better if they were in charge. They came to see themselves as a good greater than God and, by an act of pride expressed through disobedience, they chose themselves rather than God as the most important being in the universe. Their bad decision made it impossible for them to regain permanent membership in God's heavenly city there and then; but, unlike the fallen angels, they were not irrevocably blocked from someday becoming citizens. Salvation was still a possibility but only through the intervention of a power greater than themselves. They could choose hell on their own but they had to be supported by God if ever they were to reach heaven. Their situation was sad but not beyond redemption.

Redemption came through the incarnation and death of Jesus Christ, the Son of God, who became human in order to save the race. This, for Augustine, was the most important event in human history — indeed, more important than creation itself. The act of love that was creation was performed for beings who had never existed and hence could be described as innocent in their nothingness. Salvation was an act of love whereby those who had turned away from God, who had become aliens if not indeed enemies, were created once again as children of God. To be sure, humans were still wounded by their past experience, sometimes confused in mind and weak in will, but at least now they had the *chance* of making the right choice of God above all. They needed continuous divine support to do so, but at least they had the chance and also the assurance that God wanted to give the necessary help.

The rest of human history in time would be the story of the continuing conflict in each individual human heart between the love of God and the love of non-God. Augustine believed that some would make the correct decision but that, unfortunately, some would not. Change of allegiance was possible up to the moment of death, but at that moment each individual's fate would be sealed. Those who chose to turn away from God would at death become permanent citizens in the earthly city, a hell that would last forever. Those who chose God by a saintly life or at least by a life that ended with repentance, became forever after citizens of the heavenly city, that one place where they could find perfect happiness and have the permanent vision of the God who created them. Time now would be finished, but the two cities would go on forever with no increase or decrease in membership.

Augustine's philosophy of history is obviously *linear*. The first humans had a chance to maintain their original innocence and once they failed there was no going back. Sin could always be forgiven but it could never be forgotten or erased and the woundedness that it caused in the species could be healed but not eliminated in future generations. The coming of Christ was also a historical event never to be repeated. Once his redemptive death occurred, humans had again the possibility of heaven, but whether they would confirm themselves as members of the city of God or the earthly city was up to them. Their final decision for heaven or hell could not be reviewed. Once made, the judgment on their lives was irrevocable.[5]

Augustine sees the history of any individual as being *progressive* in that each one has (with the help of God) at least a chance to achieve a perfectly happy life. It is also progressive in accomplishing God's plan for creation. At the end of time human history will achieve the providential purpose set for it by God, to reflect in a finite way the infinite perfection of God. But Augustine does not consider the history of the human race in time to be similarly progressive. There is no earthly utopia towards which the race is inevitably moving. Humans will be "cracked" until the end of time and the presence of those cracks means that sin, selfishness, and silliness will always be a part of the human experience this side of death.

---

5. Augustine does not mince words in rejecting the ancient cyclic theories of history, calling them a "mockery of the truth" (*The City of God*, 12.14).

But even with all of its negative features, every moment of human history has an infinite *value*. At every moment of time the individual is able to strive for the ultimate perfection that can come after death. At every moment of time the created universe reflects the glory of the God who made it after his own image and who continues to support its existence and guide its destiny. Despite the pessimist's lament, it is indeed better for a human to exist than not. Despite all of the tribulations and failures of human beings, none of them are useless and each remains one of the greatest wonders of the world.[6]

There are both external and internal forces that move human history. The external force is neither chance nor fate; it is the providential care of God for his creation. The internal energies that drive history are the desires and the loves of the individuals who make it up. That love which Augustine declares has drawn him through the various phases of his life is also the driving force impelling communities of humans towards the city of God or the earthly city.[7] It determines the good or bad events of time and also the final membership of the eternal cities that exist now outside of time and will exist after time is no more.

The complete lists of citizens in the city of God and the earthly city will be fixed only at the end of time. Only the fallen and saved angels have permanently determined their citizenship. The challenge offered to the angels at the beginning of time was given only once and those who failed and those who passed that test were irrevocably bound by the effects of their decision. The case is quite different for humans still living this side of death. No final judgment has been made. Everyone has a chance for a change of heart as long as there is life.

This being said, it is true that sometimes one can make an educated guess about the direction of a life from characteristic day by day activities. Those who are moving towards full citizenship in the city of God live this life as pilgrims. This world is for them a place they must pass through in order to reach their true home in heaven. They do not become attached to the goods they experience in this life. They rejoice in love, friendship, good health, the feeling of accomplishment in a work well done, the beauty of the world around them; but they rejoice in these as goods to be *used* along the way, not as the goal of their life. They are able to recognize that there is only one good that can be *enjoyed* for its own sake: the goodness that is

6. *Free Choice*, 3.23.66; *The City of God*, 10.12.
7. *Confessions*, 13.9.19; *The City of God*, 14.28.

God. All other goods are good only because they reflect some aspect of this infinite goodness and because, when appropriately loved as *useful* goods, they can aid one in finally coming to possess the infinite good.[8] On the other hand, those who reflect the values of the earthly city are perfectly happy making their home here. Those moving towards the eternal "Jerusalem" (Augustine's symbolic name for God's city) are constantly looking to the future for their final happiness; the lovers of the earthly city (the symbolic "Babylon") seek only the peace and happiness that this life can give and direct all their efforts to achieving that peace.[9]

On a day by day basis, there are many differences between those living in accord with the ideals of the city of God and those who seem dedicated only to the earthly city. Those aiming at the city of God glory only in God and seek personal glory only from God. They rejoice in the power of God rather than in their own power. In their earthly societies they seek a community in which ruler and ruled serve each other in love. Citizens of the earthly city act in a quite different fashion. They glory in themselves and seek an affirmation of their glorious state through the approval of other human beings. Gathered together in political society, they respect only the power that they can achieve on earth and seek to enhance that power by subjugating others. Their societies are characterized more by domination of the weak by the strong than by a loving relationship among friends.[10]

Although the perfection of the city of God and the earthly city are never realized here on earth, their "shadows" can sometimes be detected in individuals and societies throughout history. Augustine traces the march of the two cities historically in books 11-18 of *The City of God*. Certain events have special importance:

1. Cain's murder of his brother and the building of the first city;
2. the attempt to construct the tower of Babel;
3. the founding of Babylon and the ascendancy of Assyria as a world power;
4. the rise of Rome;

8. On the distinction between "goods meant to be used" and "goods to be enjoyed for themselves" see *Christian Doctrine*, 1.3.3–1.7.7; 1.22.20–1.22.21.

9. *Commentary on Psalm 136*, 2 and 3.

10. *The City of God*, 14.28. For a comparison of the two cities as they exist in time, see Johannes van Oort, *Jerusalem and Babylon: A Study into Augustine's "City of God"* (Leiden: E. J. Brill, 1991), pp. 129ff.

5. the coming of Christ and the beginning of the Christian Church, a mystical union in which Christ is the head and the community of believers is the body.

The story of the two cities on earth begins in Eden with the creation of the first humans. In those idyllic days before human sin Adam and Eve lived as family, experiencing true "oneness of heart" with each other and with God. Unfortunately, this did not last. The first humans used their great gift of freedom to destroy their paradise by disobeying the one and only rule that God imposed. As a result, those who at first had been "shadows" of the city of God on earth now became reflections of the values of the earthly city. In their pride-filled disobedience they imitated the perversity that had caused the fall of Lucifer: they preferred a "non-God" (themselves) to the true God. By free choice they turned away from the heavens to create their own paradise on earth and every human born thereafter was destined to share their desperate condition of being separated from God. They would be born as "strangers" rather than as friends of God, incapable on their own of ever climbing back to the heights where God had meant them to be. Born as members of the earthly city, they could become members of the heavenly city now only by special divine intervention.[11]

This was the condition in which the first children born of human intercourse began their lives. From the first moment of their conception Cain and Abel shared the woundedness and weakness of their fallen parents. They were unable to see beyond the good that this earth could provide, seeking their happiness in the respect accorded them by humans rather than in the love bestowed by God. But soon the paths of the two sons diverged. For reasons known to God alone, Abel was rescued and predestined to become the first person "born of man" to be a citizen of the heavenly city. He became a shepherd — wandering across the earth, owning none of it, living off the good things provided in passing pastures, testifying by his pilgrim life to his status as a citizen of heaven. The unfortunate Cain was left to his own devices. He was not called to the heavens and could only try to make a home for himself on earth. He became a tiller of the soil, seeking his fortune and honor in whatever fruits the land could yield.

---

11. *The City of God,* 15.1. Augustine seems to suggest that while the city of God exists on earth only in shadow form, the earthly city exists more concretely in those individuals and societies which dominate others and who are in turn dominated by their thirst for power (15.2; 1. preface).

But Cain still retained faith in God and joined with his brother in of-fering sacrifice. To his dismay (and consequent anger) his brother's sacri-fice was accepted with praise while his was rejected. We can only speculate on the reasons for God's rejection. It was not because of Cain's lack of faith. He believed in God and valued God's opinion. When he brought his offering to God, he hoped that he would receive some recognition, but he did not. Could it be that Abel's offering was more precious? It is true that Abel's sacrifice is said to have been from the "best" of his herd and that no similar statement was made about the quality of the "fruits of the soil" of-fered by Cain. Perhaps Cain's problem was that he saw his gift as a repre-sentation of himself, as being the fruits of *his* labors in the fields, *his* wise planning, and for this he expected some reward for what he alone had ac-complished. His ego was so entangled in the goods he offered that their re-jection seemed to him to be a rejection of himself, a symbolic assertion that he was of less value than his brother. His hurt became anger and then envy, demonstrating the truth of Augustine's aphorism that "anger grown stale becomes hatred."[12] Whatever the reasons for Cain's rejection, it caused him to become crestfallen and resentful. Soon after, he killed his brother in a fit of envious rage and was condemned by God to become a restless wanderer on earth. He then joined with others of like mind in es-tablishing the first civil society, a city-state named after his son Henoch.[13]

Augustine interpreted the story of Cain and Abel as the symbolic be-ginning of the history of the "two cities" here on earth. The wandering shepherd Abel was the spiritual father of all those faithful souls who there-after would live as pilgrims on earth, frequently persecuted for their dedi-cation to God, living "in bondage" because they were separated from the only home they could ever know, the heavenly city that awaited them be-yond death. Those who gathered around Cain in the first city were quite different. Cain formed his community from humans dominated by the vices of the earthly city. Created by a murderer as a home for all those who sought a permanent place here on earth, it was a society of those who sought only earthly goods and these for selfish reasons. Considering the character of the citizens of that first city, Augustine thought it quite appro-priate to name it after its first king, Henoch, the son of Cain. "Henoch"

---

12. *Sermon 114a,* 6. Augustine gives his own interpretation of the reason for the rejection of Cain's sacrifice. Simply put, "there was no love" (*Commentary on the Letter of John to the Parthians,* 5.8).

13. *The City of God,* 15.5.

means "dedicated" and the city that he ruled was truly a society of those who were "dedicated" to and at home in this world. They did not consider themselves to be pilgrims on earth, much less exiles. They were home and were quite satisfied with whatever passing peace and happiness this world could provide.[14]

The passions that dominated the citizens of the city of Henoch were very different from the ideals of those living on earth as "shadow-citizens" of the city of God. These latter traced their spiritual roots to Seth, Cain's second brother. As was the case with Cain's son Henoch, Seth's very name reflected the community that would follow his example. "Seth" means "resurrection" and symbolized all those throughout history who would seek their ultimate good in the land beyond death where the souls of the just would be reunited with their bodies in the heavenly city. Thus Enos, the son of Seth, was literally a "son of resurrection" and he is described in Sacred Scripture as one who "hoped to call on the name of the Lord." He was, along with Abel and Seth, the first of those descendants of Adam and Eve to look to the future for their salvation and to hope here and now for the divine assistance to achieve it. The communities formed by the sons and daughters of Seth would be quite different from Henoch, the city of Cain. Henoch was a city of "belongings," filled with those who belonged to this world, whose main concern was to gather for themselves as many "belongings" as possible. The descendants of Seth gathered in earthly cities of "longings," longings for heaven and final union with God.[15]

With the coming of Noah, a descendant of Seth, there was a new beginning. The earth was covered by a great flood. Of the humans alive at that time only Noah, his wife, and his three sons with their wives survived. One would think that after such a catastrophe those who had come through safely would be absolutely dedicated to God since all of the objects of their earthly desires had been literally washed away. Moreover, remembering those humans who had literally "missed the boat" and per-

---

14. *The City of God,* 15.17. See Peter Brown, *The Body and Society* (New York: Columbia University Press, 1988), p. 405.

15. *The City of God,* 15.18; 15.21. The descendants of Cain and Seth were not long to exist as separate clans. They intermarried and soon each became affected by the spirit of the other. Augustine writes that some of the "shadow-citizens" of the heavenly city became infected with the earthly passions of their spouses. On the other hand, it is not unlikely that at least some of the earthy "Cainites" were turned towards higher things by the gentle example of the "Sethites" whom they had come to love. See *The City of God,* 15.22.

ished should suggest to any thinking person that life indeed was contingent, that life was as Augustine later described it: a rushing river plummeting towards the great falls of death.[16] The pious Noah and his wife were faithful followers of God's commands, but it would seem that they had no more luck with their children than had Adam and Eve.

The line of citizens of the heavenly city was continued through Noah in the families of his sons Shem and Japheth, but the earthy city began again in the line of the third son, Ham. The line of Shem produced such spiritual heroes as Abraham, Isaac, Jacob, Moses, David and, finally, Mary — who was destined to be the mother of Jesus Christ. Augustine was of the opinion that the holy Shem and Japheth symbolized the Jews and gentiles who would later come to be members of the mystical body of Christ, the Church.[17] Quite different was the destiny of the children of Ham, a lineage that was cursed because of Ham's disrespect for his father. In two generations it produced Nemrod, the architect of the tower of Babel and the founder of Babylon, the city that for Augustine symbolized the earthly city existing in time.[18]

Augustine considered Nemrod's attempt to build the tower of Babel as the most dramatic manifestation of the values of the earthly city since Cain's city of Henoch.[19] The godless pride of its builders was evident in their planning:

> They said to one another, "Come, let us mold bricks and harden them with fire. Let us build ourselves a city and a tower with its top in the sky and so make a name for ourselves. Otherwise we shall be scattered all over the earth."[20]

The reaction of God was quick and effective:

> The Lord came down to see the city and the tower that the men had built. Then the Lord said: "If now, while they are one people, all speaking the same language, they have started to do this, nothing will later stop them from doing whatever they presume to do. Let us then go down and there confuse their language, so that one will not understand what

16. *Commentary on Psalm 109,* 20.
17. *The City of God,* 16.2.
18. *Ibid.,* 16.3.
19. *Ibid.,* 16.10.
20. Genesis 1:3-4.

21

another says." Thus the Lord scattered them from there all over the earth, and they stopped building the city.[21]

Augustine saw the whole project as an example of humanity's some-time unholy pride in itself. Humans took earth and, using only their own tools and their own abilities, attempted to build something that would be much more than a permanent home for themselves on earth. Their dream was to build a city which indeed would reach to the sky, a city where they would be able to touch heaven through their own powers. The reason for such a venture was not a pious desire to be with God; rather it was to make a name for themselves. They all spoke the same language in that they shared a common desire to make a personal home for themselves as individuals in a "safe" place on earth, a place which would dominate the rest of the world and thereby win the honor that comes with being feared.[22] The whole venture had a tragic ending because it was based on a misconception that one can reach heaven on one's own, that one can touch God by climbing over others. Nemrod's terrible mistake was that he did not realize that the way to build a highway to heaven is not by attempting to take the place of the Lord but by exhibiting a humility which lifts up the heart towards the Lord.

Considering the tower-builder's drive to dominate others, Augustine considered the punishment inflicted on Nemrod to be quite fitting:

> Since it is the tongue that is the usual way a person expresses a domi-neering command, this pride was punished in such a way that the man who refused to understand and obey the commands of God could not be understood by men when he tried to command them. Thus was the plot foiled. Since no one could understand him, they abandoned him and he could associate only with those who would come to understand him. Thus were nations divided by language barriers and scattered over the earth.[23]

21. Genesis 11:5-8. An interesting comparison may be made between the scene at Babel and the story of Peter's first sermon after the resurrection of Jesus (Acts 2:14-41). At Babel all the builders were seeking their own glory and the result was the break-down of the one common language they had previously shared. At Peter's first sermon many people of many nations with many different languages shared a common focus on God and thus were able to understand Peter's words even though they were not spo-ken in their native tongues. The difference suggests the truth of Augustine's axiom that pride divides but charity brings together. See *Sermon 46*, 18.

22. *The City of God*, 16.4.

23. *Ibid.*

The confusion that resulted is not surprising. It is difficult, if not impossible, for humans to form a common bond with each other if they cannot understand each other's language. Two humans of differing language are worse off than two dumb animals, even of different kinds. Even though their social nature may naturally drive them together, they cannot tell each other what they think. They are alienated because they know the other is thinking (and perhaps even thinking about them) but it is impossible to open the gates to understanding, and this inability is disturbing. Of course we humans cannot open up channels of communication with dumb animals either; but we do not expect to. It is the frustration of expectation and desire that makes us somewhat upset when we find ourselves in the presence of another human being who speaks a different language. As Augustine remarks: "That is why a man is more at home with his dog than with a foreigner."[24]

The desire for personal glory that motivated the builders of Babel separated them from the rest of the world and even from each other. Glorification of self shuts out even fellow citizens and coworkers. Such selfishness destroys all possibility of a "oneness of heart" that is the mark of membership in the heavenly city. Love of self and one's own security and honor separates. Shared love of God, even among humans who are radically diverse, is a door that opens to love of the other. Individuals can love each other in and through their love for the same God. The punishment of confusion of language was a fitting conclusion to a venture of those already separated from God and each other by their personal earthly ambitions. They could no longer be friends since friendship implies understanding, and how can one understand another when one cannot even understand the words that are used? These who were seeking a permanent home on earth found themselves in a true Babylon (a land of confusion) and very soon went their separate ways.[25] These were not "children of

24. *Ibid.*, 19.7.

25. Augustine sees a continuation of confusion in the excessive tolerance of any and all opinions in those societies that have turned away from God. Speaking about the various opinions of ancient philosophers on the nature of the universe, he says: "Tell me! Has any people or senate or any person with some authority in the godless society ever bothered to look closely at the results of such philosophical wrangling with the intention of accepting certain unchanging principles and condemning any opinion to the contrary? Has it not rather been the case that such godless societies have given up all critical analysis and have simply accepted all contrary ideas from whatever source and clutched them frantically to its heart? No wonder, then, that the earthly city [wherever it appears] has been given that name which symbolizes confusion: Babylon" (*The City of God*, 18.42).

God" but "children of the earth" and in their efforts to become permanent residents in some secure place in the world they became, instead, wanderers — aliens on their own chosen earth.[26]

The two actual cities of Babylon and Jerusalem became for Augustine the symbolic representations of the two supratemporal cities making their way through time. There was a certain fittingness in his choice. Jerusalem was the holy city of the chosen people, the capital of the nation promised to the Jews as they made their long trek out of Egypt. It was for them that place on earth where God was most powerfully manifested, the place of the Ark of Covenant which symbolized the special relationship between God and his people. In Jerusalem Solomon built a great temple as a permanent home for the sacred Ark and as the center of religious worship for the Jewish people. In Jerusalem, and especially in its great temple, the wandering Jew could find a home away from home and be reminded of the heavenly home where finally there would be eternal rest.[27] Although this earthly Jerusalem was sometimes conquered and even destroyed by the pagan forces of non-God, it always stood as the object of desire for those pre-Christian "children of God," a place that reminded them of God's graciousness to them on earth and, even more, reminded them of that other, celestial city which was meant to be their eternal resting place.

Babylon was likewise used by Augustine as a symbol of a supraterrestrial society. It stood for that earthly city that was made up of all those who loved some non-God more than God. The real Babylon had its beginning in those humans who attempted to build a tower to heaven so that they might become like gods. Their goal was personal glory but their project failed when they fell into a confusion of speech. The city that they thereafter formed memorialized that confusion by its very name: *Babylon.* For a time it was the capital of Assyria, the most powerful kingdom of the ancient world and (according to Augustine) the society "in which the

26. *Ibid.,* 16.5.

27. Augustine remarks that God gave the actual city of Jerusalem to his chosen people "as a type and symbol with a special meaning to an earthbound, materially minded community who, even though they worshipped the one God, still desired from him little more than earthly prosperity" (*Sermon 346B,* 1). Cranz writes that as a historical nation Israel remained closer to the earthly city than the city of God. Only in its prophetic character as a pilgrim people now held in bondage could it be called a "shadow" of the heavenly city (F. Edward Cranz, "*De Civitate Dei* 15.2 and Augustine's Idea of the Christian Society," in *Augustine: A Collection of Critical Essays,* ed. Robert A. Markus [New York: Doubleday, 1972], p. 407).

domination of the godless city was at its height."[28] It was for a time a place of exile for the chosen people, just as existence on earth is a time of exile for those who belong in the city of God. The exiled Jews, in their yearning for their homeland, represented all children of God who are for a time forced to live in a world dominated by the ideals of the earthly city. They were faced with the challenge of living in the midst of a worldly city without being suffocated by it and losing their desire for their true home. In order to live on earth they had to participate in the earthly life of the secular city. In order to eventually live in the heavenly city they had to avoid being consumed by the earthly goods and earthly ambitions and earthly values that formed their present environment. To live as true citizens of the heavenly city on earth they were challenged to bring their own values into the life of the secular city, to carry Jerusalem to Babylon and, perhaps, save it.

To some extent this is what had happened to the Rome of Augustine's day. Christianity had moved from persecution through tolerance to dominance, from hiding from secular power to using secular power to promote its own interests. At the same time Rome remained a "secular" society driven by values far different from those of the city of God. In *The City of God* Augustine argued that it was the continuation of Rome's pagan values, not its support of Christianity, that caused its downfall. Even after more than a hundred years under the rule of Christian emperors, Augustine still felt justified in saying that Babylon had been the first Rome and that Rome was closer to being a second Babylon than an earthly anticipation of the city of God.[29]

At the same time, though Rome was not an essential instrument in accomplishing God's providential plan for his pilgrim people, neither was it "a satanic obstacle to its realization."[30] Like every other political society,

28. *The City of God*, 16.17; *Commentary on Psalm 64*, 2. In his *City of God* Augustine spends much time tracing the history of Assyria and Rome because, in his opinion, these were the two kingdoms on earth most representative of the values of the earthly city. See *The City of God*, 18.2.

29. *Ibid.*, 16.17; 18.2; 18.22; 18.27.

30. Markus points out that Augustine disagreed both with those who maintained that the state as represented by Rome was antithetical to Christianity and also with those who saw Rome as God's instrument for the Christianization of the world. He writes: "He [Augustine] could accept neither the hostility and opposition to Rome inculcated by the apocalyptic view (for example, the Donatists) nor the near identification of Christianity and the Roman Empire involved in the Eusebian view" (R. A.

Rome came into existence under God's providence either to test his chosen people by creating an environment of secularism, greed, immorality, and turbulence antithetical to heavenly values; or, occasionally, to support those values by tolerating their existence and by providing that temporal peace and order which were conducive to a pleasant, fruitful existence on earth.

Rome was a second Babylon as much in its dedication to earthly values as it was in its vices, and only in this sense can it be said to be closer to an emblem of the "earthly city" than the city of God on earth. In the same way a church (and specifically the Catholic Church), dedicated to the service of God, can be said to be that temporal society which comes closest to being the earthly representation of the heavenly city.[31] But it was not a particular social structure, be it state or church, which made its members citizens of either supratemporal "city." It was the love of the individuals who made it up. And though the secular orientation of the state, seeking temporal peace and prosperity, and the religious orientation of Church, seeking eternal salvation of its members, made it easier for one dedicated to the former to be consumed by earthly affairs and for one dedicated to the lat-

---

Markus, *Saeculum* [Cambridge: Cambridge University Press, 1970], p. 56). Some have suggested that in fact Augustine proposed a "third city" somewhere between the city of God and the earthly city, a secular state which was concerned only about temporal peace and which took no stand either for or against God. For a summary of this debate see van Oort, *op. cit.*, pp. 151-53. See also Peter Hawkins, "Polemical Counterpoint in *De Civitate Dei*," *Augustinian Studies*, vol. 6 (1975), pp. 97-106. See also C. Journet, "Les trois cités: celle de Dieu, celle de l'homme, celle du diable," *Nova et Vetera*, vol. 33 (1958), pp. 25-48; Henri-Irenée Marrou, "Civitas Dei, Civitas Terrena: num tertium quid?" *Studia Patristica*, vol. 2 (1957), pp. 342-45. Goar maintains that Augustine had little respect for the pagan virtues of the noble Romans and indeed had little respect for Rome itself. See Robert J. Goar, "Reflections on some Anti-Roman Elements in *De Civitate Dei*, Books 1-5," *Augustinian Studies*, vol. 19 (1988), pp. 71-84. See also *Commentary on Psalm 98*, 4; *Commentary on Psalm 121*, 4.

31. Barrow sums up Augustine's views on church and state as follows: "He treats the church in its best aspects and in its best moments, not as identical with, but as representative of the city of God. But under other aspects (for example its many unrighteous members) he treats it as sharply divided from the city of God. In the same way he occasionally speaks of political societies (the state) as the earthly city. But this is only because, speaking generally, states historically have shown little interest in the city of God. It is not because states *by their very nature* are parts of the earthly city. See R. H. Barrow, *Introduction to St. Augustine: "The City of God"* (London: Faber & Faber, 1950), pp. 157-58. See James Dougherty, "The Sacred City and the City of God," *Augustinian Studies*, vol. 10 (1979), pp. 81-90.

ter to be interested primarily in the affairs of heaven, it did not follow that particular individuals would reflect the dedication of their particular society. As Augustine observed, "There are few human beings who are totally irreligious, just as there are few who are deeply religious."[32] As a result, he was not embarrassed in the least to praise the virtues of those noble Romans who (though for the less than noble motive of personal honor) sacrificed personal gain for the good of the commonwealth.[33] Nor did he hesitate to note that in his day the church was filled with "Christians" who had their own personal agendas for seeking Christ, so many indeed that Jesus was scarcely ever sought for his own sake.[34] The virtues of the noble pagan Romans and the vices of the self-serving Christians had to be admitted and dealt with because they seemed so contradictory to the ideals of their respective societies. The heavenly city may be held up as a goal of the Catholic Church, but the future citizens of the city of God are those who belong to the spiritual society of the "people of God," and that community is not necessarily coextensive with the Church. Indeed, as Augustine observes, the two cities were mixed together from the very beginning of time and will be so even till its end.[35] At any moment in time, if one is looking for those who are destined for permanent membership in the city of God (or, for that matter, membership in the earthly city in hell), it is important to realize that: "Many who seem outside are really inside and many who seem inside are really outside."[36]

For those aspiring to be saints in heaven, the reality of living on this earth will always be a tale of two cities. As we shall examine in later chapters, these future saints may "dream of Jerusalem" but they must first deal with "Babylon." While they can and should long for the life that is to come, they must live each day in the midst of the secular city. Against those who would demand separation from any taint of earthly matters, Augustine

---

32. *Sermon 69*, 3.

33. *The City of God*, 5.15; *Letter 138*, 3.17. See Eugene TeSelle, *Augustine the Theologian* (New York: Herder, 1970), pp. 272ff.

34. *Commentary on the Gospel of John*, 25.10.2.

35. *Commentary on Psalm 64*, 2; *The City of God*, 16.11.

36. *Commentary on Psalm 106*, 14. Speaking about members of the church, Augustine remarks that some are motivated by true love for God and others are not; it is impossible for anyone other than God and the person to determine what is the predominant motive (*Commentary on the Letter of John to the Parthians*, 5.7). See Herbert Deane, *The Political and Social Ideas of St. Augustine* (New York: Columbia University Press, 1963), pp. 36-37).

took the very reasonable stance that the pilgrim people should take advantage of the "good things" provided by the "Babylons" and "Romes" of the day and even, where possible, should participate in their governance with a view to making even the most earth-bound society closer to that ideal human community where humans are joined together with God in a friendship that causes a true oneness of heart.

The citizens of the heavenly Jerusalem, while continuing their exile on earth, should follow the directions that God gave to the chosen people exiled in the real Babylon:

> They were commanded to pray for those by whom they were held captive and in the midst of the peace provided to hope for continuing peace so that they might beget children, build houses and plant gardens and vineyards.[37]

The Church of Christ (the people of God) is in a similar exile now under the rule of earthly kings. As long as the laws of the land do not contravene what is owed to God, they should be given due respect. Christians should serve their temporal rulers with patience and fidelity and pray for them that they themselves may be converted to service of God. Through such pious kings peace is given to the Church, a temporal peace to be sure but a peace nonetheless that gives the quiet necessary for building the spiritual temples of God in the human heart, planting the gardens and vineyards which produce fruit for eternity.[38] In Augustine's view, there never will be a truly Christian empire even though there may be from time to time Christian emperors and kings. There is nothing wrong in enjoying the advantages of such enlightened rulers and, indeed, there is nothing wrong in taking advantage of whatever peace even the worst "Babylon" provides. But one must not come to depend on such earthly peace. Even in the most tolerant societies the people of God suffer persecution within from being in an alien land, constantly tempted to relish the pleasures of the here and now and to forget about their destiny and true home.[39]

37. *Catechizing the Uninstructed*, 21.37. See *The City of God*, 19.26; 19.17.

38. TeSelle disagrees with those who hold that Augustine believed that political life has no positive value. See Eugene TeSelle, "Toward an Augustinian Politics," *Journal of Religious Ethics*, vol. 16 (1988), pp. 87-108; "Civic Vision in Augustine's *City of God*," *Thought*, vol. 62 (1987), pp. 268-80.

39. See Richard Dougherty, "Christian and Citizen: The Tension in St. Augustine's *De Civitate Dei*," in *Collectanea Augustiniana*, ed. Joseph Schnaubelt and Frederick VanFleteren (New York: Peter Lang, 1990), pp. 205-24.

The membership of neither supratemporal city is fixed as long as time continues. Therefore, the task for all people is to discover how they can win citizenship in the city of God, how they can avoid eternal condemnation in the earthly city. But to accomplish this one must know what to do and how to recognize obstacles along the way. The discipline that guides humans in their continuing struggle is the science of ethics, the subject to be examined in the next chapter.

CHAPTER 3

Ethics

I. The Questions Raised by Ethics

The science of ethics seeks to answer the basic question of the human being facing a life of multiple possibilities. The question is simply this: "What should I do? How should I act in this particular situation?"

This simple question leads to other questions that are not so simple, questions that form the basis of the science of ethics. We constantly speak about *good* actions that *should* be done and *evil* actions that *should* be avoided. We praise some humans as being *good people* and others as being *evil*. To justify such assertions we must be able to give some answer to the three following questions:

1. What is "good?" What are the characteristics that make one course of action "good" while others are "not-good" or "evil"?
2. Why should I do the "good"? Assuming that I have discovered that a particular course of action is good, while its opposite is evil, what is the justification for saying that I *must* do the good and avoid the evil? We seem to assume the truth of the principle: "Do good; avoid evil!" But can that assertion be supported by reasons, reasons why "I am bound by moral obligation"?
3. Finally, since the aim of ethics is not to make laws for law's sake but rather to give guidelines so that each individual can become a "good" person, what are the essential characteristics of the "good" person?

30

A moral system is said to be *objective* if it maintains that the answers to the questions "What is good?" "Why be good?" "What is a good person?" are to be discovered rather than contrived by individual human beings. It affirms that statements that take the form "X is a morally good act," "You ought to do x," have a truth value, and that the criteria for discovering whether the proposition is true or false are to be found in the real world, a world which for the most part the individual cannot create or control.

There is general agreement that when we make statements of the form "X is a good act," we do more than describe a factual situation. We also note our approval of the act and hold out the act as worthy of being imitated. But is there a reasonable justification for our approval, for our claim that this act should be done and that its opposite should not be done? Certainly over the history of the human race many criteria for goodness have been offered. Egoism argued that an act is good if it promotes "my" best interest. Utilitarianism demurred, saying that the good act must result in the greatest happiness of the greatest number. Some have argued that the good act is that which society agrees is good, either by a quasi-contract or simply by custom. For Hitler the good act was that which brought about the purification of the race; for Marx it was that act that led to the classless society. Kant argued that a good act was one that came from a good will, one that sought to follow the dictates of rational nature. Aquinas, following in the tradition of Plato and Aristotle, held that the good act was one that moved the individual towards her/his proper goal, which was to be the best human being possible. To say that some act is good for a human to perform means that it leads to an environment in which that human can flourish.[1]

It would seem logical to say that the "perfecting" nature of the act must in some way depend on one's nature, one's place in the universe — with all the relationships that this entails. Put simply, we must have some knowledge of *what* human beings are before we can say what is good or bad for them, what will make them more or less perfect. If such knowledge is impossible, ethical assertions from this perspective become meaningless.[2] But perfect knowledge is not required. Even minimal knowledge of

1. For an example of this position see Thomas Aquinas, *Disputed Questions Concerning Truth,* q.21, a.1, corpus.

2. For a discussion of this problem see Mary Mothersill, "Duty," in the *Encyclopedia of Philosophy,* ed. Paul Edwards (New York: Macmillan, 1967), vol. 2, pp. 444ff.

my position in reality is enough to begin my moral venture. Knowing that I have a body and a mind suggests that I should always act consistently with that fact, giving neither too much nor too little attention to either. Knowing that I have acquired relationships to others through family or contract means that I should act out the course of action that such relationships entail. If I am employed, I should work at my job. If I am married, I should be faithful to my spouse. If I have children, I should nourish and protect and love them to the best of my ability. I will be made better by doing the "right" thing and the "right" thing will be dictated by the position I hold in the universe. "A good act is one that makes more perfect" seems like a sensible statement and it is not empty of meaning as long as I have some sense of what it is to be a human being and, more specifically, to be the individual person that I am.

Knowing *what* is good does not give an answer to the second question "Why be good?" Luckily, most people will not make an issue of the "Why?" if you can show them an answer to the "What?" They will agree that the fundamental principle of ethics — "Do good; avoid evil" — should be followed if someone could only convince them of the nature of good and evil. However the question of "Why should I do this and not that?" is a legitimate question. In ordinary life one is usually answered with a motivating reason, an incentive that will sway the person to freely choose to do this rather than that. For example, a child refusing to eat supper and saying "Why must I?" may be moved to eat by threat of loss of an allowance. But this is not a justifying reason, a reason that would support the imposition of obligation, giving reasons why this child is doing something "wrong" in not obeying. For a truly complete and objective ethics some answer must be given to the question "Why be good?" and like the answer to the question "What is good?" it should be firmly rooted in reality. Examples of such reality-based justifications are a contract whereby person "a" agrees to follow the rules set down by person "b" or a subordination established by the nature of things whereby one person is truly subject in some respects to the will of some "other," be it a society, an individual human, or God.

Further, for a completely objective system of morality it is important that the obligation be a categorical imperative ("Do this!") rather than a hypothetical imperative ("Do this if you want to please me!"). In the latter case the recipient of the command still has it within her/his power to make a non-blamable choice. If the person is not interested in pleasing me, then the command loses all force. Ethics then becomes a game something like etiquette, a game that one can choose to play or not without being blamed.[3]

The problem in giving moral commands is precisely in establishing the "justifying reason," a reason that can provide a sound basis for the asserted moral obligation. We certainly can give motivating reasons to people to get them to act in this way or that, reasons that will influence them to act in the way we wish them to act; but can we justify the obligation we impose, give reasons rooted in the nature of reality itself such that we can truly say that "You should do this because if you do not, you are guilty of evil?"

It is obvious that if we cannot answer the questions "What is good?" and "Why be good?" we cannot give a sensible answer to the question "What is a good human being?" It seems intuitively true to say that a good person will be one who does good things and avoids bad things. A good person is one who has developed a habit of doing good. Only by answering the first two questions can we explain why temperance is a virtue and intemperance is a vice, why selfishness is wrong and altruism is right, why love is good and hatred bad.

In the pages that follow we shall explore how Augustine attempted to answer such questions as these.

II. Augustine's Ethical Theory[4]

A. *The Meaning of Happiness*

Happiness is one of those aspects of reality that needs no long explanation. All humans have an understanding of the term even if they do not share much of the reality. Consequently, when Augustine speaks about happi-

---

3. Phillipa Foot, "Morality as a System of Hypothetical Imperatives," *Philosophical Review,* vol. 81, no. 3 (July 1972), p. 312.

4. As Babcock observes, Augustine never dealt with ethical theory as a separate discipline. There is no one work where he specifically addresses the questions that serve as the structure for this chapter: "What is good?" "Why be good?" "What are the characteristics of a good person?" The structure of this chapter should not be taken as an "Augustinian structure" but only as a convenient way of organizing Augustine's reflections on ethical issues. See William S. Babcock, "Introduction," *The Ethics of St. Augustine,* ed. William S. Babcock (Atlanta: Scholars Press, 1991), pp. 3-4. See P. Gregorio Armas, *La Moral de San Agustin* (Madrid: Difusoria del Libro, 1954) for useful texts.

ness, he seems to assume that everyone knows what he is talking about. He gives a working definition of happiness almost as an aside in the preface of book five of *The City of God,* saying that it is "the full possession of all that the heart can long for." Scholastic philosophers would later give a more technical definition which says about the same thing: "Happiness is the conscious satisfaction of all innate appetites."

Some of our appetites are innate in that they flow from our human nature itself. Others are acquired in that they result from our free choices or from our life experiences. The desire for food and drink is a natural appetite. The appetite for an addictive drug is an acquired appetite. Although satisfaction of acquired appetites plays a part in our happiness now, such satisfaction is not essential to our being happy. If we have acquired appetites, we can also suppress them. But innate appetites cannot be suppressed. We cannot "will away" hunger or thirst. To be happy our only option is to satisfy our natural hungers. It would seem reasonable to say that in the satisfaction of such appetites not only are we made happy, we are also made better. Health results from the rational satisfaction of our natural needs.

Although unconscious beings may be described analogously as having "natural appetites" (the tree whose leaves turn towards the sun and whose roots search for water; the falling rock which seeks equilibrium in the midst of the competing forces that affect it), their condition upon satisfaction of these "appetites" is not properly called "happiness" because it is not a conscious state. A tree in a nourishing environment may be called healthy but it is not happy. A rock that has achieved its proper place may be at rest but it is not at peace. Though Augustine shows concern for the preservation of nature and the health of the animal kingdom, his discussion of "happiness" is restricted to "rational beings," especially those members of the human race who are still living this side of death, those still striving to achieve perfect happiness.

Degrees of happiness are possible and the extent of our happiness or unhappiness depends on the extent of the satisfaction of our desires. The definitions suggested by Augustine and later philosophers in speaking about "perfect and permanent" satisfaction of all desires are thus connected to "perfect happiness" or beatitude. Beatitude is not simply feeling good today; it is feeling good forever. Such permanent happiness is what Augustine means by the word "happiness" in all of his discussions; beatitude is what humans strive for and, until they achieve it, they are not perfectly satisfied. If present happiness will inevitably come to an end, there is still something more to be desired.

In one of his earliest examinations of the happy life, Augustine takes it as beyond question that everyone wants to be happy, and he repeats this sentiment frequently throughout the rest of his writings.[5] Our thirst for happiness is not caused by chance or by our arbitrary decision. We can choose whether we shall "desire" the pleasure of smoking by choosing to build up the habit. We are not born with a cigarette in our mouth. But we cannot choose whether we shall "desire" happiness. We do not begin our existence like a straight stick caught between the alternatives (being happy/being unhappy), with such indifference to either that we could easily choose either one. From the very beginning, we are like a concave mouth already hungering for happiness.

The great mystery is how this passion for perfect happiness came to be in the human psyche. Obviously none have experienced such perfect satisfaction; if they had they would no longer be searching for something more. Indeed it almost seems that some people have had no experience of happiness at all. Where then does this desire for an unknown, an unexperienced state come from? The only answer that makes any sense is that humans are born with it. Just as there is an inborn desire to live — such that some humans will even choose to live miserably rather than not to live at all — so the desire for perfect happiness must flow from human nature itself.[6]

Indeed, the only logical explanation for the human hunger for happiness is that God wanted it to be so; it is a desire "which the supremely good and unchangeable blessed Creator has implanted in the will."[7] The divine decision that the human should desire happiness was an integral part of the decision to make the human a rational animal, a being with the capacity to know the good and to desire the good. The human desire for happiness is as unchanging as the nature of the human being. To be rational implies the capacity and need to know the "true" and to desire the "good." God could have made humans such that they would not seek hap-

---

5. *The Happy Life*, 1.10. Other citations on the universal desire for happiness are the following: *The Morals of the Catholic Church and the Morals of the Manicheans*, 1.3.4; *The Trinity*, 13.4.7; *Confessions*, 10.21.31; *Sermon 150*, 4. In *The City of God* (19.1) Augustine suggests that the only reason for doing philosophy or anything else is in order to be happy.

6. See Augustine, *The City of God*, 11.26-27. Augustine explores the mystery of the human desire for the as yet unexperienced *perfect* happiness in his *Confessions* (10.20.29; 10.21.31). See William S. Babcock, "*Cupiditas* and *Caritas*: The Early Augustine on Love and Human Fulfillment," in *The Ethics of Augustine, op. cit.*, pp. 39-40.

7. *The Trinity*, 13.8.11.

piness only by making them something other than rational animals. But this was not done, and the fact that human beings do exist as beings with a desire for happiness must be described as a *good*, since they were made this way by God and "all that God creates is good."[8]

The consoling fact implied in all this is that perfect happiness must be possible for human beings. It is inconsistent with an acknowledgment of God's goodness to maintain that he brought human beings into existence with a desire that could not be fulfilled. Perhaps (as Augustine believed) humans later made such happiness impossible by turning away from God, but the first humans did not begin to exist that way. If they had been created with an uncontrollable thirst that was impossible to satisfy, this would indeed have been the height of cruelty. To so condemn the individual to a life of misery would represent a horrifying creation, one that was simply incompatible with the goodness of the Creator.

The fact that all humans want to be happy does not answer the more difficult question: "What will make humans happy?" To say, as Augustine says, that happiness consists in the full possession of all that we love, does not answer the question either. To "love" something is nothing other than to desire that something for its own sake. Love is thus a kind of motion or action and the motion is always towards a "something."[9] The benefit and also the peril of love is that when we achieve what we love we are changed in a much more radical way than when we simply "know" the object of our love. To know a lovely thing is not to become it. There remains a radical difference between the knower and the thing known. However when we love that known thing and come to possess it, we somehow become that thing. That which is loved necessarily affects with itself that which loves it. To love the earth is to become earthy; to love the eternal heaven is even now to anticipate the joys of eternity.[10]

It follows that what humans love and how they love will have an immense effect on their search for happiness. To possess what you desire will not always bring happiness. As Augustine observes:

> Humans love many different things and when they seem to have all that they desire, we are accustomed to call them happy. But we can be happy

8. *Letter 140*, 2.4.

9. Augustine writes: "Love is a kind of motion and all motion is towards a something. To love is nothing other than to desire something for its own sake" (*83 Diverse Questions*, 35.1). See *Soliloquies*, 1.13.22.

10. *The Trinity*, 11.2.5; *83 Diverse Questions*, 35.2.

only if we are loving what ought to be loved. Happiness does not consist simply in having what we happen to love. We sometimes are made more unhappy by having what we love than in not having it. When unhappy persons love something hurtful, they are made even more unhappy.[11]

Even when humans love truly good things (Augustine lists such things as large families with blameless and attractive sons and daughters, an abundance and peace in both family and society), the happiness that results can only be incomplete and tinged with sadness because it is temporal.[12] It will end with death and even as we enjoy its possession, we fear its loss.[13]

Even though we may not know exactly what will bring perfect happiness, we do know some of its characteristics. For example:

1. True happiness is a *conscious* state of satisfaction based on *knowledge* of what is true. The object that will bring happiness must be known and be "true," not a fiction created by our passion or confused imagination.[14]

2. If we are to be happy, it is not enough to "know" the good and to desire it. It must be *possessed* through love, a force that drives us towards immersion in the object loved, which indeed results in our becoming one with the object loved.[15]

3. Since we are made into that which we love, we cannot be happy if we do not have that truly good thing which we love nor can we be happy when we do have something that is bad for us.[16]

11. *Commentary on Psalm 26*, 7. Augustine adds that a truly "happy-making" good must be one that can be possessed whenever one wants it. It is not enough to love; one needs "to have and to hold" what one loves. See *Free Choice*, 1.11.22; 1.15.33.

12. *Commentary on Psalm 143*, 18. This is not to deny that there are many things in this world which are truly good and which contribute to our happiness. Augustine lists some of the things that obviously contributed to his happiness in *The City of God* (19.13).

13. *The Happy Life*, 2.11. Augustine writes: "Unquestionably the only cause for fear lies in the fact that what is loved might be lost, once acquired; or might not be acquired, once hoped for" (*83 Diverse Questions*, 62).

14. *Free Choice*, 2.13; *The Happy Life*, 4.34. Though possession of our proper good (the good that is meant for us) is the cause of happiness, knowledge of the good is a precondition. To be happy one must be wise; one must have a balanced mind (*The Happy Life*, 4.33). To be happy one must indeed possess the highest good but this good is *known* and possessed in that truth that is called wisdom (*Free Choice*, 2.9.26).

15. *Commentary on Psalm 143*, 18. See Etienne Gilson, *The Christian Philosophy of Saint Augustine*, trans. L. E. M. Lynch (New York: Random House, 1960), pp. 8-9.

16. *The Morals of the Catholic Church and the Morals of the Manicheans*, 1.3.4.

4. Since we are made into that which we possess through love, it is logical to assume that perfect happiness cannot come from loving something less than ourselves (which makes us less) or even loving something at the same level as ourselves (which changes us in no radical way). Happiness can come only through the possession of that which is *best* for us and that best can only be something that is superior to us. This leads to the conclusion that our perfect happiness will come only if we come into conscious possession of God.[17]

5. Finally, the possession of this *best* object must be permanent. Even if we possessed all that was good in the universe but knew that we would or even could lose it at anytime, there would still be something more that would make us even more happy. This would be the assurance that the ecstasy we experience now in the possession of our greatest love will never end. If life ended in oblivion at death, we would of course not be unhappy in that condition; we would be nothing at all. But if at *this* moment in time we are happy but are conscious that this happy state will someday end, we cannot be other than a bit dejected. Our present happiness is tinged with heartache over what will come. For happiness to be perfect, it must be permanent.[18]

B. Augustine's Answer to the Question "What Is Good?"

It is clear that Augustine believed that "perfect happiness" is the ultimate *subjective* good, that perfect feeling of fulfillment in the individual that would seek nothing more. But what is that *objective good* which, when possessed, will bring about such perfect fulfillment? The conclusion that Augustine comes to at the end of his discussion of happiness makes it clear that this objective good is not determined by an arbitrary decision made by human beings or even by God. It is determined rather by what it is to be human, by the wants and needs that are rooted in human nature, by what it means to be a "perfect" human. As we have seen, Augustine concludes that the individual human will be perfectly happy if and only if he/she

---

17. *Ibid.*; see *Free Choice*, 2.13.36. Augustine repeats in many places the theme that happiness depends on the possession of God. For example, *The Morals of the Catholic Church and the Morals of the Manicheans*, 1.6.10; *83 Diverse Questions*, 2; *Confessions*, 10.22.32.

18. *The Trinity*, 13.7.10; *Sermon 359A*, 4.

loves and possesses that which is best for human beings and possesses it forever without fear of loss.[19]

The phrase "best for human beings" needs clarification. It is clear from Augustine's analysis of happiness that a particular good is not made "best" for me simply because I desire it. I can desire things which are not truly good for me at all. Wishing will not make it be what it is not. Something is "best" or "not best" for me because of the nature of things. There is a definite hierarchy in reality and I have a very defined place in that hierarchy. Thus, when Augustine comes to describe the human soul, he gives a quasi-spatial description: "God alone is better than it, the angels are equal to it, and all the rest of creation is below it."[20] My place as a human being is thus in the middle of reality. Some parts are above me and some are below me. Augustine concludes from this that happiness can come only from the possession of a good that is greater than human beings and, indeed, is that good than which there is no greater.

The principle that we are made happy only by possession of that which is best for us leads Augustine to the conviction that we will only be made perfectly happy when we achieve permanent possession of God, the infinite being, the being that encompasses all good in every possible world.[21] Thus, the possession of God is the goal of the ethical life and this is not because of the will of humans or even because God specifically commands it to be that way. It is because of the reality that is God and the reality that is the human being. It is in the very nature of things that God should be the ultimate good which will bring humans perfect happiness

---

19. Augustine discusses various opinions from Greek and Latin philosophy on the "supreme good" that must be achieved for humans to be perfectly happy in *The City of God*, 19.1-4. In *Sermon 150* he criticizes the Epicurean and Stoic positions.

20. *The Quantity of the Soul*, 34.78.

21. Thus Augustine writes: "Just now our love can only drive us towards God and make us live well; if we reach God after death we shall live not only well but happily" (*The Morals of the Catholic Church and the Morals of the Manicheans*, 1.6.10). See *Confessions*, 10.22.32. A suggestion of Augustine's answer to the question "What is Good?" can be found in *The City of God* (8.8) where he describes ethics as the science which deals with that supreme good towards which all human actions are (or should be) directed. The definition implies two facts. First, actions which are properly described as "human" actions naturally tend towards a specific goal and in moving towards that goal they exercise their proper function. Thus, for example, the act of eating has as its proper goal the health of the person and when exercised in an appropriate way it achieves that goal. Second, the goal of all human actions taken together is the supreme good for human beings. Once it is achieved no further good is sought.

when possessed. Once humans were created in their particular place in the really existing world, they could do nothing other than "look to the heavens" to find the source of perfect happiness. Augustine's famous observation that "You have made us for yourself, O God, and our hearts are restless till they rest in you" is much more than a simple prayer; it is a statement of fact.[22]

What this "rest" in God will be like remains a mystery until it is actually experienced. The only analogy offered by Augustine is that of an eye rejoicing in light, bathed in that reality for which it had been made and to which it is perfectly adapted.[23] But resting in God is much more than this. The eye surrounded and immersed in light does not become light, but we humans in possession of the Infinite Loved One are affected in a much more dramatic way. We become "better" because we become in some mysterious way the "best." As Augustine says, he would never dare make such a claim without the support of Sacred Scripture:

> Do you love God? What shall I say: "You will become God?" I dare not say this on my own. But let us listen to the scripture where it is written: "I have said 'You are gods and sons of the most high.'"[24]

The answer to the question "What is the proper end for human beings, that object which all humans should strive to possess?" is clear. It is nothing less than God, the supreme being. Any human action will be a *good* action that leads towards that end, and concretely such actions will be those that respect the order of reality. In the words of Augustine:

> Everything God created is good. The rational soul performs good action when it observes the order of creation, when it chooses the greater over the lesser, the higher over the lower, spiritual values over material goods, eternal realities over those that last only in time.[25]

---

22. *Confessions*, 1.1.1. Other texts that expand on this point include the following: *Commentary on Psalm 134*, 6; *On Lying*, 1.18.13.

23. *The City of God*, 8.8.

24. *Commentary on the Letter of John to the Parthians*, 2.14. For Augustine the conclusion was obvious: "It is good for me to stick to God. He is complete goodness. But do you wish for something more? I am saddened by your wishing. My friends, what more do you wish for? There is nothing better than to be 'glued' to God" (*Commentary on Psalm 62*, 36).

25. *Free Choice*, 1.8.18; 1.15.32.

The fundamental principle answering the question "What is *the good?*" thus becomes:

> The morally good act will be that which is in accord with the order of the universe.

Some have suggested that Augustine answered the question from a divine voluntarist perspective, saying that a good act is good because God wills it to be good.[26] In my view it is more accurate to say that moral good depends on the will of God only indirectly — that is, on God's will creating the universe as it actually exists with human beings made to be finite beings of spirit and matter in a universe composed of pure spirits, pure matter, and an infinite being who is superior to and rules all the rest. God could not have made a universe in which it was "good" for humans to act like God or to live pretending that they had no soul or no body, dedicating themselves to a harsh asceticism or to the pleasures of material existence. The essence of the immoral act is disordered love. The sin of Adam was to feel so important that he no longer needed God. The sin of Judas was to believe that his sin was so important that it was unforgivable. Adam made too much of himself. Judas made too little. In both cases there was a sin against reality. In both instances the human being was unable to achieve what was best for him because he lived in a fantasy land created by his disordered love. Indeed, it is not inaccurate to say that Augustine would de-

---

26. Vernon Bourke, for example, has suggested that Augustine moved from an early natural law position to a position of legal voluntarism, ". . . the view that the source and standard of moral good is the will of some legislator." He refers to *Sermon 124* (no. 3) where Augustine says: "Justice is whatever God wills" and *The City of God* (21.7.1) where Augustine writes: "The whole point of being Almighty is that God has the power to do whatever He wills to do." (See Vernon Bourke, "Voluntarism in Augustine's Ethico-Legal Thought," *Augustinian Studies,* vol. 1 [1970], pp. 3, 7.) However, the last statement is made in the context of arguing that God has the power to suspend the ordinary laws of nature which would demand that the bodies of the damned be consumed and not burn for eternity. And even the first statement is not directly applicable to the question "What is good?" but rather refers to issues such as "Was it unjust for Abraham to take the life of Isaac?" I have argued against identifying Augustine as a divine voluntarist in "Augustine on Divine Voluntarism," *Angelicum,* vol. 64 (1987), pp. 424-36. Koterski is correct when he notes the movement in Augustine's ethical theory over his long life, at least in his appreciation of the human inability to do good without the grace of God. But throughout these changes he remained convinced that morality was based on the order of the universe, an order that was unchanging. See Joseph W. Koterski, "St. Augustine on the Moral Law," *Augustinian Studies,* vol. 11 (1980), p. 65.

scribe sin as being in the *wrong place* at the wrong time and would describe hell as being in the wrong place for all time. The penalty seems especially fitting considering the nature of the crime.

Could the order of this actual world, and thus the content of the moral law, have been different? Are there possible worlds in which our "evil" would become "good" or at least morally indifferent? God is omnipotent, but omnipotence does not mean the power to do the impossible. In his *The Trinity* (1.6.9) Augustine describes the real world as including two radically different components: God and those things created by God out of nothing. Certainly God's decision to create was a free act, as was his decision to create this rather than that. The elements and therefore the hierarchy in created being could have been different. God could have made a world without angels or a world without human beings or a world in which there were only angels and humans. He could have made a world where there was only one human being and where such obligations as justice and charity towards others would not exist. The nature of moral good thus does indeed depend on the will of God in the sense that it depends on the actual world which God freely chose to create. But once that world exists with its particular order, the determination of moral good comes proximately from that order and the characteristic of "being good" cannot be changed without changing that order. God could not have created a world in which it was not morally evil to blaspheme the Creator, pretending that the creature was more than the Creator. God could not have created a being of mind and body where it was morally permissible for the latter to rule the former. God could not have created a multitude of human beings with identical natures and value and then allowed humans to treat each other as though all were not of equal value and dignity. To do any of these things would contradict the order built into the nature of things and the orderly rules for creation that follow from the Creator's nature as exemplary cause of all that is. Morally good actions are therefore those that are in accord with the order of the universe and only remotely those that God wills in choosing to make this universe the way it is in actuality.

C. Augustine's Answer to the Question: "Why Be Good?"

To be able to tell a person why an action is good does not tell them why they have an obligation to perform the good. The concept of "obligation," like the concept of "good," is a defining element in any system of ethics. Of all the various disciplines, ethics is the only one that moves beyond a description of what is to an assertion of what should be. To know that one can make water by combining oxygen and hydrogen carries no implication that one should or should not make water, but to say that violating a contract is a moral evil leads immediately to the assertion that one should avoid such violation.

Moral obligation rests on law, the imposition of the will of a superior upon an inferior, a ruler on a subject. For a law to be justifiable there must be some reason given why the superior has been designated as superior, why the ruler has the right to rule. The reason may be the free choice of a group of humans, as for example in a sorority or fraternity where the members elect their president and then stipulate that "in this area of life we shall follow your orders." It may also be rooted in an ontological superiority, one based on the nature of reality. Thus we justify making dogs our pets and using animals and plants for our purposes by claiming that we belong to a higher order of reality than they do. A law is nothing more than a guide showing others what they should or should not do. Free beings are not forced to follow this guide, but if they do disobey and the law is a valid law, they can be said to be "in the wrong" because they are not doing what they *should* do. Law is the only instrument which can move ethics beyond a hypothetical imperative ("Do this if you wish to be happy!") to a truly categorical imperative ("Do this!"). Augustine argued that we have a natural need to be united to God, but is there an obligation to be so united? How can we move from the proposition "We tend naturally to God" to the proposition "We are *obliged* freely to choose to tend towards God?"[27] To justify obligation one must justify subordination and, indeed, since we are speaking about moral rules for every aspect of human life, we must find a superior who is not simply above every individual human being but also above the human race itself. Some have suggested that such absolute authority can be found in the state or in human society itself, that these human groupings are essentially superior to every human individual in every aspect of his/her life. Others, like Augustine, have pointed to God as the source of moral obligation.

27. See Bernard Roland-Gosselin, "St. Augustine's System of Morals," in *A Monument to St. Augustine,* edited by M. D'Arcy (New York: Sheed and Ward, 1930), p. 233. For a general discussion of the problem of justifying moral obligation, see my article, "The Problem of Justifying Moral Obligation: An Aspect of the Moral Argument for the Existence of God," *Proceedings of the American Catholic Philosophical Association,* vol. 49 (1975), pp. 72-81.

According to Augustine the first rule or law of the universe, governing both free and non-free creatures, is the eternal law. He describes it as "the divine reason or the will of God commanding that the order of nature be preserved and forbidding that it be disturbed."[28]

For Augustine the moral law (in later centuries called "natural law") was nothing more than that aspect of eternal law which applied to human beings as free, rational beings who had the power to choose not to follow the law, that is, to love in a disorderly way.[29] Although it was impossible for any human being to follow the moral law without the help of God's grace, the law itself was nevertheless present to the mind of every person who took the time to consider it. As Augustine says:

> Through the ineffable and sublime management of all things by divine providence, natural law is transcribed upon the rational soul so that in the conduct of their life on earth humans can discover how to act in such a way that their actions reflect the will of God.[30]

There is no question that God has the superiority in being that justifies the authority to impose the moral law, but to establish that God was sufficiently interested in the human race to impose such a law is a more complex task. Augustine turned to Sacred Scripture for his proof. There it

28. *Against Faustus the Manichean*, 22.27. See *Free Choice*, 1.6. Fortin notes that for Augustine morality rests on reason in two ways. First, it depends on God's mind establishing and imposing a plan on the universe, a plan that makes sense and is wise. In a secondary sense morality rests on the human mind which is able to discover this order and intuit within itself the law that dictates its observance (Ernest Fortin, "Augustine and the Problem of Human Goodness," *University of Dayton Review*, vol. 22, no. 3 [Summer 1994], p. 187). On the fittingness of an ordered universe in which the inferior is subject to the superior, see Augustine *Commentary on Psalm 46*, 10; *Commentary on Psalm 143*, 6.

29. *Free Choice*, 1.6.15.

30. *83 Diverse Questions*, 53.2. See *Commentary on Psalm 57*, 1. Augustine suggests that one of the reasons it is important for humans to "know thyself" is because only by knowing ourselves can we come to knowledge of the eternal rules of justice that are imprinted on our hearts much like the imprint of a ring on soft wax (*The Trinity*, 10.5.7; 14.15.21). He firmly believed that God speaks to all human beings through their conscience, revealing the basic moral rules (*A Commentary on the Lord's Sermon on the Mount*, 2.9.12). Miethe comments: "St. Augustine, by introducing the fundamental concept of a theistic eternal cosmic law, laid the foundation for all natural law ethics in the centuries to come" (Terry L. Miethe, "Natural Law, the Synderesis Rule, and St. Augustine," *Augustinian Studies*, vol. 11 [1980], p. 95).

was made abundantly clear that God was involved in the destiny of the human race by his providential care. In the Old Testament it is recorded that God gave ten commandments to his servant Moses and the New Testament testifies that the incarnate God, Jesus Christ, promulgated a law of love which ordered humans to love God above all and their neighbors as themselves. One might also argue that if God had not imposed these laws, he should have; that for God "not to make law" guiding free creatures would be inconsistent with his nature as an infinitely perfect being. To give the human race a thirst for heaven without giving directions on how to get there would seem at least imprudent and at worst unkind.

The primary expression of moral law is the eternal law itself. From it are derived other principles which begin to apply the general rule about "keeping order" to specific areas of life. Immediately flowing from it is the general principle of justice, commanding that we treat every existing thing with the respect due it because of its place in the universe. This rule implies that lower things should be subject to higher things, that equality should be preserved among things which are equal, that temporal affairs should be subordinate to those which are eternal, that the corruptible be recognized as being inferior to that which is incorruptible.[31]

The law of charity follows as an application of justice to a person's relationship to God, other humans, and all things desirable. It commands that one should love all that is good but in an orderly way. Here Augustine distinguishes between goods that are loved as useful means to an end and those goods that should be enjoyed for their own sake. Only God is in the latter category and all other loves must hold a subordinate position. Thus, to love God and neighbor properly means to enjoy God for his own sake and one's neighbor for the sake of God.[32] Applying the

31. *Letter 140*, 2.4.

32. *Christian Doctrine*, 3.10.16; 1.4.22. On the distinction between goods that are properly enjoyed *(frui)* for their own sake and those loved as goods to be used *(uti)* for higher ends see *ibid.*, 1.22.20 and also *The Morals of the Catholic Church and the Morals of the Manicheans*, 1.37. In the latter work Augustine writes: "It is unnecessary for me to say more about morally good action. God is the highest good for the human being. It clearly follows that since living a good life is nothing more than to seek to possess this highest good, then living a good life is nothing else than to love God with one's whole heart and soul and mind" (1.25). See also *Commentary on Psalm 89*, 17. In the *Confessions* (10.37) Augustine writes: "You command us not only to be continent, that is, to withdraw our affections from some things; you also command justice through which we bestow our love on other things. Thus, it is not your desire that we should love you only; we must love our neighbor also."

principle of charity specifically to fellow humans, Augustine pronounces the so-called *Golden Rule:* "Do not do to another what you would not want done to yourself."[33]

The principles of justice ("Give all their due") and charity ("Love all things as they should be loved") are the foundation for all other moral rules. Thus, for example, the commandments of the Decalogue regulate our love for God and others, the first three forbidding actions which do not recognize the superiority of God, the last seven forbidding the ways in which we harm each other in body and in spirit.

D. The Characteristics of the Good Person

The various regulations of the moral law are not aimed at obliging obedience to law for its own sake. Their real purpose is to guide humans in the development of those characteristics which can make them into truly *good* human beings. The primary concern of ethics is not *the good in general* or making *good laws*. Its aim is to give direction in the making of *good people*. This was Augustine's purpose in writing and speaking about ethical matters. Doing good is commendable, but becoming a good person is absolutely necessary. A good person is not constituted by performing this or that good act or even in having one or two virtues, habits of doing good. Good people are those who possess so many virtues so perfectly that in every situation they will have an inclination or tendency to do what should be done. The goal of ethics is not good action or good habits; it is to help form a person of *good character.*

Augustine believed that the central virtue that must be the foundation of all other virtues is the virtue of *charity,* the habit of loving well. He found his justification both in the teachings of the New Testament and in an examination of the human condition as it is now and how it could be after death. Just now the human being lives in a middle ground between success and failure. It is still possible this side of death for any of us to pursue and achieve the goal for which we were created, perfect happiness in union with the infinite good who is God. One pursues this good by love, by a desire for something for its own sake. Day by day the course of our love is not predetermined in any one direction. We are free, which means that as we view the multitude of good things in our daily

33. *Commentary on the Gospel of John,* 49.12; *Commentary on Psalm 57,* 1.

lives, we could move towards any of them by our love. The challenge and temptation of this life is created by the many good things in our daily experience that are worthy of desire. God, of course, is infinitely good but all of creation (in that it reflects the perfection of its Creator) is also good and desirable. We spend our time in the midst of competing goods that pull us this way and that. The path that we ultimately take will depend on which good we come to love more at that particular moment. As Augustine so aptly describes it: "My love is my weight; it carries me wheresoever I go."[34]

The good person is one who is moving towards the ultimate goal for all humans: union with God. The force driving this movement is orderly love, or desire, for the goods experienced. As Augustine observes:

> When we ask how good a man is we do not ask what he believes or hopes but what he loves. Indeed, every commandment has the same goal: namely, charity.[35]

To love God above all is the first requirement, but this does not mean that one should not love created things. As Augustine told his friends one day:

> I don't want you doing no loving at all, but I want your loving to be rightly ordered. Put heavenly things before earthly ones, immortal things before mortal, eternal things before temporal and put the Lord before everything else.[36]

The reason for his advice was his conviction that a good life is not created by holding back love from anything that is worthy of love but rather by loving all things, God and creatures, as they should be loved. Indeed, degrees of holiness are measured by the extent, fervor and orderliness of

---

34. *Confessions*, 13.9; *The City of God*, 11.28; *Letter 55*, 10.18.

35. *Enchiridion on Faith, Hope, and Charity*, 31.117; 32.121. As we shall see, Augustine did not believe that perfect charity (which includes love of the true God) was possible without faith. But, as he says in *Sermon 90* (no. 8), it is unfortunately possible for a person to have faith and no love.

36. *Sermon 335C*, 13. Carney is correct in his description of Augustine's moral theory as a "double matrix ethic." It rests on love, but this love must be grounded in truth. Moral action does not consist in loving every sort of thing in any sort of way. Truth is the root of "the good" in that the good act is one where one loves in accord with the actual order of the universe. See Frederick S. Carney, "The Structure of Augustine's Ethic," *The Ethics of St. Augustine, op. cit.*, p. 11.

one's love. Sin or moral fault is nothing other than not loving what should be loved or loving it less than it should be loved.[37]

Only through a life of ordered love can humans achieve the perfect happiness that comes with the possession of God. Love is like a "wedding garment" required for entrance to the heavenly banquet; it is absolutely necessary for salvation.[38] Our journey to the heavens is by our desire, our love. It is for this reason that Augustine gave the following advice to his friends: "If you wish to come to God, do not be slow to love because we run to God not with our feet but with our affection."[39]

It follows that it is not enough simply *to perform* acts which are in accord with the order of the universe. To be "forced" to be just or to give to the poor out of fear is not especially noble. The implication of such actions is that we would not do them if the force or fear was not present. A truly good act is characterized by obedience to the law with no desire to do otherwise under any circumstances.[40] Augustine considered keeping a law out of fear of punishment rather than from a desire to be righteous to be an "unfree" act and not an observance of law at all. No fruit is good which does not grow from the root of love, and this root is not present if we do not "delight" in doing the righteous act.[41]

It is in light of this conviction that one must understand Augustine's famous statement: "Love, and do what you want!"[42] One obvious purpose of the phrase is to emphasize the importance of motive in performing any action. But this does not mean that Augustine was saying that motive, acting out of a spirit of love, was the *only* factor in determining the morality of an action. There are many sorts of love and some of them are perverse and "out of order." When Augustine speaks about love in this text and in similar texts he is speaking about the highest form of ordered love, that

37. *The Perfection of Justice,* 6.15; 3.8. See also *Letter 137,* 5.17; *Nature and Grace,* 70.84.

38. *Sermon 90,* 6. For a more complete discussion of the place of grace and freedom in the performance of the good act see my *Augustine's World: An Introduction to His Speculative Philosophy* (Lanham, MD: University Press of America, 1996), pp. 139-66.

39. *Commentary on the Gospel of John,* 26.8.2.

40. *Against Two Letters of the Pelagians,* 1.10.19; 2.9.21. Augustine writes: "What good do we do if we do not love? And how can we not do good if we love? Even though it seems that the commands of God are fulfilled by one who does them out of fear rather than from love, there can be no good work where there is no love" (*The Grace of Christ and Original Sin,* 1.26.27).

41. *The Spirit and the Letter,* 14.26.

42. *Commentary on the Letter of John to the Parthians,* 7.8.

love whereby one chooses God over all things. He is saying that if we truly love God with an all-consuming love, we will never *want* to act against eternal law by disturbing the order of the universe. Nothing but good can come from what Augustine calls "the root of love." Only good can come when the source of every activity is the love of God.

Charity, the foundation for the good life, expresses itself through many other virtues.[43] Thus, temperance is love giving itself wholeheartedly to that which it loves, preserving itself whole and unblemished for God. Fortitude is love enduring all things willingly for the sake of that which is loved, enduring all things willingly for the sake of God. Justice is love serving only that one who is loved, serving God alone and, therefore, ruling well those things subject to human beings. Prudence is love choosing wisely between that which helps and that which hinders, discriminating correctly between those things that lead towards God and those which stand in the way. Indeed, true virtue is nothing else than the perfect love of God.[44]

Two virtues are of special importance as preconditions for anyone to have perfectly ordered charity. The first of these is humility. This is the root of true charity because before one can love in an orderly way one must accept one's place in reality, making oneself neither more nor less than what one actually is. As Augustine remarks:

> The Son of God came to this earth as a human being and became humble. You too are commanded to be humble but this does not mean denying your humanity, thinking you are no better than a beast in the field. God indeed *became* a human being but you, a human being, must recognize that you are just that: a human being. Humility for you consists in knowing exactly who you are.[45]

43. A complete discussion of Augustine's ascetical and mystical philosophy (how the individual searches for God in this life, a description of the way of perfection, the obstacles standing in the way of a person's spiritual development) is far beyond the scope of this volume. It must wait for another book at another time, a volume specifically dedicated to Augustine's teaching on individual spirituality.

44. *The Morals of the Catholic Church and the Morals of the Manicheans*, 1.15.25. As Davis notes, the determining factor between good and evil in any human action is whether or not the act is driven by the love of God and is in accord with the will of God, the one who must be loved above all. See G. Scott Davis, "The Structure and Function of the Virtues in the Moral Theology of St. Augustine," *Studia Ephemeridis "Augustinianum,"* no. 26 (Rome: Patristic Institute "Augustinianum," 1987), vol. 3, p. 12.

45. *Commentary on the Gospel of John*, 25.16.2. For an extensive treatment of Augustine's teaching on humility see Michael Cardinal Pellegrino, *Give What You Com-*

True humility is thus contrary to both pride and despair and this explains why it is so important. Those who claim to know everything and to have the highest prudence will never be able to see the true God because they think themselves to be divine.[46] Pride is the sickness that is part of all sin; humility is the one medicine that can cure it. In a picturesque analogy, Augustine describes the proud as being blocked from entering heaven through the "narrow gate" because they are too swollen, too filled with themselves. The swelling must be brought down and humility is the only medicine that can do that.[47] Like the tree, humans must fix their roots deep in the ground before they can lift their arms to touch the sky. In trying to reach the heights without a love growing from humility, humans challenge the wind without having any roots. The result is not surprising: they crash to the earth rather than grow towards heaven.[48]

Humility does not mean ceasing to value oneself. Even though the world may consider a person to be the refuse of creation, that person is still the best reflection of the Creator in the universe. Thus, there is nothing wrong in praising ourselves as long as we praise ourselves as the work of God, praising ourselves not because we are this or that kind of person but because we are God's creation, praising ourselves not because we have this or that gift but because God works through our gifts (whatever they are) to accomplish his purpose in the world.[49] The terrible mistake of the builders of Babel was that they thought that they could build a "highway to heaven" through their own power and skill. They did not realize that the only way to discover such an exalted path is from a humble perspective.[50]

The second virtue that is a precondition for the perfection of charity is faith. In *The City of God* and in his debate with Julian the Pelagian, Augustine was confronted with the question of whether true charity was pos-

---

mand: Augustine's Reflections on the Christian Life (New York: Catholic Book Publishing, 1975), pp. 37-70.

46. *Sermon 57*, 8. Augustine's advice to those who want to contact God is very simple: "Don't go seeking God either in caverns or on mountains. Have lowliness in your heart, and God will raise you up to as high an altitude as you could want. He will even come to you and be with you in your bedroom" (*Sermon 45*, 7).

47. See *Sermon 142*, 2-11.

48. *Sermon 114*, 4. Augustine suggests that this is the reason Christ chose fishermen rather than people of importance to be his first apostles. They were humble. They were not filled up with themselves. There was thus much room for the grace that God wished to pour into them (*Sermon 87*, 12).

49. *Commentary on Psalm 144*, 7.

50. *The City of God*, 16.4.

sible without the gift of faith in the person and teaching of Jesus Christ. Was the "noble pagan" a contradiction in terms? Augustine believed it was if by "noble" one meant one who could be saved and by "pagan" one meant the unbeliever. His argument was based on his interpretation of the Scripture teaching on what was necessary for salvation. He read there that the truly good action is one that flowed from love. This love has to be manifested in two ways. First of all, "what" is done (what later scholastics would call the "moral object") must be in accord with the order of the universe. Secondly, the "why" (the motive for acting) must be the love of God. Any action performed from a noble motive other than the love of God cannot be described as being "less good." At best it is "less evil" than an act done with a truly perverse intent. The so-called virtues of the "noble pagan" are in fact as far from true virtue as vices are from virtues. Augustine makes the point to Julian in the following words:

> You know that virtues must be distinguished from vices, not by their functions but by their ends. The function is *that* which is to be done; the end is *that for which* it is done. When a man does something in which he does not seem to sin, yet does not do it because of that for which he ought to do it, he is guilty of sinning. Whatever good is done by man, when it is not done for the purpose for which true wisdom commands it be done, it may seem good from what it accomplishes, but if the motivation is not right, it is a sin.[51]

A person who performs good acts will eventually be saved, not because of what is done but because in the doing God is loved above all. Such saving love is expressed by obeying the will of God out of love for God. It is possible that an unbeliever could recognize and obey some of the dictates of the moral law which is imprinted on the hearts of all humans, believer and unbeliever alike. But how can a person act out of love for the true God when that God is not explicitly recognized? Augustine concludes that it cannot be done:

51. *Against Julian the Heretic*, 4.3.19-21. Augustine illustrates his point through the examples of a flute player and a miser. The flute player may dedicate himself to a continent life but only out of ambition, reserving his strength so as to win a contest. The miser may appear on the surface to be very temperate in his use of material goods but only because he is driven by greed. One would hardly call either man virtuous even though what each was doing would be called virtue if done out of love of God. See *ibid.*, 4.3.18. Augustine sums up his position in *Sermon 142*, 13: "Great actions done without charity are useless."

Works cannot be counted as good before there is faith. Where there is no faith there is no good work. It is the intention that makes the work good and faith directs the intention.[52]

Virtues are genuine only when the one doing the apparently virtuous act believes in God. The works of unbelievers cannot be done with a truly good will because an unbelieving and ungodly will is not a good will. To live a truly good life, one that will lead to salvation, one must recognize the one true God.[53]

This is the message that Augustine received from his reading of Scripture. Belief in Christ is necessary. To say otherwise would lessen the importance of Christ's life and death in God's scheme of salvation. As Augustine tells Julian:

> Christ died in vain if one without faith in Christ could by reason or some other means come to true virtue, true justice, true wisdom. If the will of a human being can achieve justice on its own by simply acting in accord with nature, then Christ died in vain because anything that can bring about true justice must also give entry to the kingdom of God.[54]

The last phrase is crucial. If the truly just (good) act leads to the making of the truly good person, it must also lead that person to the kingdom of God. Christianity teaches that it is only by the death of Christ that such a goal becomes possible. Salvation results in seeing God face to face, but to achieve that lofty experience humans must be lifted up. They need not only the grace to perform acts in accord with the universe's order; they also need an uplifting grace, the grace of faith whereby they are able to believe even now in that hidden God whom they are destined to someday see.

The apparent virtues of the non-believer cannot have this uplifting effect. Although noble pagans may do "right," they cannot do so in a way which will raise them to heaven. Every true virtue must lead towards the proper end of human beings, citizenship in the city of God.[55] There is only one way to enter that kingdom; one must pass through the sheep-gate that is Christ. How can those get through that gate who do not even know where it is? It is true that noble pagans might commit no murder, theft, or adultery,

52. *Commentary on Psalm 31/2,* 4.
53. *The City of God,* 19.4.1; *Against Julian the Heretic,* 4.3.33; *83 Diverse Questions,* 35.2.
54. *Against Julian the Heretic,* 4.3.20.
55. *On the Spirit and the Letter,* 28.48; *The City of God,* 5.2.

that they might have only good desires, honor their parents, bear injuries patiently, even give all their goods to the poor. But since these acts are not done out of a love for the true God, they cannot be a means of salvation. Augustine interpreted the harsh rule of Paul in his letter to the Romans (14:23) as being unambiguous and universally true: "All that does not proceed from faith is sin."[56] Considering Augustine's conviction of the absolute need for faith as a basis for charity it is understandable that he was so passionate about preaching about faith in Christ and so intolerant of those who would preach against it and cause disunity. In his view, such disruptive activity was much worse than killing the body; it was killing the soul.[57]

56. *Against Two Letters of the Pelagians*, 3.5.14; 3.7.23. See also *Commentary on the Gospel of John*, 45.10.2. Augustine makes it clear that the excuse of the unbelievers that they have never heard of Christ is not a sufficient reason for them to claim salvation (*Commentary on the Gospel of John*, 89.3.1). He admits that there are many non-Christians who are living good lives but, unfortunately, they are running on a path that is distant from the one and only way to salvation, the way that leads through that Christ who clearly declared himself to be to be "the Way, the Truth, and the Life" (John 14:6). Though one must honor such noble pagans for their efforts, it would be better for them to "limp and stagger on the right way, than to walk strongly and vigorously off the way" (*Sermon 141*, 4). Augustine was led to this sad conclusion (and it saddened him too) by his narrow interpretation of the ways in which one could "go through Christ" to achieve salvation. For mature adults the one and only way was through explicit faith in Jesus Christ.

57. *On Order*, 2.10.29. It should be remembered that Augustine's emphasis on the necessity of faith for salvation occurred for the most part in the midst of his passionate response to the humanism of the pagans and Pelagians. He had no incentive, and indeed it would have been counterproductive to his argument, to develop a doctrine of an "implicit" saving faith in all those who through no fault of their own did not believe in Christianity but who lived lives of ordered love. However, in other parts of his writing (especially in his *Commentary on the Letter of John to the Parthians*), we find emphasis on the very scriptural texts which prompted later Christians to recognize that there were paths to salvation other than baptism, faith, and martyrdom, that indeed everyone who would be saved would only be saved through Jesus Christ, but that God was not limited in the ways in which that passage could be effected. Augustine himself seemed to leave that door open by suggesting that the spiritual heroes of the Old Testament received a private and personal revelation of Christ. An even larger opening for the working of God's redeeming will is suggested by a statement which he made in one of his earliest works and which was never retracted: "God's merciful assistance reaches out to all people in a more abundant fashion than we could ever imagine." This view is reflected in the current teaching of the Catholic Church: "Every man who is ignorant of the Gospel of Christ and of his Church, but seeks truth and does the will of God in accord with his understanding of it can be saved" (*Catechism of the Catholic Church* [Vatican City: Libreria Editrice Vaticana, 1994], no. 1260).

III. Concluding Thought: Hopeful Optimism

Vernon Bourke has described Augustine as a "cheerful personality" whose reputation has suffered from those who have overemphasized his sometimes pessimistic view of life. He writes:

> To my mind this looking forward to better things to come under divine providence is more characteristic of St. Augustine during most of his life than are the expressions of discouragement that sometimes appear in his anti-Pelagian works.[58]

Perhaps the source of that cheer was his conviction that the human thirst for happiness is a need created by a providential God who cares. It follows that perfect happiness is possible to achieve and that it can be achieved by doing good in this life with the help of the grace of God. Augustine believed that whatever ultimate success he would achieve as a human being was dependent more on God's will than his own, but for him this was a cause for joy. The experience of his own passionate nature and the turmoil in the lives of others convinced him that humans, left to their own devices, have a tendency to make horrendous decisions. Better by far to place human salvation in the hands of a loving, all-powerful God rather than depending on the strength of wounded human freedom.

58. Vernon Bourke, *Joy in Augustine's Ethics* (Villanova, PA: Villanova University Press, 1979), pp. 17-18.

CHAPTER 4

Friendship and Society

I. Introduction: The Human as Social Animal

It is a fact that humans spend most of their lives in relationships with others of their kind and these relationships involve more than just being in the same place at the same time, as when people are gathered together in a subway train, moving in the same direction but unknown and uncaring about each other. Human beings gather in all sorts of societies: families, nations, and innumerable purely voluntary associations. When one begins to develop a social philosophy examining the features of the various organizations in which humans find themselves, the first question that needs to be addressed is whether such "gatherings" are natural to the human species. Are they expressions of what is best about human beings or the result of what is worst? Are they true "goods," goods which lead to the perfection of the individuals, or are they signs of human weakness? Are they, in essence, goods which perfect or are they merely the lesser of two evils?

Certainly sociability is not characteristic of every species. Turtles, for example, seem to have no intense interaction beyond the passing contact between male and female necessary to insure the continuation of the tribe. Tiny turtles emerging on some desolate beach from their incubating holes show little or no concern for their fellows as they make their mad dash for survival in the distant ocean. It is true that they are not especially aggressive towards each other. They do not eat their young or each other, as some other more violent species seem to do. They are just socially indifferent, apparently, by their very nature.

Is the human a non-social animal of this kind? Some have said this, and much more. Hobbes described the "natural" human being as an animal driven by self-interest, suspicious of and (where possible) aggressive towards others of its kind.[1] Nietzsche maintained that anti-social attitudes are the best characteristics of a human being, not the worst. Only the weak seek others in society; the strong relish isolation, coming together only to accomplish a joint action furthering their individual will to power.[2] Society stands in the way of the purposes of the "*Superman*" and is best done away with to clear the ground for the truly superior human being to develop.

Of course many others have taken a quite opposite view on the human need for society. Those following in the traditions of Socrates, Plato, and Aristotle have generally agreed that society for humans is a good thing. Without going so far as Marx or Hegel, who suggest that the whole value of the individual comes from the collective, people such as Aquinas and Locke argue that the full perfection of the individual physically, intellectually, and spiritually depends on a healthy relationship to others.

This is the view taken by Augustine. The life of the truly wise human being is social both on earth and in heaven.[3] The sad paradox is that humans frequently do not behave very sociably. In the words of Augustine: "There is nothing so social by nature or so anti-social by sin as a human being."[4] But this sad truth does not belie the fact that humans *are* social; it only means that when they do not act sociably they are being untrue to their nature. We humans live in society because we are *driven* to so live. Our social groupings are expressions of what is best in us, not what is worst. Augustine was convinced that the imperfection in all human societies comes from a defect in individual human beings; it is not a sign that living in society is unnatural.

Augustine believed that our social nature is a true good. We are perfected as humans by our love for other humans. We are made happy when that love is returned, and the most important expression of such reciprocal love is the love of friendship. As he declares:

1. Thomas Hobbes, *Leviathan*, 13.
2. Friedreich Nietzsche, *The Genealogy of Morals*, 18.
3. "By the very laws of nature, a human seems to be forced into fellowship and, as far as possible, into peace with fellow humans" (*The City of God*, 19.12). "The life of virtue, that is the *best* life for a human now, is a life united to others in society. It is only through this drive to society that the ideal state for the human race, the city of God, becomes possible" (*ibid.*, 19.5). See also *The Good of Marriage*, 1.1; *Commentary on Psalm 54*, 9.
4. *The City of God*, 12.28.

In this world two things are essential: a healthy life and friendship. God created humans so that they might exist and live: this is life. But if they are not to remain solitary, there must be friendship.[5]

Friendship is the highest expression of a person's social nature; it is also the solid foundation for any society. The more a society becomes a society of friends, the more perfect it becomes as a society. But this is a hard task, certainly impossible for all (and perhaps any) society on earth. The difficulty becomes apparent once one begins to consider what is necessary in order to be a friend.

II. The Nature and Characteristics of Friendship[6]

A. The Need and Value of Friendship

Augustine frankly admitted his need for friends throughout his long life. As a middle-aged man he reflected upon those early days of his life when he was consumed with desire for fame, fortune, and sexual pleasure:

> Without friends even the happiness of the senses which I then possessed would have been impossible, no matter how great the abundance of carnal pleasures might be. I loved these friends for their own sakes and I felt that I was loved in return by them for my own sake.[7]

He remembered the feeling of emptiness and despair he felt when he lost a dear friend in death, a friend whom he was desperately trying to convert from Christianity to his Manichean views. He finally was able to overcome his sorrow through the company of others who came to be with him:

> The consolation of other friends did the most to repair the damage and give me strength after the death of my friend. The interchange between us captured my mind: conversations and joking, doing favors for each other, reading together good books, being foolish and being serious to-

---

5. *Sermon 299D*, 1.

6. For a comprehensive study of Augustine's views on friendship, showing its roots in classical literature and the modifications coming from his Christian faith, see Carolinne White, *Christian Friendship in the Fourth Century* (Cambridge: Cambridge University Press, 1992), pp. 185-217.

7. *Confessions*, 6.16.26.

gether, disagreeing without hatred almost as though I was debating with myself, sometimes falling into disagreement but thereby remembering in how many things we agreed, teaching and learning from each other, waiting impatiently for the absent to return and rejoicing when they did. These and so many other like signs coming from the hearts of friends are shown through their eyes and mouths and speech and a thousand little gestures. All of these expressions of friendship brought our hearts together like bundled kindling, making one out of many.[8]

The same depth of feeling for the loss of a love was reflected later on when, now as a believing Christian, he lost his mother Monica in death. Again he was paralyzed with grief, surviving only because of the Christian community of friends that surrounded him.[9] Augustine believed that the loss of a friend was one of the terrible burdens of this life and having a friend present was one of the best supports for enduring such burdens. As an old man, looking back over the joys and sorrows of his life, he mused: "What is there to console us in this human society so full of errors and trials except the truth and mutual love of true and good friends?"[10]

Love is the vital force which unites friends or seeks to unite them.[11] Augustine believed that we experience such friendly love from our earliest days. As he told his listeners one day, "The first thing a baby sees when opening its eyes are its parents, and life begins with their friendship."[12] If we are lucky, family friendship is a reality that lasts a lifetime and we spend our days searching for others with whom we can find the depths of trust and caring and security that we experienced within our own family. When we find it, a new splendid phase of our life opens up. Not only do we learn new things through the experiences of our new-found love; through love, the old accustomed patterns of our life suddenly become new. We see them now in a completely different light as we share them with our loved one for the first time.[13] If we can find a few such loves to be our friends in a lifetime we are truly gifted. Augustine describes their effect in a letter to his friend Proba:

---

8. *Confessions,* 4.8.13.
9. See *Confessions,* 9.11-13.
10. *The City of God,* 19.8.
11. *The Trinity,* 8.10.
12. *Sermon 9,* 7.
13. See *Catechizing the Uninstructed,* 1.12.17.

These good people seem to spread no small comfort about them even in this life. For, if poverty pinches, if grief saddens, if physical pain unnerves us, if exile darkens our lives, if any other misfortune fills us with foreboding, let good people be present to us, people who know how to "rejoice with those who rejoice" as well as to "weep with those who weep" (Rom. 12:15), people who are skilled in helpful words and banter. If such people are with us then in large measure our bitter trials become less bitter, the heavy burdens become lighter, perceived obstacles are faced and overcome.[14]

Augustine was convinced that human beings cannot enjoy the fullness of happiness in this life and in the next if they are by themselves, if there is no one they care about or anyone who cares for them. Friends can help us through our days of sadness; they make possible our days of joy. As Augustine observes: "It is hard to laugh when you are by yourself."[15]

B. The Characteristics of Friendship

Augustine agrees with Cicero that friendship involves both an intellectual and affective element. There is a substantial "thinking alike" on temporal and eternal affairs, on goals and values. But friendship does not stop with such bland consensus. There is also a true affection for the other and a benevolence (a "wishing well") directed to the other. Friendship is not just a meeting of minds. It is a union of hearts, a *concordia*.[16] Augustine believed that this impulse to be driven together as friends had its roots in our origin. We are not simply members of the same species; we are family united by common ancestry. We are bound together by blood.[17]

The harmony that comes from friendship rests on order: "an arrangement of equal and unequal things which gives to each its proper place."[18] This is necessary because no two humans are alike. Order makes a "oneness of heart" possible even between the greater and lesser. Not only can we love things much above us and much below us, we can also become

14. *Letter 130*, 2.4.
15. *Confessions*, 2.9.17.
16. *Against the Academics*, 3.6.13; *Letter 258*, 1.
17. *The Good of Marriage*, 1.1. See R. Canning, "Augustine on the Identity of the Neighbour," *Augustiniana*, vol. 36 (1986), nos. 3-4, pp. 182-83.
18. *The City of God*, 19.13.1.

friends to them. This is so because friendship does not depend on our status. Our common understanding of the universe, our common desire for the same goals, and our mutual care for each other can bridge many gaps.

Order (and, by extension, *friendship*) does not preclude subordination and it is good that it does not because every friendship implies some relationship of greater to lesser. If I differ from you by characteristic "x," in that respect I am either "better" or "worse" than you depending on whether "x" is a perfection or imperfection relative to being human. If this is so and if friendship depends on a proper ordering, our friendship will *demand* subordination of lesser to greater. There cannot be order where the lesser is *not subordinate* to the greater and without such order there can be no true friendship between beings that are different.[19] That friendship is an ordered concord suggests that Augustine did not demand (nor could he) that friends be exactly alike in all respects. Being somewhat different does not stand in the way of friendship as long as this is not a difference in hearts. This *oneness in heart* is the essential requirement for any peace in human relationships and is thereby the root of whatever happiness a human derives from life in society.

Concord between friends is more than simply agreeing with each other; it involves a *caring* for each other, a mutual desire that good should come to the other. It is based on an altruistic love, a love which values the good that is in the friend rather than the good that the friend can give.[20] Such love is a matter of the spirit rather than of the body and consequently if the love is strong, the friendship can even endure lengthy physical absence. As Augustine writes to two recently converted Donatist priests who came to visit him only to find him absent:

19. *Free Choice*, 1.8.18. That such subordination is not antithetical to friendship is suggested by Augustine's assertion that, "In heaven we shall be friends with our bodies" even though our bodies will still be subordinate to us as persons of soul and body (*Sermon 155*, 14; see *The City of God*, 22.30.1). Again, it seems likely that the God who walked with humans in Eden was a friend to them despite his infinite superiority. When humans rejected that friendship, that same God went so far as to become friends again with them in order to rescue them. As Augustine says: "When Christ was far away from us (as is an immortal and good Creator from mortal and sinful creatures), he bridged the gap by coming down to us as a neighbor" (*Sermon 171*, 3.3). See *Commentary on Psalm 118*, 12.5; Canning, *op. cit.*, p. 187. There is no question that God is always far superior to every human being, but despite this distance a *concordia*, a "unity of affection and knowledge," is possible between them. Indeed, such union is the goal of human life and the essential condition for eternal happiness.

20. *The Trinity*, 8.10.

Your coming to see me has given me joy, but do not let my absence cause you sadness. Even if my absence were as far as the most distant lands, we should still be united through Christ. If we lived together in the same house, we certainly would be said to be together. But how much more are we together, when we are joined together as members of the one body of Christ, the Church?[21]

Augustine's point is well taken. We humans can live in the same building but still be strangers to each other, not knowing or caring what is happening to the one next to us. On the other hand, when we truly love others and are joined to them by affection, they are never far from us in spirit even though they may be physically distant. Even death cannot stand in the way of our "oneness of heart." Sometimes we are closer to departed loved ones than to the strangers we live with in one common house.

At the same time Augustine freely admits the sadness that grips our hearts when our friends are physically distant from us. When we love another with the depths of our being, absence does not make our hearts grow fonder; it cannot because our love is already at its most extreme. Absence only makes tears flow more easily. Thus, Augustine writes to his absent friend Novatus that he suffers from ". . . pangs of longing which tear me apart because those who are fastened to me by the bond of the strongest and sweetest friendship are not here physically present to me."[22] To another friend he writes:

> My great and only joy is that I am unable to avoid delight when you are with me and I am unable to avoid sorrow when you are far away. My only consolation now comes from bravely accepting my sadness.[23]

Perhaps some of this romantic rhetoric can be written off as literary hyperbole, but there is little doubt that its source is the emptiness Augustine felt in his heart whenever he was separated from a loved one: his common-law wife sent back to Africa for the sake of his career, his mother and son separated from him by death, the numerous friends of the next forty years who were with him for a time but who then moved on to new ventures.

The essential element in friendship is a *concordia*, a *oneness in heart* manifested in some harmony in thinking and a warm caring for the

21. *Letter 142, 1.*
22. *Letter 84, 1.*
23. *Letter 27, 1.*

other. But for such "oneness in heart" to exist, friendship must possess a number of attributes. The first of these is *reciprocity*. We can love many things without any return of love, but to be a friend to someone demands that they also be friends to us. When love ceases to be reciprocal, friendship ceases.[24] To have such reciprocity demands some sort of *equality* in our love. We love the other as ourselves and neither more nor less than ourselves. The eyes of friendship neither look down nor look up to a friend; they look *at* the friend. Like a delicate rake caressing soft sand, the love of friendship has a leveling power, smoothing out the differences which come from our being unique individuals. We must love both ourselves and our friends in the same way, not as ends in themselves but as means whereby we can together each achieve our one eternal good: God himself.[25]

Characteristic of friendship is *benevolence*, wishing our friends well, but this will always be incomplete unless we wish above all for their salvation. Wishing all the best for our friends implies wishing them to be united to God and praying that this will happen. Just as we truly love ourselves only when we strive to be one with God, so our true love for neighbors is shown in our desire to bring them to God.[26] The purest friendship between humans occurs when we love the other because of the good we see in them, the good which is the reflection of the good God who is the exemplar for each of us. Augustine expresses it this way:

> He truly loves a friend who loves God in the friend, either because God is actually present in the friend or in order that God may be so present. This is true love. If we love another for another reason, we hate them more than love them.[27]

Augustine's point is that love cannot be present when we cease to respect our friend's place in creation. Only God can be enjoyed in and for himself. We must enjoy our human friends for the sake of God, "loving the love of God in them."[28] For the fullness of friendship to be realized, there

24. *The Trinity*, 9.4.6. See *Faith in Things That Are Not Seen*, 1.2.4; *Against Two Letters of the Pelagians*, 1.1.
25. *Christian Doctrine*, 1.22.20-1; *Soliloquies*, 1.8. See Marie McNamara, *Friends and Friendship for Saint Augustine* (Staten Island, NY: Alba House, 1964), p. 286.
26. *Christian Doctrine*, 1.27.28.
27. *Sermon 336*, 2.2.
28. *Against Faustus the Manichean*, 22.78.

must be some agreement on matters divine, a common conviction about the nature of God and about the necessity of seeking union with God.[29] As Augustine says: "To love the neighbor in the right way demands that we act towards them in such a way that they come to love God with all their heart, soul, and mind."[30] True friendship depends on God being the glue that binds friends together. This is the reason one can speak of the universal friendship of the heavenly city. We are joined together there because we are all "glued" to God and, through him, "glued" to each other. We lose ourselves in God, become drunk with his fullness, and thereby destroy the boundaries that separate one from another.[31]

A sad necessity of friendship in this life is that we must be always prepared to bear the burdens of our friends. In its ideal state friendship is the enjoyment of the other in good times — where we move toward others not because they need us but because we rejoice in them. As Augustine remarks, "Love is more precious when it issues from the richness of beneficence rather than from the burning arid desert of need."[32] This is so because a love based on the richness of our friends is not tempted to subordinate them because of their need for us. It simply rejoices in being with them because of the good that they contain, most especially the special presence and the image of God found in them alone. In this life, however, the ideal state where there are no needs among friends does not last very long, if it exists at all. Bad things happen and it is then that the love of friends is tested. As Augustine observes, the love that we shower on friends

---

29. *Letter 258*, 2.

30. *Christian Doctrine*, 1.22.21. In a letter to Marcianus, recently converted to Christianity but not yet baptized, and described by Augustine as "my oldest friend," Augustine writes — after quoting with approval Cicero's definition (*Laelius de Amicitia*, 6.20): "Thus it happens that there can be no full and true agreement about things human among friends who disagree about things divine, for it necessarily follows that he who despises things divine esteems things human otherwise than as he should and that whoever does not love Him who has made man has not learned to love man rightly" (*Letter 258*, 1-2). See J. McEvoy, "*Anima una et cor unum:* Friendship and Spiritual Unity in Augustine," *Recherches de Théologie ancienne et médiévale*, vol. 53 (1986), pp. 76-77.

31. *Confessions*, 4.47. See *Commentary on Psalm 62*, 17; *Commentary on Psalm 35*, 14. Another reason for basing our friendship with our human loved ones in Christ is that it is only in Christ that our friendship can be eternal. Even as members of the city of God in heaven we remain temporal, contingent beings. Our only security is still in that one who is eternal and who supports our contingent existence through his loving power. See *Against Two Letters of the Pelagians*, 1.1.

32. *Catechizing the Uninstructed*, 1.4.7.

in good times is *proven* in bad times.[33] Friends may be delightfully sunny and breezy in good times but if they go away at the first threat of a storm, they are not true friends at all.

Accepting the moments of strength and weakness that we share with our friends is an aspect of another essential quality of friendship. Friendship must be based on *truth*. Two human beings cannot be brought together as friends without some agreement about the goods they want, the goals that they have in common. Their love can overcome a difference of opinion on minor issues but in important things, the nature of reality, the demands of love, obligations towards each other, they must be bound together by the truth of the matter.[34] At very least their friendship must have some understanding of the *reality* of the *person* who is the other. There is no such thing as anonymous friendship. If I do not know the reality that is my friends, if they do not know the real me, there is the danger that the friendship is a fantasy based on a fiction. Friendship cannot be established on ignorance or error. As Augustine says: "A person must be a friend of truth before they can be a friend to any human being."[35]

To achieve this mutual truth about each other there must be *frankness,* a frankness which enables us to dare to pour out all of our plans and gives us the freedom to tell our friends what bothers us about them.[36] Such frankness is necessarily imperfect in this life. I may be able to experience the physical presence of my friends but I cannot see that inner core of spirit where their friendship has its home.[37] This is not strange. We do not even know ourselves too well, much less others. Each individual is a well of darkness surrounded by thick walls and these walls cannot be pierced completely by love nor can they be scaled by words. In speaking about his lifelong friend Alypius, Augustine observes:

33. *Faith in Things That Are Not Seen,* 1.1.3. Augustine uses an interesting analogy to make his point. Referring to an experience that was no doubt known well by his North African readers, he points out that when a herd of deer crosses a rushing stream, each one will take its turn at the head of the pack to break the force of the water for the others. When finally exhausted, the leader then goes back to the rear where it can benefit from the protection of the others. So too for humans, each one is sometimes called to bear the burden for others, but there will also be a time when he or she needs the support of those others. See *83 Diverse Questions,* 71.1.

34. *83 Diverse Questions,* 31.3. See *Faith in Things That Are Not Seen,* 2.4.

35. *Letter 155,* 1.1.

36. *83 Diverse Questions,* 71.6. See *Letter 82,* 36; *Sermon 87,* 12.15. *Commentary on the Letter of John to the Parthians,* 7.11.

37. See *Confessions,* 10.5.7.

Since I do not know myself, what shame can I possibly inflict on a friend when I say he is unknown to me, especially when . . . as I believe . . . he himself does not know himself?[38]

He makes a similar point writing to his somewhat abrasive friend, Jerome:

How unreliable is knowledge based on sentiments of present friends when there is no foreknowledge of what they shall be in the future. But why grieve over this; I don't even know my own future.[39]

In his letter to the gentle and saintly Proba, he returns to the same theme:

Nothing is friendly to us without friends. But where on earth is such a one to be found, one whose mind and character can give such a security? We don't even know where we shall be tomorrow, much less the where-abouts of someone else who is now our friend.[40]

Thinking about the difficulty in distinguishing friend from foe and in even understanding those who are true friends, Augustine cries out almost in despair:

How confused it all is! One who seems to be an enemy turns out to be a friend and those whom we thought our good friends in fact are our worst enemies.[41]

Because the mystery that is present in all humans and especially in that "other" that we meet for the first time, we must be cautious about too

---

38. *Soliloquies*, 1.3.8. Other passages that make the same point about the difficulty in truly getting to know ourselves and others include the following: "In this journey of our earthly life, each one carries his own heart, and each heart is closed to every other" (*Commentary on Psalm 55*, 9). "Humans can speak. They can be seen to move their limbs and their words can be heard. But who can penetrate their thoughts; who can see their heart?" (*Commentary on Psalm 16*, 13). Speaking about the difficulties in teaching and learning, Augustine remarks: "Not even love itself is powerful enough to tear apart that massive fleshy darkness and touch that eternal light from which even passing things receive their sparkle" (*Catechizing the Uninstructed*, 1.2.4). "I do not know what you are thinking and you do not know what I am thinking. Only our own spirit (and the Holy Spirit of God) is witness to our thoughts, and indeed God knows things about us that even we do not know about ourselves" (*Commentary on the Gospel of John*, 32.7.5).

39. *Letter 73*, 3.6.

40. *Letter 130*, 2.4. See Carolinne White, *op. cit.*, p. 205.

41. *Sermon 49*, 4.4.

quickly judging strangers to be friend or foe. But at the same time we must not be overly wary, refusing to accept anyone as a friend until they prove themselves friendly to us beyond a shadow of a doubt. The paradox is that we can never be completely sure of the heart of another, but the only way truly to know another is by opening our heart to them as a friend.[42]

Since we cannot know what is going on inside others, friendship must be based on *trust*. Only in heaven will we have perfect knowledge of others. Only there will we see the thoughts of others which now only God can see. Only there will no one seek to conceal his or her thoughts because only there will there be no evil thoughts.[43] Just now we must make do, knowing as best we can and trusting for the rest, realizing that our inability to communicate perfectly is no one's fault. In order to have friends we must first believe in them and in order to keep friends we must continue to trust them. We must take chances on others and friendship is too important to human life not to take such chances. It is bad enough to betray a trust, but it is worse still to refuse ever to trust again. In Augustine's view such caution, far from being prudent, is hateful.[44]

It is a fact that true friendship is rare. There are many obstacles to the trust that is needed, perhaps the most pervasive being our fascination with earthly things. Even though we may be believing Christians, we still spend much of our time fighting about things of earth, "wishing to be earthy."[45] This difficulty in being open to and trusting others led Augustine to the conclusion that in this life one can achieve perfect friendship only with the help of God. Friendship is a God-given gift, realized only when humans are glued together by the charity poured into their hearts by the Holy Spirit.[46]

Despite our troubles in having even one good friend, Augustine forbids limiting our friendship to a select few. Our openness to friendship

---

42. "A man is known only through friendship" (*83 Diverse Questions*, 71.5). "If someone wishes to know the will of a person who is not a friend, everyone would scoff at his impudence and foolishness" (*Commentary on Genesis against the Manicheans*, 1.2.4).

43. *Sermon 243*, 5. See *Sermon 306*, 9.

44. *Faith in Things That Are Not Seen*, 2.4. See *83 Diverse Questions*, 71.6.

45. *Sermon 359*, 1-2.

46. *Confessions*, 4.4.7. McNamara comments: "For him, the only true friendship is sent by God to those who love each other in Him. This is the heart of Augustine's conception of friendship and his great innovation. It is God alone who can join two persons to each other. In other words friendship is beyond the scope of human control" (Marie McNamara, *op. cit.*, pp. 220-21).

must be universal, including all those to whom our love is due. Since love is due all members of the human race, we must be prepared to be friends with anyone who shares our common nature.[47] There are obvious practical problems in achieving such breadth. We can love all (desiring that good that is present in every human) but can we realistically be friends with all humans? What we love is somewhat within our power to control, but we cannot "make" friends. Love does not depend on similarity or reciprocity or intimate knowledge of the other or a common love of God, or a trust that supports a mutual "baring of soul." Friendship does.

Augustine must have realized this practical impossibility, and therefore his contention that friendship must be universal can mean only something like the following. Although we cannot actually be friends with everyone just now, we can still desire such universality as a goal and work towards it. Though the reality of friendship with all will occur only in heaven when we will be able to see the fullness of the presence of God in ourselves and every other human, the desire for this and the effort to extend it as far as possible can begin here. We will not meet every human in a lifetime, but we can strive to make every human we meet a friend. We can avoid rejecting out of hand anyone who offers to be our friend. At very least we can deem them worthy of our friendship and try to bring them to a point where mutual, truthful, frank, and trusting friendship is possible.[48] We must love all humans, some because they are friends, others in order that they might become friends. Indeed, Augustine goes so far as to claim that when an enemy is loved in this fashion, fellowship has already begun. We love them as friends not because they are our friends just now; rather it is because that is what we hope they someday shall be.[49]

We must love all humans and we are meant to be friends with all hu-

---

47. "It [friendship] must include all those to whom love and affection are due. It may go out more readily to some, more slowly to others, but it must reach even to our enemies for whom we are commanded to pray. The conclusion is simply this: there is no member of the human species to whom love is not due, either because they return our love or at least because we are united to them through our common nature as human beings" (*Letter 130*, 13).

48. *83 Diverse Questions*, 71.6. Augustine goes on to say that we should not be dismayed by the apparent bad qualities of others nor should we be overawed by their good qualities. We should be prepared to reach out in friendship to those who perhaps do not dare to approach us because of our supposedly "lofty" position. The strong must put up with the weak and not take themselves too seriously. The weak must not think too highly of the strong nor think too little of themselves.

49. *Commentary on the Letter of John to the Parthians*, 1.9; 8.10.

mans and we can have the beginnings of this friendship even with those who are quite different if we share a common purpose, if there is a *concordia* regarding goals. In fact, if two humans share the common purpose of serving God and loving God, there is already present a solid foundation for the fullness of friendship.[50] All other reasons for friendships (being of the same age, experience, interests, and so forth) are not as important as the indwelling of the Holy Spirit in each. What a friend loves in a friend is the divine in them. And this presence of the divine is given by God to every human who tries to love. In the words of Christ, "Where two or three are gathered together in my name, there am I in the midst of them." (Matt 18:20) This becoming one with each other in Christ will only be realized in heaven but it is certainly a worthwhile goal for humans still living on earth. Working for it before death insures its realization after death.[51]

III. Authority in a Society of Friends

Augustine's dream for the human race was that we would be related to each other as friends in every society that we form. The problem is that in the various societies we form on earth there always seems to be an authority, one who is set apart and given the power to rule the others. In the city of God existing in heaven there will of course be the ultimate divine authority, God, ruling all in love. But when humans take up a position of authority in earthly societies, it seems that their exalted position contradicts the equality that is the core of a friendly relationship. We can look up to or bow down to authority, but how can we truly be friends with them? How can you be a friend to someone who has the power to make decisions that *must* be followed? If authority stands in the way of friendship, then the effort to make society a society of friends is a useless task. Augustine did not believe that authority and friendship were mutually exclusive and it was possible, at least in some degree, to make every society based on friendship. In order to explore his contention it will be helpful to begin by saying something about the nature of society and the various functions performed by authority in society.

A useful description of *society* is that it is a moral union of two or more persons striving for a common good by cooperative activity. It is a

50. *Ibid.,* 6.10.
51. *Ibid.,* 10.3.

stable union of rational, free beings and is based on a choice to work together for a common purpose. In fact every society has in place some system which distinguishes the leaders from those led, the ruler from those ruled. The basis for the distinction is the existence of authority. It is certainly possible (but by no means assured) that members of a society will arrive at an unforced consensus on a common goal and a common means to achieve it, but it seems highly unlikely that this will happen all the time and perhaps will happen none of the time if the society is large and complex. When agreement does not follow discussion, in order for the society to move forward there will be a need for someone to take charge, someone who has the power to say, "This is the goal and this is the way in which we shall achieve it." But is such authority necessary in every society? Is the need for authority based on a defect in the members of a society, or is it rooted in the very nature of all societies?

The analysis by Yves Simon is a helpful tool in exploring such questions. He defines authority as an active power of a person which is exercised through a command and is to be taken as a rule of conduct by the freewill of another.[52] The following points seem implied in this definition.

1. Authority can reside only in rational beings since the exercise of authority involves deliberation and choice.
2. Authority is exercised through a command, a categorical imperative. It depends only on the will of the legitimate authority. It does not merely "recommend" a course of action. It forcefully "directs" action.
3. Authority may use persuasion or coercion to get the subject to follow the direction. Of course it is also possible that neither of these is necessary. Those subject to authority may accept and follow the command freely as soon as it is understood.
4. Authority and its exercise through command do not destroy the freedom of the individual. If autonomy means only that individuals take responsibility for their action, then there is no contradiction in asserting both that each person is free and that there is an authoritative command. The action of authority does not determine action; it guides it. To preserve freedom it is enough that the individual be able

---

52. Yves Simon, *The Nature and Functions of Authority* (Milwaukee: Marquette University Press, 1940), p. 7. My discussion of authority depends heavily on this work and other works of Simon contained in the bibliography.

to obey or disobey commands. It is not necessary to be free of all commands.

5. Authority implies some type of subordination of subject to superior. Otherwise it is difficult to justify the claim that some persons in a society can impose their will on the others. It would seem that if I can impose my will on you so that I can "command" you to "do x," then in that "x" aspect of your life, at least, you must be subordinate to me.

Simon identifies two ways in which such subordination can come about. Subordination that is *de facto* flows from the nature of things, as in the authority of parent over the young child. In the parent/child relationship the authority is based on two facts: (1) the act of generation or adoption whereby this adult acquires responsibility for this child; (2) the inability of the child to care for itself. This second fact suggests that the full exercise of parental authority over child (telling them what to eat, when to go to bed, and so forth) will not be forever. It will cease as soon as the dependence ceases. Parents of adult offspring may have a continuing right to their love and respect but they have no longer any right to impose their will on their children. Even in the case of the child who is a minor, the authority of the parent is limited. It does not cover every aspect of the child's life. Parents have no authority to decide whom their children will marry, what career they will pursue, what they will believe in.[53]

The second type of subordination is *de jure,* established by a quasi-contract between the ruler and ruled. The authority of the ruler to demand certain acts from the subjects is freely given by the subjects themselves. The rule of leaders in such voluntary societies as fraternities and sororities would be an example of such *de jure* authority. Once individuals form such a voluntary society they bind themselves to the rules and methods of governance agreed to by the group. As individuals they cannot change those rules. If they become disenchanted, they have only one legitimate option: to exercise their freedom and leave the group.

The first form of subordination implies an inequality that is in the *nature of things.* The second is a form of subordination created by people who are *equal by nature* but who have chosen to make themselves subordi-

---

53. Augustine maintained that the command of every lawful authority was based on the authority of God himself. Thus he says that "A father's word must be listened to as God's word" (*Commentary on Psalm 70,* 1.2). This view seems consistent with his belief that the only subordination of humans rooted in the nature of things was that of humans as created beings subordinate to their Creator.

nate for the sake of a goal which they themselves have determined. The resolution of the question about conflict between friendship and authority, whether there can ever be a true society of friends, depends on whether either or both of these forms of subordination clash with the equality that is present in any true friendship. Of course the problem is solved if "authority" (and the subordination implied) is not a necessary element in society, if it is possible to have a complex society in which truly "everyone is free" and "no one is in charge." But is this possible?

Here again Simon's analysis is helpful. He identifies two general functions of authority in society.[54] At times authority performs a *substitutional* function when it substitutes for some deficiency present in the one that is ruled. But also authority in society has certain *essential* functions which do not imply that the subjects ruled have some defect in knowledge or ability to make decisions that would make their direction by others necessary. Simon lists various instances of these two functions.

There is the *substitutional* function exercised by authority in the order of theoretical truth: for example, the authority of teacher over pupil. This function presupposes a lack of knowledge in the pupil, a lack which the teacher overcomes by instruction.

There is the *substitutional* function exercised by authority in guiding immature and/or will-defective individuals towards their proper good. This is an exercise of quasi-parental authority over those who do not have the sense or do not have the inclination to choose "well" on their own. Thus a parent exercises authority over a minor child who as yet is not able to make sensible decisions about everyday necessities: what to eat, when to go to sleep, where to play, and so forth. Other examples are the medical professional's exercise of authority over an institutionalized severely retarded adult and the civil ruler's exercise of authority over criminals who perversely choose to break the laws of the society.

There is the *substitutional* function exercised by authority in the unification of action towards the common good when the means to the common good is in fact uniquely determined: that is, there is only one way to achieve the common goal. If all humans were perfect in intellect and will they would automatically see that there is only one way to the goal and would freely choose that way. But in a society of imperfect humans, authority must sometimes substitute for a stubborn lack of agreement and

54. See Yves Simon, *Philosophy of Democratic Government* (Chicago: University of Chicago Press, 1951), p. 61.

an unreasonable unwillingness to choose the one and only way to the goal to which all have committed themselves.

There is the *essential* function exercised by authority in the unification of action for the common good when the means to the common good is not uniquely determined. Simon argues that this is a common phenomenon in complex societies. Even if there is a consensus in a state that all should work for prosperity and peace, it is unlikely that there will be common agreement on the best way to reach this goal. There usually are a multitude of ways of proceeding and all of them are possible. Even if all citizens had the ability to understand the situation and were all gifted with the prudence that moved them to choose the best way to achieve the common good, they would still disagree precisely because there is no one best way. All would look at the problem from their own particular point of view, formed by their peculiar personality and history. The fact that I cannot see a problem as you see it does not imply that there is anything wrong with either of us. It just means that we are different persons. Such a diversity suggests that there will always be a difference of opinion on the way to achieve the goal of society. Even in the best society there is a natural basis for divergence in prudential choice about means. Thus, when authority steps in to say "We shall go this way!" this is an essential function demanded in any society where agreement cannot be reached. It does not imply a deficiency in the members of the society. It simply reflects that the society is made up of different, free, rational beings who are likely to see a complex problem in different ways. I suspect that even Adam and Eve might have disagreed about the best place to go on vacation from paradise.

Finally there is what Simon calls the *most essential* function of authority in willing the common good *materially* considered: that is, the common good viewed "as a whole." We will the common good *formally* when we will a particular good which serves to foster the common good. Simon explains the difference through the example of an efficient and productive school. In such a school a teacher of Latin wills the success of the whole school program by willing to teach Latin as perfectly as possible. The "whole" concentration of the teacher is on this particular subject and by that unswerving focus the individual contributes to the good of the school. The common good is willed materially when it is willed independently of any particular good. Thus the principal of the school wills the good of the whole school apart from any special interest in any special subject or aspect of the school. The Latin teacher wills the common good in and through a particular viewpoint of the common good, the common good seen through the eyes of a Latin teacher. The principal wills the common good as a whole, taking into account all aspects of that good. Simon argues that a society would not be well served if all its members were concerned about the *whole*. It is better that they perfect their own little contribution to that good and leave concern for the totality to those who govern the whole and whose primary function is to take the universal viewpoint. The common good is furthered better by all individuals dedicating themselves to one facet, one occupation in a society. In so doing they are still willing the common good but only formally, by willing to do their particular job as perfectly as possible. If each one had to will the common good materially the result would be mediocrity. The individual functions would not be performed with the attention that would insure their perfection. A school will not prosper if the faculty is more concerned about governance than about teaching the individual disciplines. Neither is it well-served by administrators whose interest and attention is directed at only one aspect of the school. The ideal in any society is to have a band of experts being guided to one end by one who is a non-expert in their fields but who has skill in directing the efforts of a diverse group of experts towards a common goal. As Simon writes:

> No part of the land will be thoroughly tilled unless each laborer has a distinct field to plow. And no function will be exercised with thoroughness unless my function (say, that of teaching Latin) is distinct from any other function and is thereby particularized. But if my function is a particular one, if, in other words, the good with which I am concerned is but a particular aspect of the common good, then it is necessary that there be above me, a person or a group of persons properly concerned, not only formally but also materially, with the whole of the common good.[55]

IV. Augustine and the Friendly Society

Augustine agrees with Cicero that some subordination of one to another is natural. It is just and proper that the soul rule the body, that God rule hu-

---

55. *Ibid.*, p. 47. Aquinas seems to be saying the same thing as Simon when he observes that no society can endure unless it possesses some principal person or group whose main duty is to provide for the common good. See *On the Rule of Princes*, 1.1.

mans, and that the civil ruler have sovereignty over a community when such authority serves the good of the community.[56] Unnatural subordination among humans occurs when the ruler seeks to make everyone and everything serve himself, denying the natural equality among humans and pretending to be God Almighty.[57] Augustine maintains that when the subordination of one human to another occurs within the context of friendship, its harshness is softened. In its exercise it respects the equality and dignity and goodness of the other that is demanded by the social bond. Although true authority is present, an authority that assumes some sort of superior/inferior relationship, there is no denigration of the subject. As Augustine observes:

> Where charity is not present, the command of the authority is bitter. But where charity exists, the one who commands does so with sweetness and the charity makes the very work to be almost no work at all for the one who is commanded, even though in truth the subject is bound to some task.[58]

We are called to love each other as friends not in order to consume each other, losing our identity in our attachment, but in order to enjoy each other as separate but joined individuals. When some inequality is present, for example between teacher and pupil, the rule of the superior should be a loving rule. Though there is a real inequality in knowledge, friendship must flow from the equality and goodness shared by all members of the human race because of being equally images of God. The authority that is exercised in the context of such leveling love seeks to remedy the accidental inequality of the inferior and therefore is more a service to the ruled than a privilege of the ruler. Augustine believed that the teacher who wishes that the student remain always as a learner and never achieve equality in knowledge is not truly a teacher. A parent who wishes that a child never become mature is not truly a parent. A king

56. *The City of God*, 19.21. Speaking about the family specifically, Augustine lays down a rule which he clearly believed was applicable to any society. He writes: "In the home of the religious person, those who command serve those whom they appear to rule. They rule out of concern and compassion for those for whom they must care" (*ibid.*, 19.14).

57. *Ibid.*, 19.12.

58. *Commentary on the Letter of John to the Parthians*, 9.1. Elsewhere Augustine writes: "Whatever is burdensome in a command is made light to one who loves" (*Commentary on Psalm 67*, 18).

who relishes sovereignty for the joy of being in charge is not worthy of the name "king."[59]

But is there not a conflict between authority and friendship at least in those situations where the exercise of authority is substitutional? For example, can a parent treat a child as a friend without ceasing to be a good parent? Does trying to be "pals" conflict with being a parent? Augustine would likely respond in the following way. First, friendship in this life will always be imperfect. It will be a matter of degree since in fact it will depend on conditions (e.g., reciprocity, frankness/truth, equality) which will be verified only "more or less" in any relationship. Only in heaven will these conditions be realized perfectly. Only then will there be perfect frankness/ truth between humans and perfect reciprocity of love in the fullness of God's presence perceived to be present in the other.

Secondly, if other persons (for example, children) are in fact dependent, it would be an unfriendly act on the part of the parent to treat them as if they were not. The truth of friendship demands that we recognize in the friend that which is equal to oneself and that which is unequal. A teacher must recognize the ignorance (and perhaps lack of motivation) in students in order to "love them so that they might become friends." Parents must recognize that while their children are equal to them in being *imago dei,* they nevertheless need a lot of help if they are to reach a stage where they can stand on their own two feet in this life and know how to go successfully into the next. The burden of being a parent is precisely the obligation to recognize the inequality of children and to help them to mature toward equality. Similarly, it is the duty of the sovereign in a state to recognize the fact that a complex community of free beings is not likely to reach consensus on many things on their own. Nor is it likely, in a society made up of somewhat cracked citizens, that everyone will always joyously obey every law promoting the common good. Sooner or later the sovereign will need to intervene to remedy the discord. Someone *must* make a decision if the common good is to be achieved and it would be a severe disservice to the community for the ruler to refuse to exercise that authority. In

---

59. Augustine writes: "As long as he, the student, is slow, he learns from you. You seem to be the superior, because you are the teacher; he the inferior, because he is the learner. If you do not wish him to be your equal, you wish to have him always a learner. But if you wish to have him always a learner, you will be an envious teacher. And if you are an envious teacher, how can you be described as a teacher at all?" (*Commentary on the Letter of John to the Parthians,* 8.8.). For Augustine's description of the ideal civil ruler see *City of God,* 5.24.

any society the friendly love of the superior must sometimes be expressed through command; in such a society the friendly love of the subjects is found in their obedience out of love to a directive that is for the good of the community but which here and now is not their preference.

How Augustine's ideal of a society being a community of friends applies to the family and the state will be addressed in the chapters that follow. As we shall see, he considers both what is ideal and also what is unfortunately too often real in the efforts of humans to get along in these two premier societies. In both family and state, one may dream of the heaven of Jerusalem only to find that day by day life is filled with the turmoil of Babylon.

CHAPTER 5

The Family: A Society of Friends

I. Introduction

A. Influences on Augustine's Teaching

Augustine's views on marriage and the family have both a practical and theoretical foundation. The theoretical foundation came from the teachings that he found in the pages of the Bible, especially in the writings of St. Paul. The points that he chose to emphasize from such texts were dictated by practical considerations. Included in the latter were the needs of the people he served in Hippo and the specific theological opponents he faced from time to time. Thus, in his earlier writings he had to deal with the contention of the Manicheans that marriage and intercourse were by their very nature expressions of an evil principle rampant in the world. Later, his opponents were the Pelagians who argued that marriage as it exists now is not radically different from the way it was in the innocence of Eden. Against the Manicheans he stressed the goodness of marriage and procreation; against the Pelagians he pointed out the inability of humans in their present wounded condition to live chastely in marriage without the grace of God.

Augustine's thinking about marriage and the family was also influenced by his experience of his own family and the ordinary families of his day, families that typically included a husband and wife, children, and a large extended family of grandparents and in-laws, uncles and aunts, nephews and nieces, and cousins of various degrees of consanguinity. In many households "family" also embraced servants, who could be freemen or slaves. The *pater familiae*, the one who was the leader of the group, had responsibilities towards all of these and was owed respect from each and every one. Thus, when Augustine became the leader in his own extended family and established himself in a good position at the Imperial Court in Milan, it was not unexpected that eventually he would be joined by his common-law wife, his son, his widowed mother, his older brother, and assorted relatives who traveled from North Africa to join him.

When Augustine was a young boy, his family was typical of the lower middle class family of Tagaste. His father, Patricius, was a minor bureaucrat holding a position of some respect but little money in the civil service of his town. A hard-working, mostly good-natured pagan, he left the religious training of his children to their mother. At the same time he was dedicated to making provision for their success in life, working tirelessly to scrape together the funds necessary to insure a good education for them. Both Augustine and his brother Navigius were provided with funds necessary for an education that could be the door to a noble profession. Augustine's sister (given the name Perpetua by tradition) was given a dowry sufficient to insure a respectable marriage. Patricius was eventually baptized a Christian but during his days as a pagan he apparently was not especially faithful to his wife. At home he was sometimes overcome with rage and stopped short of beating his wife only because of her skill in dealing with him when he was in the throes of his passion.

Augustine's mother, Monica, was a strong and clever woman. As a young wife she was able to survive the suspicions of a dominating live-in mother-in-law, the gossip of vindictive servants, the temper of her husband, and the intellectual and sometimes immoral roaming of her increasingly wayward son. She had the persevering power to endure and a patience that enabled her to bide her time through her husband's occasional outbursts and her son's seemingly permanent flight from Christianity. She was practical and accepted life as it was dealt to her. She did not reject her son when he strayed but at the same time she made it clear that she would not put up with him when, as a proud born-again Manichean, he knocked on her door expecting to be met with open arms and free room and board. She remained ambitious for him and did all she could to further both his earthly career and his spiritual development. She prayed for him constantly, but on a more mundane level she was not above advising him in his adolescence to dabble in sex if he must but at least to avoid a marriage that could hurt his career (which Augustine immediately did, entering into a "common-law" marriage with a woman much below his station in life). Later on it was probably with the blessing of Monica that he sent away this woman who had been faithful to him for eleven years and who had given him a son. The reason for her dismissal was far from noble. She stood in the way of a marriage of convenience to a girl of noble rank, a union that would promote Augustine's career at the imperial court.

Augustine's knowledge of husband-wife relations came from watching Monica and Patricius, from his personal experience with the good woman who was the mother of his son, and from his innumerable contacts with the good and bad marriages of the people he served as pastor for forty years. His understanding of parent-child relationships included both his experiences with his mother and father and with his own son Adeodatus. He understood the position of servants in his family when he was a child and was aware of the problems of slavery and servitude as they existed generally in the North Africa of his day. As a consequence, when he came to write about the family, he spoke not only about what the ideal family should be, but also about how one could live and improve the less than perfect families that actually existed. His dream for every family was that each one somehow and someday would become a society of friends.

B. The Forms of Society

A society is something more than a group of people who move in the same direction. A true society is a group whose members not only choose their direction but also choose to be a member of *this particular group* moving in the chosen direction. They are related to each other in a much more formal way than, for example, the riders on a train going from one city to another. Though riders on a moving train are voluntarily pursuing a common goal through common means, they do not constitute a society because their only relationship with each other is physical, not formal. Family members making the same trip by the same means have something more, an intimate relationship to each other. They are not simply fellow-travelers; they are a traveling society.

Every society is in some sense voluntary, the creation of a free-will decision on the part of its members. Some (like a bridge-club) are *completely voluntary*, the only force driving the members together is a free, somewhat arbitrary, choice. Some societies seem to have deeper roots than just free choice. These are *natural* societies. Saying that a particular society is "natural" can mean two things. A society may be said to be natural in that it is demanded for the fulfillment and for the perfection of human nature. The society is as much a natural expression of human nature as is friendship. The society called the "city of God" by Augustine is such a natural society. It fulfills a natural need in a human being. It is the one and only place where people can achieve the full perfection of their humanity. Its opposite society, the earthly city, fills no such natural need. Indeed, it is antithetical to human needs and this is the reason for the sufferings it causes. Its members are forever out of place, out of that one place where they can be eternally happy. Though the absence of love present among the damned makes it questionable whether they can form any sort of society, it is obvious that if a society exists in hell, it cannot be natural. It is not the natural fruit of human nature; it only becomes necessary as a reaction to the sin of rational beings (angels and humans) who have turned away from God.

The first question addressed in this chapter is whether Augustine believed that marriage and the family are the natural fruit of human nature or social constructs (like slavery) made necessary by human sinfulness. Is the family a society that perfects human nature or is it a society that exemplifies that nature's imperfection?

II. Augustine's Views on Marriage and the Family

A. The Nature and Goods of Marriage

Augustine believed that one of the strongest arguments for marriage and family being a truly good institution is that it was created by God himself at the beginning of the human race.[1] The family existed before any sin existed and, more importantly, it existed because God wanted it to exist. He draws a further argument from the New Testament story of the wedding feast at Cana. The active participation of the Incarnate God in the celebration suggests that such a festive event is one that not only expresses the best of humanity but was even enjoyed by God himself.[2]

---

1. The following texts reflect Augustine's view that marriage is a divine institution: *The Good of Marriage*, 1.1; *The City of God*, 14.22; *Commentary on the Gospel of John*, 10.2.2; *Marriage and Concupiscence*, 1.1; *Against Two Letters of the Pelagians*, 1.5.

2. See *The Good of Marriage*, 3.3; *Commentary on the Gospel of John*, 9.2.

The goodness of marriage and the family is confirmed by the good things it accomplishes even now in humanity's wounded condition. Augustine lists the following:

1. *Proles:* the procreation of children;
2. *Fides:* the fidelity of the spouses to each other;
3. *Sacramentum:* an element of sacredness reflected in the indissoluble commitment of husband and wife to each other until death.

In addition to these primary goods there is also the secondary good of providing a remedy for the somewhat wild sexual desires troubling humans since their fall from grace. Channeling this desire towards procreation makes something creative out of something that is often destructive. Moreover the fidelity and permanence of the marriage bond establishes a strong foundation for a true society of friends, human beings united in mutual care for each other.[3]

Although the institution of marriage and the family accomplishes these many good things, it was primarily instituted to continue and increase the human race, to produce *proles,* offspring. Augustine believed that this increase was made necessary because of angelic sin. God had determined the number of free creatures who would be future citizens of the city of God. When Satan and his followers rejected their invitation, this left many spaces vacant. Since in God's plan there would be no new creation of angels, the vacancies in the heavenly city could only be filled by the other type of created free beings: human beings. Since a great number of angels had rejected God's invitation, it would take more humans than the two first formed by God to fill up the quota. Propagation of the species was therefore necessary. Augustine also suggests a second reason for human procreation. When humans sinned, God determined that their salvation would be accomplished by the Word becoming flesh and redeeming humankind by his death. But this would not happen right away. Therefore a number of generations of humans were necessary in order to establish the human family of the Savior who was also the Son of God.[4]

3. Augustine speaks of the goods of marriage in various places, sometimes using slightly different words. For example, *The Good of Marriage,* 24.32; *Marriage and Concupiscence,* 1.11.13; *Holy Virginity,* 12.12; *A Literal Commentary on Genesis,* 9.7.12; *The Good of Widowhood,* 4.5; *The Grace of Christ and Original Sin,* 34.39.

4. Augustine believed that in his day the time had come for humans to think seriously about remaining continent in their marriage for the sake of the kingdom —

Humans had nothing to do with the creation of the first two humans. God was the active agent in the formation of body and soul of Adam and Eve. However, God wanted humans to participate actively in the continuation of the race. In his plan, the souls of future generations would come from him, but the formation of the human bodies would be accomplished through an intimate physical joining of male and female. Each one would make their own special contribution to the formation of a child who would be different from both, not only in soul, but also in the material elements (in modern terms, the "DNA") which established its bodily characteristics. In order to implement this plan, God made human beings with a strong desire for coitus. Just as hunger and thirst were given so that humans could maintain their health, so the impulse towards physical intercourse was given to insure the health of the race. And just as the pleasure from satisfied hunger and thirst is made noble by the good end that it accomplishes, so too the passion that accompanies intercourse is made holy by the great good that the act can accomplish, the formation of new human beings in a crucible of love. God did not want this creative act to be simply a cold, mechanical union of bodies. It was to be accomplished through an intimate loving act of friends who would reach out to embrace each other and the child that they had helped to create. From the first moment of their existence, man and woman were bound together by flesh and by love. Eden was not a "singles bar." It was a marriage bower where that first human couple quickly added a commitment of spirit to their common flesh. To their blood-relationship they supplied love, and that bonding of heart was more intimate and important than any physical intercourse that might follow.[5]

---

still united to each other by a union of hearts but developing their personal sanctity by an unwavering focus on the love of God. Since Christ had already come, there was no longer a need to create ancestors for him. And, as far as the need to fill the empty spaces in the city of God was concerned, it seemed to him that this would happen more quickly if humans avoided the distractions of the *concupiscentia carnis* and directed all their passion toward God. Now that Christ had come and humanity had been redeemed, the only remaining great event would be the end of time when the faithful would be rewarded for their holy lives. He saw no good reason for delaying that date with glory.

5. Augustine recognized that in humanity's present fallen state, intercourse is often desired simply for the pleasure involved with no intention or desire for children. Following St. Paul (1 Cor 7:5), he considered such practice to be morally wrong but only slightly so. Indeed, he argues that married persons (even if there had been a previous agreement to remain continent) should accede to their partner's demand for inter-

Although procreation was the primary reason for the creation of the family, the essential element in the family is something else entirely. In Augustine's view marriage is constituted by a commitment between husband and wife where each gives oneself to the other in a spiritual bond expressed through friendship. Augustine's position makes good sense. Certainly no one would say that a man and woman are married because they share a physical intercourse. A true family is formed not by a passing physical encounter but by a permanent spiritual union of hearts. This conviction led Augustine to insist that a marriage can exist even when the union is infertile by reason of age, illness, or a free mutual decision of the partners to remain continent for good reasons. A marriage can exist without children, but it cannot and does not exist where there is no union of hearts.[6]

Even though he usually puts procreation first in his list of the goods of marriage, Augustine maintained that the essential characteristic of a valid marriage is that it be a union of friends, a friendship solidified by *fidelity to one's spouse (fides)* and the *permanence of the commitment (sacramentum)*. One can have friends without getting married, but the bond of friendship between those who are married is of a special kind. First, of all it is *exclusive.* To be married to another means not only that one will not give one's body to another but that one will not give one's "married love" to another. One who is married may have many other loves, love

---

course lest they be driven to adultery. In his words, "If they choose to go beyond the limits set by the matrimonial bargain, don't let them go beyond the limits of the matrimonial bed" (*Sermon 51*, 22). See *Enchiridion on Faith, Hope, and Charity,* 21.78. As Edmund Hill notes, Augustine's position was common in his day. Hill goes on to suggest that this viewpoint owed more to the spirit of times coming from Roman and Hellenistic sources than from Old Testament teachings. See Edmund Hill, O.P., trans. and notes, *Sermons,* part 3 of *The Works of St. Augustine: A Translation for the 21st Century,* ed. John E. Rotelle, O.S.A. (New York: New City Press, 1991), vol. 3, p. 47, fn. 55.

6. The following texts show that Augustine did not believe that the generation of children is the only good achieved by marriage: "I do not believe that marriage is good solely because of the procreation of children. There is also a natural association between the sexes" (*The Good of Marriage,* 3.3). "There could have been some kind of real and loving union, where yet one rules and one obeys, even without sexual intercourse" (*ibid.,* 1.1). See *The Morals of the Catholic Church and the Morals of the Manicheans,* 1.30.63. Finally, in a letter to Ecdicia (*Letter 262*), he reminds her that the concord and solemn relationship of husband and wife is the essential element in Christian marriage even when there is no sexual intercourse. Apparently she had taken a vow of continence (against her husband's wishes and thereby driving him to adultery) and had begun to act as though the marriage was over, dressing like a widow and distributing family property to passing monks.

of children, love of parents, love of ordinary friends; but the love bestowed on these others cannot be of the same sort that one gives to one's spouse. There is a special oneness of heart that cannot and must not be shared with another without damaging the marriage bond. The fidelity demanded of a married couple is a fidelity expressed through the preservation of chastity; chastity in this context means a special giving of body and soul to each other and to none other.

Chastity for a married couple means that they express their sexuality through intercourse only with each other. Adultery can never be justified because each spouse has already given sexual rights to the other through the marriage contract. They no longer can give themselves to another person physically because in truth they have already given themselves to their loved one. Their loved one owns their physical affection and to give it to another would be akin to stealing. Augustine speaks often of this *physical* fidelity, stressing especially that there is no difference between husband and wife in the obligation to avoid adultery. However it is clear that he did not believe that the obligation of fidelity is satisfied simply by physical fidelity. *Spiritual* fidelity is also required. The marriage bond, that special union of hearts in friendship, means something much more than not having intercourse with another. To be faithful to one's spouse, one must be faithful in body and spirit.[7] Although each human will have many loves in a lifetime, the love of husband and wife is a special love that cannot be given to another. To steal the affection of a married person away from his or her spouse is as much a violation of fidelity as is adultery, perhaps even a worse violation. To give one's body to another can be remedied; such giving is not necessarily forever. But when one gives one's special love to another, that love which is the very foundation of the marriage bond, it is at least difficult and possibly impossible to retrieve it. The marriage is seriously wounded because its root has been destroyed. The union of hearts has been destroyed. The good of *fidelity (fides)* is no more.

The third good of marriage (called by Augustine *sacramentum*) adds a new characteristic to the fidelity of the spouses, the property of being *unchangeable,* meaning not only that the bond will never terminate but also

---

7. Augustine describes fidelity as a "great spiritual good to which one sacrifices all earthly goods and even life itself" (*The Good of Marriage*, 4.4). He continues: "Fidelity involves the whole of the shared life of the spouses, especially in their obligation to support each other's weakness" (*ibid.*, 6.6). See Émile Schmitt, *Le mariage chrétien dans l'oeuvre de Saint Augustin* (Paris: Études Augustiniennes, 1983), p. 270.

that it *cannot* be terminated. Even though Augustine's primary (but not exclusive) reference is to marriage between validly baptized Christians, he clearly is not speaking about the sacrament of matrimony defined by later generations as "an outward sign instituted by Christ to give grace."[8] Though he frequently speaks about the sacraments of baptism and eucharist and has vague references to four others, he never speaks about marriage in this formally "sacramental" sense. When he speaks about marriage as a sacrament (a sacred sign), he uses the word in its most broad meaning as something which points to a reality that pertains more to heaven than to earth.[9] It is in this same sense that he describes as *sacraments* some of the practices of Old Testament Judaism that anticipated or prophesied the coming of Christ.

Marriage is a sacred sign *(sacramentum)* because the permanent fidelity of the husband and wife reflects an unending love which will exist in its fullness only in the heavenly city. This sacred character is not contained in the attribute of "fidelity" that is the essence of the marriage contract. It adds something new. Fidelity implies only that the contracting parties will be faithful to the contract as long as the contract exists. It does not imply that the contract will be forever. To say that the fidelity of love between friends is indissoluble adds a mysterious property, a special character of faithfulness between the spouses which makes their union unchangeable in this life. The union thereby becomes a sacred sign of a more exalted union, the union of Christ with his church. When loving spouses pledge themselves to each other "till death do us part," they imitate Christ's pledge to be forever united to those he loves.[10] The indissoluble loving union between one man and one woman in marriage is also a sign that prophesies

---

8. As Schmitt notes *(op. cit.,* pp. 224-25), when Augustine wrote *The Good of Marriage* in 401, he seemed to limit the good of *sacramentum* to marriage between Christians. This view is suggested by the following passage: "Therefore, the good of marriage among all nations and all men resides in its being a cause of generation *(causa generationis)* and in the spouses' fidelity of chastity *(in fide castitatis).* In marriages among members of the people of God, however, there is an additional good: the sanctity of the sacrament *(sanctitate sacramenti)* (*The Good of Marriage,* 24.32). When he was in the midst of his debates with the Pelagians some years later, he seems to modify this opinion, saying that the sacred character *(sacramentum)* of marriage is found *especially* (and therefore not exclusively) in the marriages of Christians. See *Faith and Works,* 7.10; *Marriage and Concupiscence,* 1.10.11; *Against Julian the Heretic,* 5.12.46.

9. *The City of God,* 10.5; *Letter 138,* 1.7.

10. *Marriage and Concupiscence,* 1.10.11. For a description of the special union between Christ and the church see *Commentary on the Gospel of John,* 8.4.1-3.

the future when the saints are with God in the heavenly city.[11] Marriage thus points to the heavens in two ways: reminding humanity of the union that exists even now between Christ and his church, and giving a foretaste of the joy that will be experienced by the faithful when joined forever with God after death.

The holiness of God's unchanging love for his church and every individual destined to be a citizen of the heavenly city, makes the marriage bond that signifies it a holy contract. Unlike most other contracts that can be dissolved with the consent of participants, the sacred bond created in the marriage of those already joined to Christ through baptism must be permanent. Although physical separation of spouses is unfortunately sometimes advisable, they must still be spiritually bound to each other. Even intercourse with another for a noble purpose and with the consent of one's spouse is still adultery. Even the desire to have a child when one's spouse is infertile is no excuse, because, as Augustine remarks, "The holiness of the sacrament is more important than the fruitfulness of the womb."[12]

B. Husband and Wife: A Union of Friends

The qualities of fidelity and permanence that Augustine maintains are the essential elements of marriage indicate his conviction that every family should be a friendly society, a society where the relationships of husband to wife, parent to child, indeed, even that of master to servant, should be built on a foundation of friendship. Thus he uses the word *concordia* to stand for the essential element in friendship and uses the same word when he comes to describe the peace in the ideal home. Domestic peace is, he writes, "an ordered oneness of heart *(ordinata concordia)* in the commanding and obeying of those who are living together."[13]

11. *The Good of Marriage*, 1.8.21.
12. *Ibid.*, 18.20.
13. *The City of God*, 19.13. Elsewhere, Augustine gives a more romantic description of the friendly union between husband and wife, describing them as being "joined one to another side by side, strolling together and as one looking towards the end of their earthly journey" (*The Good of Marriage*, 1.1). In yet another place he refers to such a loving union when he prays for a peace which "is like a sweetheart and friend with whom we share our heart as in an inviolate wedding bed and in whose company we find trust and rest. May such a peace be like the beloved whose embrace comforts us and with whom we live in unbreakable friendship" (*Sermon 357*, 1).

86

In other places Augustine explains and expands on his view that the primary component of marriage is this "friendly oneness of heart." For example, he remarks that one of the reasons that faith and trust are necessary in human affairs is because without them friendship is impossible and without friendship marriage is impossible. He repeats again and again that marriage does not depend on a couple's ability to propagate; rather it depends on their ability and willingness to be one in heart.[14] The good that marriage brings to the human race and to the spouses is not restricted to the children that may be produced. It also includes the natural companionship of husband and wife.

In Eden the problem expressed in the words "It is not good for the man [Adam] to be alone" (Genesis 2:18) was not resolved by giving him a child to raise. His loneliness was cured by giving him a woman to love ("a suitable partner for him"), one to whom he could cling so as to become one body with her (*ibid.*, 2.24).[15] Eve was created first and foremost to be a companion to Adam. Because she was a woman she could bear his children; because she was a loving wife she could do away with his lonesomeness. The first man and woman were meant to be spiritual support for each other. They did not need each other to supply their material wants. God took care of that. They needed each other because they needed a friend.[16] Their relationship was first and foremost a relation between loving companions. As Augustine writes:

> The first natural bond in human society was that between husband and wife. God did not create them as strangers but made them from one and the same flesh, indicating the strength of the union between them. They were destined to be joined together, side by side, as they walked together towards a common vision.[17]

14. *Faith in Things That Are Not Seen*, 1.2.4.

15. See *The Good of Marriage*, 3.3; *The Morals of the Catholic Church and the Morals of the Manicheans*, 1.30.63. For other texts emphasizing the "friendly" and "loving" bond that should exist between husband and wife, see Schmitt, *op. cit.*, pp. 280-81. Schmitt notes (p. 269) that in his listing of the goods of marriage Augustine will frequently give equal importance to fidelity between husband and wife and propagation of children.

16. *Marriage and Concupiscence*, 1.12. See Elizabeth A. Clark, "'Adam's Only Companion': Augustine and the Early Christian Debate on Marriage," *Recherches Augustiniennes*, vol. 21 (1986), p. 154. Also see Schmitt, *op. cit.*, pp. 92-3.

17. *The Good of Marriage*, 1.1.

In Eden God joined together a man and a woman with a contract by which rights and duties towards each other were exchanged and through which they became "two in one flesh" while retaining their separate identities.

The twofold need to give the first human being a friend and to propagate the race was fulfilled by making the second human being a woman. Of course there were other possibilities and one can speculate why this particular plan was chosen. Augustine observes that if God had merely wanted to give Adam a friend, he could just as well have made the second human being a man.[18] This apparently anti-feminine statement is in reality only the innocent recognition of the fact that, if companionship is the only goal, any compatible human (man or woman) would do the trick. I am sure that Augustine would have said something analogous if the first human being had been a woman. If she needed only a friend, another woman would do nicely. Of course the sexual desire for another can reinforce the attractiveness that brings compatible people together, but by itself it cannot create the bond that makes them friends. Indeed, sometimes it can stand in the way. Augustine's conclusion is that Adam needed another human being as a friend because that's the way human beings are built. But he needed his new friend to be a woman so that with her he could accomplish God's plan to continue the race.[19]

Of course God did not need to choose this particular method of continuing the race. Generation of offspring by an intimate physical act is obviously not the only way of producing living things. For example, God could have continued to use the process that produced Eve, taking the flesh from a human being and infusing into it a newly created soul. Modern technology has demonstrated that propagation can be accomplished without a union of friends. The technology involved in cloning, ovum and semen donation, *in vitro* fertilization, and surrogate motherhood shows that human beings can potentially be produced without an intimate physical act between two people who love each other. But there is no technology that can create a friend. That God did not choose some such impersonal and antiseptic method of continuing the race suggests that he wanted to give Adam someone who would be both a friend and a "help-mate" in the noble work of continuing the race. In their common participation in that extraordinary act, the friend-

18. *A Literal Commentary on Genesis,* 9.5.9.

19. See Gerald Bonner, "Augustine's Attitude to Women and *Amicitia*," *Homo Spiritalis: Festgabe für Luc Verheijen O.S.A.,* ed. Cornelius Mayer (Würzburg: Augustinus-Verlag, 1987), pp. 259-75.

ship of the first man and woman, now fallen from paradise, was no doubt strengthened to face the difficult days ahead, days when they no longer walked with a visible God but only with each other.[20]

Children can enhance and expand the friendship that should be the foundation of family, but (as we have seen) they are not absolutely necessary for a true family to exist. That first couple and married couples thereafter could have continued to be loving companions in marriage even without offspring. The spirit of love that binds a man and woman together in marriage is not dependent on children or even on innocence. As Augustine observes, even now, after the disaster of sin, the stream of love runs deep in the hearts of humans; it takes many different forms and it can express itself in many different ways.[21]

A further indication that the marriage bond can thrive in a childless marriage can be found in the marriage of Mary and Joseph. No one would deny that their celibate marriage created a true family. Their union was without physical intercourse but this did not weaken the "oneness of heart" that was at the center of their union. Only by recognizing that marriage is essentially a joining of loving spirits can one explain the continuation (and sometimes the initiation) of the bond well after child-bearing age. Only by seeing marriage as a commitment of will and love can one understand the decision of a husband and wife who mutually pledge to live in continence so that they can express their love for each other more forcefully through their intense love for the God who in his providence brought them together, joining their hearts by meeting in common union with God.[22] Certainly there is a blessing in having children, but the first and es-

---

20. See Peter Brown, *The Body and Society* (New York: Columbia University Press, 1988), p. 403. He gives the following summary of Augustine's position: "Marriage, therefore, was an expression of the primal and enduring nature of men and women as social beings, created by God for concord."

21. *The Good of Marriage*, 16.18. See *Sermon 51*, 13.21; *Against Faustus the Manichean*, 23.8. For commentary, see Elizabeth Clark, *op. cit.*, p. 151; Peter Brown, *op. cit.*, p. 403.

22. On the marriage of Mary and Joseph, see *The Harmony of the Gospels*, 2.1.2-3. Clark (*op. cit.*, pp. 151-52) notes that Augustine was the first major western theologian to argue that Mary and Joseph had a true marriage even though they remained celibate. For Augustine's view on the marriage of elderly beyond the child-bearing age, see *The Good of Marriage*, 3.3; *Against Julian the Heretic*, 5.16.62. For his view on continent marriage entered into for religious reasons, see *Marriage and Concupiscence*, 1.11.12; *Sermon 51*, 13.21; *Letter 127*, 9; *Letter 262*, 4. For commentary, see Schmitt, *op. cit.*, p. 276.

sential blessing of marriage is to have a man and a woman pledge fidelity in love to each other, loving friends as long as both shall live.

C. Friendship between Parent and Child

Augustine believed that the love between husband and wife was the beginning of the friendly love that should permeate all of society. Friendship begins in the family. The typical middle-class family of his day was something like the family he experienced as a child. In the ideal family (and no family is ideal), love of friendship between the spouses would reach out to all members of the extended family and especially to their own children. In their children parents could find hope. One of the first gifts that God gave to innocent humanity was the ability to reproduce itself, and the fact that this gift could endure even after human sin was a sign that, although humanity may have turned its back on God, God had not given up on humanity. Throughout the "swift flow of human history," two streams meet and mix, the evil which humans do and the good things that come from God. And one of the greatest goods in this now imperfect world is the ability of human beings to form the bodies which will house new immortal souls created day in and day out by God.[23]

Unfortunately, not all human beings have this power. But this very disability teaches an important lesson about what makes a parent a parent. For those couples who are sterile, there is still the option to adopt, and Augustine insists that such adopting parents are as much true parents as those who generate through intercourse. Joseph, after all, was recognized both by Mary and by Jesus as a true foster-father and was as much a father to Jesus growing up as he would have been if Jesus had been flesh of his flesh. Indeed, Augustine continues:

> Anyone who says "Joseph should not be called a father because he did not generate Jesus," concentrates more on the sexual pleasure in the production of children than on the acceptance of children through an act of love. Joseph embraced Jesus spiritually and thereby accomplished more effectively that which others seek to achieve by their physical intimacy. Indeed, people who adopt children beget them in their heart even though they cannot generate them in the flesh.[24]

23. *The City of God*, 22.24.1.
24. *Sermon 51*, 26.

Augustine continues this point by noting that adoption has a long history in Sacred Scripture (Moses survived by being adopted) and has been accepted from the beginning of Christianity. The lesson that Augustine was teaching was that parenthood, like marriage, is more a matter of spirit than of body. To be a parent in the flesh is not as important as being one in heart with the child. It is a union of hearts that makes a human being a true parent; not the passing intimacy that generates the new physical being.

Ideally, the process of choosing, conceiving, and giving birth to a child can give a man and woman another reason for loving each other. Unfortunately, the ideal is not always realized. As was likely the case with Augustine's son Adeodatus, sometimes children are not planned. The spouses do not love them into life; they must learn to love them afterwards.[25] In most instances this indeed happens and the birth fills the parents with new joy. It expands the love of husband and wife by encouraging them to extend that love in an intimate but quite different way to their new creation. When a child comes, the mutual love between husband and wife can now express itself as father and mother joined with God in the common wondrous adventure of forming and nurturing a new human being. Even considering his less than intimate relationship with his father and the sadness resulting from his own son's early death, Augustine believed that children and family were a gift from God. His optimism is reflected in his sympathy for the sad plight of Cacus "who had no wife to exchange soft words with; no tiny children to play with; no bigger ones to keep in order; no friend whom he could enjoy."[26] This mythological monster had great power and was universally feared, but his state was truly sad in Augustine's opinion. He had no one to love. He had no one to love him. He had no friend. Augustine seems to believe that a family would have fixed all that.

This is not to say that the birth of a child is a blessing unmixed with burdens. Children impose tremendous responsibilities on the parents. From the first moment of its existence the infant is equal to and as important as every other human being in the eyes of God, but in all other ways it is unequal. It depends completely on the kindness of others for its continued existence. It does not have the physical strength, knowledge, or ratio-

---

25. Augustine writes of his own life with the mother of his child as follows: "Living with her I found out through experience the difference between the chaste restraint of a marriage entered into with the goal of having children and an alliance joined simply to satisfy lust in which children are not wanted. Still, if they come, we cannot help but love them" (*Confessions*, 4.2).

26. *The City of God*, 19.12.

nal skill to take care of itself. Augustine remarks that humans in their infancy are much more incompetent than their animal brothers and sisters. Young animals can at least identify their mothers, find the maternal breast, and begin taking nourishment almost immediately. Human infants, on the other hand, have "feet unfit for walking and hands unfit for scratching." They seem more adept at crying when hungry than finding and suckling their mother's breast. And, perhaps worst of all, their lack of physical powers is matched by a mental helplessness that prevents them from communicating to others their most basic needs.[27]

Augustine believed that it was natural for the child to be subordinate to its parents. Not only has the young child no right to rule over others; it has no ability to rule even itself. It has a defect which precludes autonomy. Hopefully, its incompetence in the skills of living will eventually disappear — but not without a lot of support, guidance, and education from those who are older and wiser.

The plus side of infantile incompetence is that the young child, like its animal confreres, is incapable of personal sin. Despite his somewhat strange and somber listing of the sins of infancy in his *Confessions* (1.19.30), Augustine did not believe that infants were personally responsible for their apparent greed and selfishness. However, he believed that such innocence was short-lived. Sooner rather than later the child becomes responsible for good and bad actions. The forty-year-old Augustine confesses that, as a young boy just starting school, he was responsible for various nefarious acts such as lying to his teachers, stealing from his parents, and cheating at games. Reflecting on these years of childhood he sees in himself the tendency towards such adult vices as wasting time on frivolity, desiring to win at all costs, and greedily grasping at earthly things. As he remembers his childhood passions, he sees in them the beginning of adult vices, vices that are different only in the greater seriousness of their effects and severity of the punishments. A child's passion for candy and ball-playing and pet animals becomes in our mature years as governors and kings the lust for gold and property and enslaved subjects.[28]

---

27. *On Merits, Remission of Sins, and Infant Baptism*, 1.35.65. See William Harmless, S.J., "Christ the Pediatrician: Infant Baptism and Christological Imagery in the Pelagian Controversy," *Augustinian Studies*, vol. 28/2 (1997), p. 31.

28. *Confessions*, 1.19.30. Augustine's memories of his early days in school strike a familiar note even today: "My delight was in play and we were punished for it by those who did just the same sort of things. However, the trifling which is punished in children is called "business" when you are an adult. And I noticed that the man who beat

Because of the growing responsibility of the child, Augustine insists that it would be a mistake to ignore bad behavior. But because of the continuing deficiencies of childhood, it would be even more terrible to attempt to treat the young child with the equality and mutuality of friendship in its strict sense. Young children share with their parents a similarity in physical characteristics, but in matters of understanding and rational choice they are not at the same level. Parents must love their minor children not *as friends* but (to use Augustine's phrase) "in order that they *might become friends.*" Parental love must be expressed by providing for children's bodily needs and by giving them guidance necessary for a developed moral life.

Augustine believed that parental love for the child must be exercised through much command and correction in the early years. There is a need for tough love, a love which holds the child somewhat responsible for the good and bad that it does. To refrain from such discipline is to invite chaos. The cure for recalcitrance is not forgetfulness, declaring to the child that worst of all insults to its humanity, "You are not responsible!" Rather it is found in law and education, the only ways of directing a being who can freely choose to do good or evil. Such demands upon us are required by our condition. Augustine, perhaps remembering his own painful experience of growing up (painful to those around him as much as to himself), remarked that he would rather die than go through it again, and for obvious reasons:

> Our infancy proves how ignorant we humans are when we begin our lives and our adolescence proves how full of folly and concupiscence we become. Indeed, if we humans were left to live as we pleased and to do everything we desired, we would indulge in the whole list of lawless and lust-filled actions including those which I have mentioned and those which I forgot to mention. This is the reason why we use fear in trying to control the wildness of growing children. This is the reason why we have teachers and school-masters with their rulers and straps and canes. In our training of even a beloved child we not infrequently follow the advice of Scripture to "beat his sides lest he grow stubborn" (Ecclesiastes 30.12).[29]

---

me for my childish actions, when he lost some petty argument with a learned associate, was more tortured by anger and jealousy than I was when I lost to one of my playmates in a game of ball" (*Confessions*, 1.9.15).

29. *The City of God*, 22.22. A little earlier in the same work Augustine writes:

Augustine rejects the argument that such punishment is not Christian, violating Christ's mandate that we should forgive others "seventy times seven times." When a child, after doing what he knows to be wrong, begs "Let me off!" we may do so the first time and even up to the fourth time, but after that it does not promote the good of the child. To use Christ's command of infinite forgiveness as an excuse for not punishing willfulness is to destroy all discipline and to allow anarchy to rule the world. Augustine's advice to parents faced with misbehaving children is to correct them first with words and then sometimes even with a cane, but then to forgive them the wrong and forget about it. Love sometimes requires harsh correction of a loved one while retaining a gentleness towards them in our heart. Like a doctor who cures an infection by cutting it out, we must not be hindered in doing for our children what needs to be done, despite their cries of pain.[30] Parents should weep more over the bad choices of their children than over their death.[31] Death in time is temporary but the eternal death caused by human malice is eternal. If parents are silent in the face of the evil done by their children, they become cooperators in their evil and possibly in their damnation.[32]

The father should be the paragon of virtue for the family, giving children an example of the truly good life. The mother has the primary responsibility for nurturing and molding the child so that they follow the path of virtue out of love rather than fear. Like Augustine's mother Monica, every mother should be the instrument by which the image of Christ is imprinted on the child's heart.[33] Every father should imitate Augustine's father Patricius in being unflagging in his efforts to provide for the needs of the family and for the education of his growing children.[34]

Such provision for the material needs of children is an obvious responsibility. Any charitable donations to good causes must wait on the ful-

---

"Boys are compelled under pain of severe punishment to learn trades or letters. But the learning to which they are driven is itself so much of a punishment in their eyes that they sometimes prefer the pain of the punishment that comes from not learning to the pain of the learning once it is mastered. Thus, given a choice as an adult either to die or to go back to growing up again, who would not rather die?" (*The City of God*, 21.14).

30. See *Sermon 83*, 8.

31. *Commentary on Psalm 37*, 24.

32. *Ibid.*

33. See *Confessions*, 3.4.8; 5.9.16.

34. *Confessions*, 2.3.5. See Peter Brown, *Augustine of Hippo* (Berkeley: University of California Press, 1967), pp. 30-31.

fillment of the obligations in justice that the parents have to support and educate their children.[35] Parents must be deeply involved in the lives of their children but also must be prepared to let them live their own lives when the proper time comes. It would be a mistake for children to make a decision about marriage or a religious vocation before they are mature enough to make such decisions, and certainly it is proper that they seek the advice of their parents in such matters.[36] But, at the same time, parents must not interfere in their children's choice of vocation or career when they are mature enough to make such decisions.[37] Although the child is truly subordinate to parents and should obey them, he or she must be obedient to God first. Children need not follow the directives of parents when they command something against God's law or even when such direction is an unwanted interference in the mature child's way of life. Just as the task of the good teacher is to lead the student to a point where they no longer need the teacher, so too the task of the good parent is to bring their child to a point where they no longer need a parent. It would be a horrible mistake for parents to wish that their children never grow up. To treat them always as children means that they will never take responsibility for their lives; to keep them as children means that they can never become true friends with their parents.

Peter Brown, commenting on Augustine's lifetime relationship with friends and family, observes that Augustine ". . . hardly ever spent a moment of his life without some friend, even some blood-relative, close by him. No thinker in the Early Church was so preoccupied with the nature of human relationships."[38] As previously mentioned, Augustine's relationship with both his parents seems to have been affectionate (though in different ways) and enduring. His mother, Monica, is mentioned often in the story of his early life and in his early dialogues. She is a good example of a parent who eventually became a friend to her grown child, sharing in both the physical and intellectual life of her son. Augustine's relationship with his father is not as intimate, perhaps because of a natural reluctance of men to express emotions or perhaps simply because Patricius had a somewhat rough and ready personality. Still, Patricius seems to have truly cared for his son and been proud of him. He apparently took him on some ex-

35. *Letter 262*, 8.
36. *Letter 254*, 1.
37. *Sermon 16a*, 12; *Commentary on Psalm 44*, 11.
38. Peter Brown, *Augustine of Hippo, op. cit.*, p. 30.

cursions, once taking his adolescent son to the public baths and bragging about his obviously developing masculinity.[39] Certainly Patricius was committed to supporting an education for his son that would allow him to be more successful in life than his father. Augustine never spoke of his father with disrespect (though, as in the case of his mother, Augustine was frank in listing some of his father's weaknesses) and he seems to have expressed true love for him when, at the end of the *Confessions* narrative, he joined father and mother together in a common prayer for their salvation.

It was proper for Augustine, as it is for every child, to pray for his parents, but children must also take care of parents when they are alive. Augustine himself kept his mother with him in her later years and was with her when she died (Patricius had died some years earlier). He believed that this lesson of caring for parents was clearly taught by Christ on his cross. One of Christ's last concerns was for the care of his mother after he was gone. Augustine advises anyone who is scandalized by Christ's seemingly harsh words to his mother at the marriage feast of Cana to remember Calvary:

> There the best of all teachers instructed his own disciples that children should diligently care for their parents. From this clear command Paul learned the lesson that he taught his disciple Timothy when he wrote, "If someone does not take care of his own and especially those of his own house, he has denied the faith and is worse than any unbeliever" (1 Tim. 5:8). And who belongs to one's house as much as the children and the parents?[40]

Augustine had too much experience of human families to believe that all family life would be idyllic, and he recounts a sad example of what can happen when the bonds of friendship and respect disappear. It is the story of an abusive son, indifferent siblings, and a mother who lost control. The son attacked his mother with insults and physical abuse and the other children did nothing to try to stop him. Finally the mother had enough. In a rage she went to the church and put a curse on all her children. The curse took effect. All of them were struck down with a mysterious, debilitating illness. Seeing what she had done, she was overcome with remorse and committed suicide. The message for all parents and children was quite clear. Children must learn to show respect and when parents become angry they must remember that

39. *Confessions*, 2.3.6.
40. *Commentary on the Gospel of John*, 119.1, 2.

they are parents. Above all, parents and children must be careful what they pray for, since it just might be given to them.[41]

Augustine's message is that we must love our families as Christ wants us to love them, not putting them above our love for God but loving them because they are loved by God. Christ loved Mary not because she was his mother but because she was a faithful daughter of God.[42] He expands on this relationship between love of family and love of God in his *City of God*:

> There is the love of the person who has loved father and mother, sons and daughters as Christ wants them loved, with a love that leads them to believe in Christ and his love, or loving them because they are one with Christ through faith and love and are already members of His Body. Love such as this has Christ as its foundation. The superstructure is not made from perishable wood and hay and straw; rather it is built with silver, gold, and precious stones. When you love someone on account of Christ, it is just impossible to love them more than Christ.[43]

A true love of family, the love that becomes a friendly "union of hearts" as children develop, extends even through death. For those who remain behind, love continues, though now tinged with grief.[44] Indeed, when we love someone in this life, our love is always tinged with the fear that someday they will leave us in death. The joy coming from a loving spouse, the joy that overcomes us when we hold our newborn child, is colored by this fear.[45] When we are gifted with a good family we do not want our loves to die before we do,[46] and sometimes we go to extraordinary lengths to keep them alive even though our sick loved one fervently wants the rest of death.[47] Augustine understood the feelings of those who lose a beloved mother, respected father, or young child. He lost all of these in the course of his lifetime. The death of his mother reduced him to paralyzed grief. He never spoke about the death of his teenaged son; perhaps because it was too painful to remember.

41. *Sermon 323*, 1. For a description of the incident see *Sermon 322*, 2.
42. *Commentary on Psalm 127*, 12.
43. *The City of God*, 21.26.4.
44. *Sermon 172*, 1.
45. *Sermon 346C*, 2.
46. *Sermon 296*, 8.
47. Augustine gives an example of such frantic love in describing a young boy who will not let his tired father go to sleep, fearing that if he sleeps he will die. See *Sermon 339*, 8; *Sermon 40*, 6; *Sermon 87*, 15.

We show our love for departed loves by our tears; we show our respect for them by taking care of their bodies and praying for their souls.[48] When his mother Monica died, Augustine's prayer for his parents gives a moving example of how the love of children should extend even beyond the grave and how the child eventually can become a true friend to those who guided, nurtured, loved, and nourished them through their formative years. Remembering the long past death of his mother and father, Augustine prayed:

> May my mother and father have peace. My Lord, inspire those who read my words to offer prayers at the altar for your servant Monica and her husband, those two through whose flesh I was brought into this life. May all my readers remember with love those who were my parents in time and who are now my brother and sister, destined someday to be fellow citizens with me in your eternal city.[49]

As long as time lasts, children may be related to parents specifically as parents, but after time is finished they will be united as fellow friends, one in heart with each other in the city of God. There the ultimate goal of marriage and the family will be realized: to be forever friends with one's spouse, one's children, and with one's Lord.

48. *On the Care of the Dead*, 3.5.
49. *Confessions*, 9.13.37.

CHAPTER 6

The Family:
Obstacles to Friendship

A. Introduction: The Problem

This chapter will examine some apparent contradictions in Augustine's teaching on marriage and the family. At the same time as he presents the ideal family as a union of friends, a society whose members are "one in heart," he seems to maintain that women are not equal to men, that in the family the wife must be subordinate to the husband, and that any truly "spiritual union of hearts" between man and woman is complicated, if not made impossible, by sexual desire. The problem can be expressed in the form of the following three objections:

1. Friendship implies equality, but in some of his writings Augustine seems to say that man and woman are not equal.
2. In his description of the family Augustine makes the wife subordinate to the authority of the husband and this seems to contradict the equal partnership that a union of friends implies.
3. The relationship between husband and wife usually includes a sexual element and this sometimes ungovernable physical drive renders impossible the pure spiritual union implied in the "oneness of heart" at the center of friendship.

Each of these objections is serious and must be considered in turn.

99

B. Objection 1: The Inequality of Women

There is no doubt that Augustine believed that women and men are made equally in the "image of God" and that this reflection of the Divine is found primarily in their rational soul.[1] Thus, it can be said of the soul of woman as well as the soul of man that "God alone is better, the angel is its equal, and all of the rest of the universe is below it."[2] In both woman and man the soul is the instrument whereby the body receives the form it takes, the order and proportion of its parts, and thereby becomes itself a true but less perfect reflection of God.[3] It follows that in that most important part of human nature, the rational soul, there is no difference in dignity between woman and man.

It is true that most men are physically stronger than most women of equal age (though women seem to have better lasting power), but this is purely a superiority in body-power, not soul-power. Augustine eventually rejected the idea that the human being is the soul, but he never doubted that it is the most important part of the human composite. The soul is the formal element in the human composite and it is through the soul that the body receives its perfections. The first woman's body may have been drawn from the body of man but her identity as the person "Eve" came from her rational soul. She was made "Eve" first and foremost by the spirit created by God. She could not be the person "Eve" without her body, but the main element in her "Eve-ness" came from her spirit. It was *there* that the prism of her person radiated her unique reflection of the glory that is God.

In Augustine's view, the physical inequality of man and woman becomes inconsequential when compared to the ways in which their spiritual equality expresses itself. Thus, he insists that there is no difference between the soul of man and soul of woman in their ability to reflect the perfections of God.[4] Male or female, all human beings can, through baptism, become equally children of God and receive the grace that gives life. The differences between man and woman are truly accidental to the essence of their humanity and the glory of their destiny.[5]

1. *A Literal Commentary on Genesis*, 3.22.34; *The Trinity*, 12.7.12. See Richard J. McGowan, "Augustine's Spiritual Equality: The Allegory of Man and Woman with Regard to *Imago Dei*," *Revue des Études Augustiniennes*, vol. 33 (1987), pp. 259-60.
2. *The Quantity of the Soul*, 34.
3. *The Immortality of the Soul*, 15.24.
4. *A Literal Commentary on Genesis*, 3.22.34. See McGowan, *op. cit.*, p. 260.
5. See Émile Schmitt, *Le mariage chrétien dans l'oeuvre de Saint Augustin* (Paris:

The equality of man and woman in their nature is reflected in their equality in rights and duties when they enter into the contract of marriage. There is an absolute equality in conjugal rights. The obligation of fidelity to marriage vows is just as serious for a husband as for a wife. Adultery is as much an evil for the wandering husband as for the unfaithful wife. At least in marriage between baptized Christians, marrying another is forbidden as long as the first spouse lives.[6] Augustine does seem to have believed that there was inequality when it came to actually *being* faithful to one's spouse. Perhaps remembering his own checkered past, he presumed that women were better than men in controlling sexual passion. His sermons about adultery were almost exclusively directed to the male members of his audience, often pleading with the husbands to try to imitate the virtue of their wives. Thus, in a sermon preached to catechumens in Hippo shortly before Easter, Augustine tells the husbands in the congregation to render the same fidelity to their wives that they demand from them: "Give them an example not a lecture!" He goes on to observe somewhat sardonically that husbands brag about infidelity as a sign that they are "real men," not seeing the paradox of claiming their strength as men by their animal weakness.[7] The opinion of the day (an opinion which, as we shall see, Augustine shared to some degree) was that men were more adept in speculative matters and that women by and large had a greater mastery of the spirituality

Études Augustiniennes, 1983), p. 288. On this page he lists numerous places where Augustine describes the various ways in which man and woman are equal. Thus, for example: they are equally images of God: *Against Faustus the Manichean,* 24.2.2; *The Christian Combat,* 11.12; *The Trinity,* 7.10; they are equally children of God: *Commentary on Psalm 26,* 2.23; *Commentary on the Lord's Sermon on the Mount,* 1.15.40; *Exposition of the Epistle to the Galatians,* 27-28; they are equally able to receive the grace of God: *The Good of Marriage,* 12.14; *Sermon 51,* 13.21. Another indication that Augustine believed that man and woman are essentially equal can be found in his description of their condition after the resurrection. Then, although every person will retain her/his sexual identity, there will be no subordination (*The City of God,* 22.17; 22.18; 15.17; *Commentary on Psalm 118,* 2). Commenting on this, Borresen writes: "Where sexual difference no longer has any purpose (since the need for procreation has ceased) and survives only on the basis of the integrity and perfection of the spiritual body, the hierarchical relationship between man and woman disappears" (Kari Elisabeth Borresen, *Subordination and Equivalence: The Nature and Role of Woman in Augustine and Thomas Aquinas,* trans. Charles Talbot [Washington, D.C.: University Press of America, 1981], p. 87).

6. *Commentary on the Lord's Sermon on the Mount,* 1.16.43. See Schmitt, *op. cit.,* p. 272.

7. *Sermon 132,* 2. See *Sermon 9,* 3.

that led to sanctity. But to those who would argue that this was a sign of masculine superiority, Augustine would likely respond by pointing out that "being good" was certainly more important for eternal happiness than knowing the nature of "being."

To summarize, Augustine believed that man and woman were absolutely equal in their human nature before God. This equality was symbolized in the formation of the first humans. Both the soul of Adam and the soul of Eve were created by God. There was no difference in the divine love that prompted the act nor in the created spirits that were its effect. The intimacy of the union between these first two humans was symbolized in the taking of the flesh of one from the other. Clearly, God's intention in taking Eve's body from the flesh of Adam was to integrate man and woman as friends, not to denigrate the woman. Man and woman were both created in the image of God. Both were united in the same flesh. It was only after they contained something of God and something of each other in their individual beings that they were told to go forth and propagate the race. Whatever difference there may have been because of their sex, it was as irrelevant to their being friends as their being of different height, color, or weight. The friendship of their union depended on their being joined in heart, not in their being identical twins.[8]

C. Objection 2: Subordination of Wife to Husband

In the chapter on friendship it was argued that some subordination of ruler to ruled is a necessary component in every society and that such subordination does not necessarily stand in the way of friendship. Applying this principle to the family, it seems reasonable to say that just as a friendly union of hearts is necessary to *constitute* the family, some subordination of ruled to ruler is necessary *to make it work.* Put simply, in the family there is need for "someone to be in charge." This is so because the family is different from a simple gathering of human beings. It is a society and as society

---

8. One must take into account Augustine's emphasis on the spiritual aspect of being human and his own troubles in controlling his sexual desires when interpreting such early statements that a good Christian must love the human being in his wife, but hate the "wife" in her (*Commentary on the Lord's Sermon on the Mount*, 1.15.41). In any case, as Canning notes, Augustine explicitly rejected such reasoning in his *Retractions* (1.9.3; 1.10.2). See R. Canning, "Augustine on the Identity of the Neighbour," *Augustiniana,* vol. 36, nos. 3-4 (1986), pp. 169-70.

it seeks to achieve goals as *community*. In a complex organization such as the family, common action towards a common good is unlikely to happen automatically. There will usually be some difference of opinion and at least sometimes such difference will only be able to be resolved by the exercise of authority.[9]

Granted that in the family, as in every other formal society, someone must be in charge, who is this person to be? If man and woman are equal in dignity in the eyes of God, who should rule and who should be ruled? The family does not seem to be a voluntary society like a fraternity or sorority where the ruler is chosen by the members. But if the subordination is not *de jure* (by choice of the members), what is the basis for saying that it is *de facto* (coming from nature)?

There is no doubt that Augustine believed that in the family, the "society of those living together where some commanded and others obeyed," wives should give way to the wishes of their husbands in matters affecting the family as long as such wishes did not violate a higher law. He also believed that this subordination was natural.[10] Thus, for example, when he comes to explain Mary's deference for Joseph, Augustine will remark that "putting man before woman is in accordance with the order established in nature by God's law."[11] Again, when asked why polygamy was allowed during the Old Testament, he points to the fact that there is a hidden law of nature whereby things that rule love singularity while things that are ruled allow for a plurality. Thus there is only one master for many servants but a servant cannot have more than one absolute master. The reference to marriage is obvious. In the beginning it was advantageous to increase the number of humans as quickly as possible and this justified a man taking many women as his wives but not a woman having many men as husbands. But added to this practical argument that polyandry would not speed up propagation in the way that polygamy would, there was a deeper reason. A family can have only one "ruler" (the husband) but the "subjects" (wives and children) can be many.[12]

9. Augustine observes that even the most disorderly of persons, the robber, wants peace at home and recognizes that the "price of peace in the family is to have someone in charge" (*The City of God*, 19.12.1).

10. Some texts that express the "natural" (rather than freely chosen) subordination of wife to husband include the following: *Questions on the Heptateuch*, 1.153; *A Commentary on Genesis against the Manicheans*, 2.11.15; *Marriage and Concupiscence*, 1.9.10.

11. *Sermon 51*, 30.

12. *The Good of Marriage*, 17.20; *Marriage and Concupiscence*, 1.9.10.

It is important to remember that in all his discussions of the relationship between man and woman in the family, beginning with Adam and Eve, Augustine was not speaking about their human nature. He was addressing their accidental status as husband and wife. Family existed from the very beginning of the human race. Adam and Eve did not come into existence as strangers. From the first moment of her creation Eve was wife and Adam was her husband. Their basic relationship to each other as human beings remained but now it was clothed in the mantle of husband-wife. If they had remained simply a man and woman, the issue of subordination would not have arisen. As individuals they would stand before God in absolute equality. The only subordination would be their individual subordination as humans to God.

Thus, the question for Augustine was not, "Why should the woman be subordinate to the man?" Rather it was, "Why in the family should the wife be subordinate to the husband?" One unpersuasive argument for favoring Adam over Eve (and thereafter husband over wife) was that the man was the first to exist. But the principle "First come, first served" — though it may make sense in determining who should get served first in a restaurant or even who should have access to scarce medical therapies — makes little sense in the choice of a ruler. A stronger argument might be made in Adam's favor from the fact that he was in some sense the "generator" of Eve. Her body was drawn out of his. That "the generator should have preference over the one generated" makes some sense, but in this case it loses some of its force when one realizes that Adam's contribution to Eve was to her less important part, her body, and in even that humble endeavor Adam has little to do with the operation. He was asleep at the time. God was the surgeon who drew Eve's body from Adam and then (and most importantly) the one who (without any contribution from the sleeping man) breathed into her that soul that was to reflect his image in creation. In any case, even if these principles worked in determining that Adam was to rule that first family, they point to no "natural" basis for Eve's subordination. She was late, not deficient. An argument based on "who came first" or "who was made from whose flesh" would have been equally valid had the first human being been the woman and the second the man.[13]

Augustine offers an argument that does not depend on time or method of origin. It is based on the principle that it is proper for the greater to rule the lesser, for example for reason to rule the bodily appe-

13. *A Literal Commentary on Genesis,* 9.5.9.

tites. However, he is far from suggesting that man should be identified with pure reason or that woman should be understood as an appetite that needs regulation. His explanation of the "natural" subordination of wife to husband is more complex. It rests on a *distinction,* an *assumption,* and a *conviction.*

The *distinction* he makes is between speculative and practical reason. Practical wisdom is the knowledge which allows us to do efficiently those things necessary in our daily life. Through it we are able to "get things done," to arrange our affairs in some logical and effective order. Speculative wisdom is the ability to see how things relate to each other, to see what the universe is like and how we fit into it. Both sorts of wisdom are necessary for the perfection of human life. We need not only to "figure things out" but also to "get through daily existence." We need both metaphysics and common sense.

The *assumption* of his argument is that speculative wisdom is the more important of the two. When people exercise this sort of wisdom, they are expressing the highest level of human powers. To use a Platonic image, they are not simply regulating their lives in the cave of ordinary experience; they are reaching beyond to the realm of the pure Ideas, the world that is far superior to the everyday shadow-world of our experience. In stressing the priority of the speculative over the practical, Augustine was in accord with the common opinion of the intellectual elite of his day. He also saw a confirmation of this priority of contemplation over action in the New Testament story of Martha and Mary. When God came to visit the home of the two good women, it was Martha who scurried about doing the little domestic things necessary to make a guest comfortable. Mary was quite satisfied simply to sit before Jesus and look into the face of the man-God. Augustine believed that on a day by day basis neither sister had captured what the best human life on earth should be like. As he wrote in his *City of God:*

> No person should be so committed to contemplation as to give no thought to the needs of a neighbor; nor should anyone be so absorbed in action as to do away with the contemplation of God.[14]

In this life the practical wisdom of Martha and the speculative wisdom of Mary are both important, but Mary's wisdom is more precious in that it is

14. *The City of God,* 19.19.

the wisdom that reaches even beyond death to that realm where there will be no practical matters to bother about.[15]

Augustine's argument for priority of husband over wife that began with the distinction between speculative and practical wisdom and the assumption that the former is better than the latter is concluded with a culturally-influenced *conviction* that, while both sorts of wisdom can be found in male and female, women are specially gifted in practical wisdom and men in speculative wisdom. If this were true (and I doubt that it is), it would follow that in the family the one who rules should be that one (the man) who is more gifted in speculative wisdom and the one who is ruled should be the one (the woman) more gifted in practical wisdom.[16]

No doubt Augustine's belief in a woman's special aptitude in practical wisdom was influenced by his own experience. Both his mother and his common-law wife seem to have been very practical women, the latter seeing to his household and his son while he (Augustine) wrestled with the problem of evil in the universe and how to make a good speech. However, it seems clear that he did not believe that any woman is totally devoid of speculative wisdom nor that every man has it.[17] During his philosophical dialogues at Cassaciacum, he praises his mother's ability to understand deep questions while his male students were wandering aimlessly on the fringes of the debate.[18] Later on, the letters he wrote through the course of

15. Luke 10:42. See *Sermon 103*, 1-6.

16. Augustine supports his conclusion through analogies with the superiority of thought over action, reason over body, spirit over flesh, which (according to Schmitt, *op. cit.*, p. 289) indicate the continuing influence of Platonism on Augustine's thought. See *Confessions*, 13.32.47; *Questions on the Heptateuch*, 1.153; *Incomplete Work against Julian*, 6.23.

17. See Gerald Bonner, "Augustine's Attitude to Women and *Amicitia*," *Homo Spiritalis: Festgabe für Luc Verheijen O.S.A.*, ed. Cornelius Mayer (Würzburg: Augustinus-Verlag, 1987), pp. 263-65.

18. *On Order*, 1.11.31; *The Happy Life*, 2.10. After noting an apparent ambivalence towards women (a later flight from women following his earlier quest for women), Roten observes that neither aspect is as radical as some make it out to be. Despite his passionate nature, he was more faithful to his common-law wife of fifteen years than most men of his time (his father, Patricius, included) would have been. Moreover, his later relationships with women were friendly if cautious (since he did not trust his still passionate nature) with no intellectual patronizing of them. He corresponded on spiritual and intellectual matters with friends like Albina, Proba, Juliana, and Fabiola. He believed that his mother acquired a thoughtful state of mind that was equivalent to that achieved through the best of philosophy. See Johann G. Roten, S.M., "Mary and Woman in Augustine," *University of Dayton Review*, vol. 22, no. 3 (Summer 1994), pp. 33-34.

his career as bishop show that he had many conversations with dedicated and intelligent women on questions of speculative wisdom. At the same time, his sometimes harsh language with male correspondents on similar abstruse matters show that he never believed that being a man was a protection from being a fool.

The principle that is at the root of his entire discussion of subordination in the family has nothing to do with being a man or being a woman. It is simply this: "An orderly society will always be one in which those with speculative wisdom rule those with practical wisdom."[19] Expressed in this fashion the principle seems very sensible. In any society there will be chaos if the leaders are more concerned about "doing something" than "thinking." There is no use in building a bridge if you don't know where you are going. Thought must always take precedence over action if the action is to be worthwhile and not haphazard. Those who have mastered the speculative wisdom which allows them to see where the society should be going and how to get there should be in charge of directing the society whatever the society may be. Whether in an actual case the person is a man or a woman seems irrelevant, especially to a person like Augustine whose life was eventually changed for the better by the grace of God and by a woman (Monica) who knew the truth about this world and the next.

The subordination of wife to husband in the family is quite different from the subordination of child to parent or of servant/slave to master.

19. It is in light of Augustine's equating the man with speculative wisdom and the woman with practical wisdom and his conviction that speculative wisdom is at a higher level than practical wisdom, that one must understand the following somewhat controversial statements. "What is worse than a house where the woman has absolute authority over the man? But upright is the house where the man commands and the woman obeys. Upright, therefore, is humanity itself when the spirit commands and the flesh serves" (*Commentary on the Gospel of John*, 2.14.3). "By just law it [virile reason] should place a limit upon its helper [the appetite which controls the body] just as man ought to rule woman and ought not to allow her to rule him. When this happens, the home is perverted and unhappy" (*A Commentary on Genesis against the Manicheans*, 2.11.15). Teske comments: "Augustine's view of the role of women is far from what would satisfy most contemporaries, not to mention contemporary feminists. On this point, as on others, one should realize that his ideas were molded by his society and culture as well as by passages in Scripture which seem to subordinate women to men. Moreover, his Platonic view of human beings led him to identify the real person with the soul or mind. Hence, differences of bodily sex are theoretically extrinsic to the real person and men and women are equal as souls." (Roland J. Teske, S.J., trans., *Saint Augustine: On Genesis* [Washington, D.C.: The Catholic University of America Press, 1991], p. 112).

The subordination of child to parent is *de facto,* that is, rooted in nature. It results from two facts. The first is the fact that the child is generated by the parents and owes them and is owed by them continuing love and respect even through its adult years. The second fact is that through its early years the child is lacking that speculative and practical wisdom which would make it competent to regulate its own life. The subordination of servant or slave to its master is a *de jure* subordination. It is caused by human choice rather than natural inequality. In the case of an employed free man, there is a contract of service freely entered into by both parties. In the case of the slave, although neither this particular master nor the social structure of slavery itself has been chosen by this particular slave, the institution itself is the result of human decisions and not nature. Augustine, unlike Aristotle and others in the ancient world, did not believe that any human by nature is the slave of another. Slavery, the total domination of one human by another, is one of the many sad effects of humanity's fall from grace. It is the result of a perversion of will rather than a law of nature.[20]

The subordination of wife to husband as interpreted by Augustine can be seen as being in some way both *de jure* and *de facto.* It is *de jure* in the sense that in an ideal situation a husband and wife enter the contract freely. But within the marriage the subordination is *de facto* in that it is based on what Augustine considered to be a factual difference in wisdom, the husband more gifted in speculative, the wife more gifted in practical. However, unlike the subordination of the infant, under normal conditions (that is, apart from illness or the disability that sometimes comes with age) neither husband nor wife is so deficient in either speculative or practical wisdom as to be unable to act as a responsible, effective, human being. The subordination does not rest on any particular natural *defect* in either party. They are just *different* and the subordination of one to the other is aimed at using most effectively the special gifts of each one for the benefit of the family.

Both husband and wife have their own special areas of expertise and Augustine makes it plain that above and beyond their equal obligation of fidelity to the other, each one serves the other by supporting the spouse's weakness.[21] While the husband is called upon to be the paragon of virtue for all and the protector of the home from outside forces, the

20. See Gervase Corcoran, O.S.A., *Saint Augustine on Slavery* (Rome: Patristic Institute "Augustinianum," 1985), p. 68.

21. *The Good of Marriage,* 6.6. See Schmitt, *op. cit.,* p. 270.

wife must see to the internal peace of the household and be the source of the moral education of the family. Schmitt summarizes their respective duties as follows:

> The husband normally has preeminence in ordering the material and spiritual responsibilities of the home. His authority is not based on merit nor on virtue but on his vocation as a man, naturally predisposed to be a protector of the family. His power as representing "Christ the Head of the Mystical Body" is above all a service. The wife has priority in ordering the plans which will structure the life of the home so that it can become more warm and bountiful. She is called to give to her mate the respectful and loving docility that is reflected in the loving respect given to Christ by his Church.[22]

Augustine holds up his mother Monica as an example of such docility. Her friends were constantly amazed that she could keep peace in a household where the husband was far from perfect.[23] Monica, as wife, made the best of a bad situation, but even in the best situation the wife has a special call to make the good home environment even better. In the exercise of their different functions husband and wife serve the other and to that extent they constantly exchange status as superior and inferior. But in all of their "giving and taking" of direction they remain equal as humans before God and should continue to be bound together by a love that makes them truly "one in heart," forming a loving union that lasts even through the disability of old age.[24]

There is no reason why the subordination of wife to husband should be an obstacle to their having such a loving unity. In an environment of love authority is exercised as service, not domination. As Augustine describes it, "When love is present commands are imposed gently and the burdens on those who must obey become light and almost negligible."[25] In homes dominated by love, those who command are those charged to have

---

22. Schmitt, *op. cit.*, p. 295. See *On Continence*, 9.23. An example of how the husband and wife should work together in the family is reflected in Augustine's instructions to husbands with regard to the disposition of property. He tells them that though they may have the *legal* power to sell or give away family goods, they should consider their wives as valuable confidants and consult with them before making such decisions. See *Commentary on the Lord's Sermon on the Mount*, 2.2.7; *Sermon 262*, 8.

23. See *Confessions*, 9.9.19.

24. *Commentary on the Lord's Sermon on the Mount*, 1.18.54.

25. *Commentary on the Letter of John to the Parthians*, 9.1.

regard for the interests of the others. In such families those who command actually are at the service of those whom they seem to order about. They rule not out of a passion for being in charge but out of duty to those they care for and compassion for those for whom they must provide.[26] Thus, when God tells husbands that they are in charge of the family, Augustine observes, he is not giving them permission to dominate; he is giving them a command to serve:

> O God, you subject women to their husbands in chaste and faithful obedience, not for the gratification of passion, but for the begetting of children and the establishment of domestic society. You set men over their wives, not to make playthings of the weaker sex, but in accordance with the laws of pure and honest love.[27]

The model for the relationship of husband and wife is the union between Christ and his church. Christ is obviously the greater partner. Indeed, the difference between the divine Christ and the human "people of God" is infinitely greater than any difference between husband and wife could be. And yet despite their radical difference, there is still a loving union. Christ, the Head, is part of the Body and his rule over the Body is one of service. Thus, in his work *On Continence* (9.22-23) written in 395

---

26. *The City of God,* 19.14. As Markus notes, this ideal of loving subordination is not always found in societies that exist in humanity's fallen state. However it was the type of subordination towards which unscathed humanity was driven by its Creator. In the original family it was natural for wife to be subject to husband. It was *not* natural for husband to dominate the wife (R. A. Markus, "Two Conceptions of Political Authority: Augustine, *De civitate dei,* xix, 14-15, and Some Thirteenth-Century Interpretations," *Journal of Theological Studies,* vol. 16, no. 1 [April 1965], pp. 74-75). Corcoran explains the subordination in Eden as follows: "What then is the nature of the subordination of the wife to her husband, or the children to their parents? In *De Genesi ad Litteram* (11.37.50) Augustine states clearly that before the Fall a man ruled his wife and she served him. At the same time, he is careful to point out that this relationship was very different from that introduced by sin to the institution of the family. Before the Fall, the relationship of service and domination was prompted by love and did not arise from an obligation imposed by status. In other words, there was no question of constraint or of duties and obligations arising out of status. From this it appears that the relationship of subordination and domination before the Fall was a relationship of giving and accepting service. There is no hint of constraint, or even of duties and obligations" (Gervase Corcoran, O.S.A., *op. cit.,* p. 62).

27. *On the Morals of the Catholic Church and the Morals of the Manicheans,* 1.30.64. See Borresen, *op. cit.,* p. 34.

against the Manicheans, Augustine uses the analogy of Christ and the church to prove the goodness of the body and the goodness of marriage. He quotes Paul (Ephesians 5:25-29), urging husbands to love their wives as Christ loves his church. This is a love whereby the husband, imitating Christ's sacrifice for his church, would deliver himself up for his wife in order to sanctify her and to present her in all her glory, holy and without blemish.

Certainly such a love, although it flows out of a subordination of one loved one to another, is not a domination that would stand in the way of a union of hearts. The subordination envisioned by God in the creation of the family is one in which the man is subordinate to Christ and the woman is subordinate to the man. This means that the perfect order of woman's subordination to man is found only when Christ, the Wisdom of God, rules the man.[28] Augustine continues the analogy in various places in which he uses the love of one's husband/wife as an example of how one should love Christ. One should love altruistically, loving not for the sake of some reward but simply because the loved one is worthy of love.[29] Our love of Christ, as with the love of a beloved spouse, should carry with it the fear that the loved one will someday leave.[30] In sum, husbands should love their wives as Christ in fact loves his church; wives should love their husbands as the church should love Christ. The intimate union of Christ and church is that of head to body and the same intimacy should be present in the love of husband for wife. The principle "No one hates his own body" is for Augustine not simply a biological argument. It stands for the way a husband should love his wife. Indeed, it points to a relationship of the highest spiritual order, the relationship between God and human race.[31]

28. *A Commentary on Genesis against the Manicheans,* 2.11.15; 2.12.16.
29. *Commentary on Psalm 55,* 17.
30. *Commentary on Psalm 127,* 8.
31. In his commentary on St. Paul's letter to the *Ephesians* (5:25-29), Augustine notes that there are three forms of unity mentioned in Paul's text: Christ and church, husband and wife, spirit and flesh. "In each of these the former cares for the latter and the latter waits on the former. All of them are good as long as the superiors act in an excellent fashion and the others act properly as subjects, thus preserving the beauty of order" (*On Continence,* 9.23). Augustine goes on to note that whereas husbands are told to love their wives as Christ loves the church and wives are told to love their husbands as the church loves Christ, in Paul's use of the earthly example of spirit and body the husbands are indeed told to love their wives as they would their own bodies, but wives are *not* given the example of the body's relationship to spirit as a model for their subor-

D. Obstacle 3: Sexual Desire

The third objection maintains that the "oneness of heart," the spiritual union that is the basis for friendship, is complicated in marriage by the powerful physical attraction of sexual desire. Augustine believed that such sexual desire and, indeed, one's sexuality itself comes from the body. Souls
have no particular sex but the persons formed by their union with a physical body do. Thus, when we truly love another human being we must love
body and soul.

Augustine did not perceive this physical side of human love as repre-
hensible. In his later years he firmly rejected the Manichean notion that everything to do with the body was evil. He also discarded the Platonic view
that the human soul had been "trapped" in the body as a punishment and
that ultimate salvation and happiness would come only when the spirit
was free of its material enclosure. His final and enduring belief was that
the human being is the composite of body and soul. Thus, the separation
of body and soul at death is the final disaster in this life and their reunion
after resurrection is the beginning of glory in the next. Humans can be
completely happy only when their body and soul are forever brought together again. Peace does not come from separation of spirit and body as
enemies; it comes from their union as friends.[32]

A person's emotional life, those appetites which are rooted in and expressed through their nature as physical beings, are as much a part of their
humanity as their intellectual life. Augustine dismissed as madness the
Stoic idea that apathy is an ideal for any human being. The ideal is not lack

---

dination. The reason is that in this life there is frequently an antagonism between body
and spirit, the body reaching out to spirit for self-satisfaction. In the relationship between Christ and the church there is a true subordination but it is a caring subordination. The relationship between spirit and flesh in this life is quite different. Sometimes
the flesh tries to take over; sometimes spirit aims at putting flesh in its place rather than
loving it in its proper place.

32. *Sermon 155*, 14. See *The City of God*, 22.30.1; *Enchiridion on Faith, Hope, and
Charity*, 1.91. Brown remarks that the fact that humans were physical beings was the
reason that "death always remained for Augustine the most bitter sign of human frailty.
It was an unnatural occurrence. Its frightening wrench revealed the strength of the
'binding force' associated with the 'sweet marriage bond of body and soul'" (*Letter 140*,
6.16; Peter Brown, *The Body and Society* [New York: Columbia University Press, 1988],
p. 405). For a general discussion of Augustine's attitude towards death, see Donald X.
Burt, "Augustine on the Authentic Approach to Death," *Augustinianum*, vol. 28, no. 3
(1988), pp. 527-63.

of fervor, but the presence of controlled fervor. He went so far as to say that without the fire of emotions in one's life it is impossible to understand the divine passion for humans and the human passion to reach the divine. As he expressed it one day to his somewhat listless listeners:

> Give me a person who is in love! They will know what I mean. But if I speak to a cold person, they will not know what I am talking about.[33]

Humanity's fallen state is not reflected in an emotional response to a pleasant or unpleasant experience, in becoming flushed with anger or pale from fear or hot with excitement. Reasonable emotional response is part of being human. Only when emotions are out of control do they point to humanity's weakened state.[34]

One must take into account Augustine's insistence on the good of the body and its functions when interpreting his warnings about the dangers of the "flesh" and "concupiscence." "Flesh" in itself can stand for something good or something bad. When Augustine uses it in its negative meaning, it stands for anything that causes a human to prefer their own desires over God's will. "Flesh" in its negative connotation is not a codeword for the human body. The human body as a creation of God is not an obstacle to divine will; it is its product. "Flesh" may sometimes stand for bodily desires gone mad but it often refers to more than the material aspects of life. It can stand for ambition, power, praise, or any other earthly thing that becomes a god for an individual.

The word "concupiscence" (like "flesh") is a neutral word that can have a bad or good connotation. In itself it means nothing more than "desire" and may be used to stand for good desires as well as bad. This is brought out in a letter written by Augustine in 421 to Atticus, the bishop of Constantinople. There he is careful to distinguish both the good and bad meanings of concupiscence as it relates to marriage. He writes:

> Because of their [the Pelagians] error they do not distinguish the concupiscence associated with marriage (the concupiscence of conjugal purity, the concupiscence for the legitimate engendering of children, the

---

33. *Commentary on the Letter of John to the Parthians*, 26.4. For a more extensive discussion of Augustine's views on the emotional and sexual life of humans see Donald X. Burt, *Augustine's World: An Introduction to His Speculative Philosophy* (Lanham, MD: University Press of America, 1996), pp. 65-72.

34. *The City of God*, 14.9.

113

concupiscence of the social body by which each sex is tied to the other) from the concupiscence of the flesh which hankers after the illicit as well as the licit indifferently.[35]

In all of these cases "concupiscence" represents the desires of a spirit in a body and in at least two of them (the desire for procreation and the desire for union of the spouses) it involves a sexual desire which clearly is not disreputable. The conclusion can only be that sexual desire is no more shameful than the desire for food and drink. Both are physical tendencies placed in human beings for reasons determined by God.[36] In their perverted, uncontrolled forms, they are evil but this is not because they are physical but because they are aspects of a much worse spiritual perversion: the perversion of pride, whereby the individual acts solely for her/his own pleasure, considering himself/herself as the most important "self" in existence. It is obvious that the use of the sexual act in this depraved way is an obstacle to friendship. The other cannot be my friend if I see him or her only as a source of pleasure. But not every sexual relationship needs to be of this sort. It is possible to have sexual intimacy with another without destroying the union of hearts that is the essence of friendship. It is possible to have sexual intercourse in which the delight of the spirit comes from one's love reaching out to the beloved spouse and the hoped for child.

---

35. *Letter 6*, 5, Robert Eno, trans., *Saint Augustine: Letters, Volume 6,* vol. 81 of *The Fathers of the Church: A New Translation* (Washington, D.C.: The Catholic University of America Press, 1989), p. 55. For helpful comments on the meaning of "flesh," "concupiscence," and "love" in Augustine see Peter Brown, *op. cit.,* p. 418; Robert Innes, "Integrating the Self through the Desire of God," *Augustinian Studies,* vol. 28, no. 1 (1997), p. 76; Oliver O'Donovan, *The Problem of Self-Love in Augustine* (New Haven: Yale University Press, 1980); Terry L. Miethe, "Augustine and Concupiscence," *Augustinian Bibliography: 1970-80* (Westport, CT: Greenwood Press, 1982), pp. 195-218. Gerald Bonner notes (p. 309) that Augustine generally uses *concupiscentia* (in the sense of *concupiscentia carnis*) as referring to a sexual desire which "by inducing the highest of all physical pleasures virtually overwhelms the whole intellect." (See *The City of God,* 14.16.) He goes on to point out that Augustine believed that this effect of sin was matched by the lust for power which infects the human psyche. In his emphasis on these two powerful desires he thus anticipates the work of Freud *(libido carnis)* and Adler *(libido dominandi).* (Gerald Bonner, "*Libido* and *Concupiscentia* in Saint Augustine," *Studia Patristica,* vol. 6, no. 4, pp. 312-14). For an extensive discussion of *libido dominandi* and *concupiscentia carnis* see Francois-Joseph Thonnard, "La notion de concupiscence en philosophie augustinienne," *Recherches Augustiniennes,* vol. 3 (1965), pp. 59-105.

36. *Sermon 51,* 23-24.

Although Augustine had doubts about whether such a holy union of body and mind between spouses is ever achieved in our present "cracked" condition, he did believe that it would have been achieved in Eden if humans had not sinned. The sexuality of the first man and woman was as much a part of their innocent nature as was their rationality. They were not pure spirits. They were body and soul humans and were drawn together as humans, body and soul. Augustine was convinced that even in their innocent days they would have propagated the race by intimate physical acts of love.[37] The only difference between then and now would have been in the way in which sexual intimacy was engaged. In Eden those first humans would have enjoyed coition in the same way as they would have enjoyed eating and drinking: temperately. They would have been moved by love for the other rather than desire for self-satisfaction. In all senses it would have been an "ordered" act, passionate but not "out of control," dominated by the "spirited" love that chooses the good of the human lover before one's own, and the good God above all.[38]

This is not to suggest that the love of the first man and woman would not have had its complications. The first sin was caused by an already disordered love. It was not a misuse of the sexual drive; it was an act of disobedience driven by pride, the wish and pretension to be just like God. Augustine suggests that Adam's overpowering friendship for Eve played a part in his cooperation in the act of disobedience. His love prompted him to climb the "tree of life" so that he might join his beloved in tasting the forbidden fruit. Certainly Adam, like Eve, was driven by a desire to "know all" and become a ruler of the universe, but he also was reluctant to let his loved one "go out on a limb" by herself. As Augustine ruefully observes, it

---

37. *The City of God*, 14.24; 14.10. See *A Literal Commentary on Genesis*, 11.42.59. David Hunter points out that in his early years Augustine interpreted the relationship of Adam and Eve as being purely spiritual. In 401, in his work *The Good of Marriage*, he admits at least the possibility that Adam and Eve eventually would have had intercourse had they remained in Eden. When he wrote his *Literal Commentary on Genesis* in 410, he shows no doubt about the full physical relationship of Adam and Eve even if they had not sinned. His final position is clearly stated in his debate with Julian towards the end of his life. There he writes: "I have never censured the union of the two sexes if it is lawfully within the boundaries of marriage. There could be no generation of human beings without such union even if no sin preceded it" (*Against Julian the Heretic*, 3.7.15). See David G. Hunter, "Augustinian Pessimism? A New Look at Augustine's Teaching on Sex, Marriage and Celibacy," *Augustinian Studies*, vol. 25 (1994), pp. 166-68.

38. *Letter 6**, 38.

may have been the first time (but certainly not the last) that a human chose a human love over the Lover that is Divine.[39]

In our present fallen condition, it is difficult for us to act out of the highest motives, motives that are highly spiritual. We are not at peace with ourselves, but this is not because of our sexuality. The war we experience is more of a war in our spirit than in our body. The central difficulty in being one in heart with another is not our sexual drive. It arises from the tendency of our wounded will to satisfy this drive in inappropriate ways, to make it a higher priority in life than it deserves to be. The task just now for us is not to exterminate sexuality but to find ways by which our perverse choices can be controlled.

For Augustine there were only two ways for this to be done. Either one must choose a life of total abstinence (continence) or choose a life of controlled exercise within the society of family. He thought the continent life was the best solution for him and in principle was a higher way of life, but only because it comes closer to the life we shall have in heaven. Both the chaste married life and the life of celibacy are good, but neither eliminates the difficulty in controlling earthly passion. Neither age nor an ascetic life in the desert nor a satisfying family life can guarantee freedom from temptation. Still, it does not follow that the dangers that surround our sexuality make it an evil any more than the perils of living make life an evil.[40]

39. *The City of God,* 14.26. On the influence of "friendly persuasion" in Adam's sin see *A Literal Commentary on Genesis,* 11.42.59. On carnal relations in Eden see *On the Grace of Christ and Original Sin,* 2.35.40; *On Marriage and Concupiscence,* 2.7.17. Helpful commentaries on these points can be found in Brown, *op. cit.,* pp. 400-408 and in Schmitt, *op. cit.,* pp. 99ff.

40. *Against Julian,* 3.11.22. See Brown, *op. cit.,* p. 419. Borresen remarks: "The goodness proper to marriage exists in its purity only in the state of innocence, an ideal which has never been fulfilled. The condition of the human race after the Fall and during the time it waits for its complete renewal, involves a sexuality that is deeply disfigured. . . . The mutual vow of continence is, therefore, the summit of love between a married couple because there everything is directed towards sacramental fidelity. Married love is intimately connected with the order of salvation. It surpasses the blessing of fertility which belongs to the order of creation and it escapes the dominion of sin" (Borresen, *op. cit.,* pp. 118-19). See *Commentary on the Lord's Sermon on the Mount,* 1.15.42; *The Good of Marriage,* 3.3; *Letter 127,* 9. Augustine writes: "The resurrection of the dead has been compared to the stars of the sky (*1 Corinthians,* 15:41-42). There will be one splendor there for virginity, another for married chastity, another for holy widowhood. They will be variously bright but they will all be there. Their brightness is unequal but they have the sky in common" (*Sermon* 132, 3). "As for us, following the faith and the sound doctrine of the holy scriptures, we refuse to say that marriage is

Augustine's conclusion is that sexuality, like every other human drive, is good in itself and does not necessarily constitute an obstacle to the "friendship" that is the foundation of the family. Indeed, it can contribute warmth and energy to the oneness of heart that friendship demands. To the very end of his life Augustine fervently defended marriage and conjugal desire against those who argued that both were somewhat disreputable. It seemed incomprehensible to him that any believing Christian could call evil the human desire that leads to the propagation of the race. As he wrote to Bishop Atticus:

> What Catholic so defends the right faith against them [the Pelagians] that he condemns marriage which the Maker and Creator of the world blessed? What Catholic would call the carnal desire present in marriage the work of the devil, since by means of it the human race would have been propagated even if no one had sinned, in order that the blessing be fulfilled: "Increase and multiply" (Genesis 1:28)? By the sin of that man in whom all have sinned, this blessing has not lost the effect of its goodness in that clear, marvelous and praiseworthy fecundity of nature which is there for all to see. What Catholic does not proclaim the works of God in every creature of soul and flesh and in contemplating them does not burst forth in a hymn to the Creator who was active, not only before the sin, but who even now does all things well?[41]

What Augustine is saying is simply this: far from being a curse, the continuing ability of a loving man and woman to join in spirit and body to produce (if God wills it) another member of the human race is a sign that God has not given up on humanity, even after their sin.

Thus, when the time came to speak to his people about their married life, Augustine never dreamed of denying them the pleasures of conjugal love. Indeed he told them that it was not only unchristian but even inhuman to deny love to a spouse:

---

a sin. Nevertheless, no matter how good it is, we put it on a lower level than the chastity of virgins and even the chastity of widows" (*Holy Virginity*, 21.21). In another place Augustine notes that the three states are reflected in the good women of the Christmas story. All of them were holy but in different ways: Elizabeth representing the virtues of marriage; Anna, those of widowhood; Mary, those of virginity. Clearly Mary is the holiest of the three. See *Sermon 196*, 2.

41. *Letter 6**, 3, Eno translation, *op. cit.*, pp. 54-55.

I do not say that you are not to love your spouse; I only say that you should love Christ more. Love in your spouse the Christ that is in them and hate in them only the obstacles to Christ's presence that you find there.[42]

To love one's spouse means to love him or her as a human being, body and soul; it means to love this *person* through a friendly union of hearts and with an affection that is rightfully expressed sometimes in a physical way. Indeed, the continuing possibility of such total love is one of the divinely sanctioned delights left to us even after the mistake of Eden.[43]

E. Concluding Thought

Augustine was convinced that the friendly relations in the family were very important for the larger society. The unity of heart found in a good marriage reaches out first to embrace other members of the family and ultimately even to all members of the human race. As Augustine told his listeners one day:

So that a human being might not be alone a system of friendship was created. Friendship begins with one's spouse and children, and from there moves on to strangers. But considering the fact that we all have the same father (Adam) and the same mother (Eve) who will be a stranger? Every human being is neighbor to every other human being. Ask nature: is this man unknown? He's still human. Is this woman an enemy? She's still human. Is this man a foe? He is still a human being. Is this woman a friend? Let her remain a friend. Is this man an enemy? Let him become a friend.[44]

---

42. *Sermon 349*, 7; 1-2.

43. Clark speculates on why Augustine did not develop this idea of companionate marriage. Her conclusion is that "it is embedded in his thought but is overshadowed by his emphasis upon the reproductive functions of marriage. His ambivalent conception of the essence of marriage, can be traced primarily to the necessities of theological controversy, for it was in the midst of controversies that he formulated his marital ethic." She also points to the view of women current at the time as being influential (Elisabeth Clark, "Adam's Only Companion: Augustine and the Early Christian Debate on Marriage," *Recherches Augustiniennes,* vol. 21 [1986], pp. 139-41).

44. *Sermon 299D*, 1.

Peace in oneself is the necessary foundation for peace in the family and, if all in the family have that inner peace, the ideal family is possible. In such a family children are subject freely to their parents and the parents in turn guide them with piety. Brothers and sisters are bound together by a spiritual bond far stronger than blood. All those related by marriage or by kinship are joined together in love. In such a family servants are attached to their masters more by joyful desire to fulfill their duties than by the necessity of their condition. Masters in turn are patient with their servants out of respect for the divine Master of all and they impose their will more by persuasion than force.[45]

A political society composed of such exceptional families will truly be at peace. Whether it can also be a society of true friends remains to be seen.

---

45. Johann Roten remarks, "If there exists authority of husbands over their wives, and for him it does exist, it is not given that husbands may act as tyrants, but that they may live together in sincere love" (*op. cit.*, p. 36). See *The Morals of the Catholic Church and the Morals of the Manicheans,* 1.30.63.

CHAPTER 7

The Nature of the State

I. Introduction

A. A Tale of Two Cities

As we have seen, the foundation of Augustine's moral and social philosophy is the law of love. Just as love is the measure of our perfection as individuals, it is also the measure of the perfection of every society: that is, the perfection or imperfection in the love of its members determines the perfection of any society. Indeed, it is the love of their members that separates the two transcendent societies, the city of God (called symbolically "Jerusalem") and the earthly city ("Babylon"). Since humans in this life are mixed and not fixed in their loves (neither all good nor all bad), none of the societies they form can be identified as perfect examples in time of either of the two transcendent cities. The supra-temporal societies of Babylon and Jerusalem exist in their fullness only in hell and heaven.

Just as individuals can freely choose to make themselves devils or, with the grace of God, choose to become saints, so too political societies can tend towards being a Babylon or a Jerusalem. If a state is dominated by the ideals of Babylon, it will seek only earthly goods and will not hesitate to use any means available, be it deceit or cruelty or aggressive war, to achieve peace by domination and to gain prosperity by theft. If a state tries to mirror the heavenly Jerusalem, its members will be united by a love akin to friendship and, while seeking necessary earthly goods, will yet live as pilgrims seeking their true good in that city of God only reached through death.

In Augustine's day (as in ours) the reality of political life involved a mixture of the values of both Babylon and Jerusalem. Every state, like the humans who are its citizens, is somewhat "cracked" and falls short of the perfection of love that can make it the best that it could be. At the same time, no state is beyond hope. Faced with this reality and this possibility, Augustine's political writings thus became a tale of two cities: the Babylon that often is and the Jerusalem that could be. For the pilgrim people struggling to live morally in the various "Babylons" of this world he provided a critical analysis of their imperfect state and practical advice on how to survive it. To those who dreamed of something better he held out a vision of the ideal state, an earthly "Jerusalem" that was based on the love of friendship.

Augustine was too much of a realist to believe that any political society, past or present, has ever achieved such perfection. As he somberly observed, in ordinary political life the wise and the pious are not usually found in seats of power and most citizens are motivated more by servile fear than friendly love in their respect for the common good.[1] He recognized the sad fact that in this real world of wounded human beings there will always be a need to judge and punish those who refuse to obey the law. From the day when Cain founded the first city, pious exhortations to civility have seldom been effective in controlling human criminal tendencies. The state, from its first beginnings, has found itself forced to deal with actions against the public good which "it must punish in order to keep peace among ignorant men."[2] Augustine seems to anticipate the pessimism of Hobbes when, looking at the society that surrounded him, he gloomily observes:

> All in the human community are driven by personal passions to pursue their private desires. Unfortunately the objects of such desires are limited and no one can ever be totally satisfied. As a result the normal condition of earthly society is one of conflict and war where the weak are oppressed by the strong.[3]

Augustine never experienced the reality of his dream of an ideal state where citizens and rulers were "one in heart," loving God above all and each other because of that love. He recognized that such perfection would

1. *The Trinity*, 2.4.9; *Letter 185*, 6.21.
2. *Free Choice*, 1.5.13.
3. *The City of God*, 18.2.

never be found this side of the heavenly "Jerusalem," the city of God in full flower. At the same time he was convinced that any political society striving for such perfection of love could be made a better state by the very effort. A Babylon trying to become a Jerusalem is infinitely better than a self-satisfied Babylon. It was for this reason that he encouraged capable young people to participate in political life and was ready and willing to support them when they became rulers. He insisted that politics was a true calling from God and that it would be a sad disservice for those qualified to give up politics for a supposedly more pious way of life. A noble king trying to achieve concord in his earthly kingdom prepares himself and others for the perfect achievement of friendship in God's city. In doing this he fulfills the will of God even in the midst of a still imperfect political society.

B. The Cultural Context

In writing about political life, Augustine had to deal with humanity as he found it, both the good and the bad. He was convinced that humans remain social animals despite their fall from grace but he also accepted the fact that in their present weakened condition their social nature does not always shine through. Every human has difficulty conquering ignorance and making good choices. As Deane notes, when Augustine says that "the laws of man's nature move him to hold fellowship and maintain peace with all men so far as in him lies,"[4] he is speaking about humans before they were wounded by sin. In our present circumstances, because of sin, the human desire to form community is frequently hampered by self-interest and the tendency to seek personal good at the expense of others.[5] Only those few humans who consistently follow the rules of love that lead to permanent citizenship in the city of God express day by day the natural comradeship which reflects the best aspect of a human being's social nature. Most humans involved in society will act as though they were not redeemed, giving in to selfishness, taking advantage of the stranger, desiring to rule over others so as to be able to dominate them.[6]

4. *Ibid.*, 19.12.

5. Herbert Deane, *The Political and Social Ideas of St. Augustine* (New York: Columbia University Press, 1963), pp. 92-93. See *Commentary on the Letter of John to the Parthians*, 2.11-14. For other somber reflections on the sometime lack of sociability among humans see *The City of God*, 12.28; 12.23.

6. See Deane, *op. cit.*, pp. 95-96.

The North African environment in which Augustine lived and worked was not conducive to creating a very sophisticated society, much less a society of saints. The ordinary folk were convinced that their destiny hinged on fate and thus were not very interested in public affairs. Their main interest was to preserve their life and to enjoy themselves as far as possible. These friendly, passionate, mostly ignorant, mostly poor and un-educated, sometimes violent people were primarily concerned with their own lives and the lives of those closest to them. They were also the raw material of political society in Augustine's day. From time to time Augustine speaks about the ideal (the ideally best ruler, the ideally best form of government, the state which fulfills all the demands of justice) but most of his writings concern what was *real* in political life, a state apparatus that had to try to bring order to a populace who most of the time acted like citizens of the earthly city rather than saints in the city of God, people who more often than not were driven by self-love and ambition for more and more pleasure and more and more goods and more and more power. Such a state had to be concerned first with preserving some semblance of external order among its rambunctious citizens; in order to accomplish this, coercive force was often necessary.[7] Creating a society of friends often had to give way to control of enemies. This was the environment in which Augustine did his thinking and writing about the state.

II. Augustine's Political Philosophy

A. Preliminary Points

In trying to understand Augustine's writings on the state, it is important to note the following points. First, he never composed a *scientific* treatment of political philosophy. His thought did not develop in the quiet of an academic study; much of it was a response to violent controversy. Much of his thinking about the state, political authority, law and punishment, war and peace, was developed in conflict with the Manicheans and Donatists, in the midst of civil insurrections, in reaction to the trauma that followed the

7. For a more complete description of the times and the people, see. F. Van der Meer, *Augustine the Bishop,* trans. Brian Battershaw and G. R. Lamb (New York: Sheed & Ward, 1961), pp. 129-98. J. E. Merdinger, *Rome and the African Church in the Time of Augustine* (New Haven: Yale University Press, 1997), pp. 3-27. Peter Brown, *Augustine of Hippo* (Berkeley: University of California Press, 1967), pp. 19-27.

sack of Rome or (towards the end of his life) in fearful anticipation of barbarian victory. In order to understand his writings at any moment in his life, it is important to understand the situation that provoked them. Also, since his thinking was inspired by the events of the day, there is no one place in the Augustinian *corpus* where one can find the *final* statement of his political philosophy. His thoughts about the state are scattered throughout his writings over the last forty years of his life.

Secondly, all of Augustine's political thought assumed that *all* humans (ruler and ruled alike) are slightly cracked. While he admits that "rule by the best" makes sense in any society, he is equally firm in his conviction that there is no group or individual who can be said to be *best* by nature. All humans share similar weakness. All must battle misdirected/uncontrolled desire (concupiscence) and an ignorance that makes it difficult for even the most "educated" to see and accept the reality of their lives. At their best, humans are the highest good in creation; at their worst they are the most destructive force the world has ever seen. Every society must take into account that its members are mixed blessings (or "mixed up" blessings) as it pursues its goal of bringing order out of disorder and peace out of conflict.

B. Nature and Purpose of the State

1. Essential Characteristics

A description of the state that is generally accepted today is that it is a perfect society whose purpose is to promote the temporal common good. It is described as a *perfect society* to indicate that a true state is not subject to any other society of the same order. Put simply, it has *sovereignty* over its own affairs. Its purpose is said to be the promotion of the *temporal* common good to differentiate it from religious societies which are concerned about the eternal good of their members.

The temporal common good that the state seeks to achieve includes two elements: peace and the prosperity of its members. In order to preserve peace it must first establish a body of laws that create internal order by regulating interaction between citizens: for example, various laws regulating the use of property and the orderly flow of traffic on highways. It also has a legitimate function in motivating its members to become good citizens through education of those of good will and a justice system to punish those of bad will. Finally, the state has a legitimate right to use whatever moral means are necessary in order to protect itself from external attack, to preserve peace through defensive war.

The state also has a proper interest in promoting public prosperity, the material conditions under which its citizens can lead a decent life as human beings. At very least this implies creating an atmosphere in which individuals can live well if they exercise their own initiative. Those political/economic philosophers who espouse the "laissez-faire" state limit the state's function to establishing such an environment. In this view, the state's task is to provide an equal opportunity for its members to earn prosperity. It has no obligation to assist individuals in finding it. Other views maintain that the state must provide positive help to individuals so that they may live well, some even going so far as demanding that the state provide for all of its citizens' needs from cradle to grave.

Finally, some argue that the state must not only help its members become good citizens; it must also encourage them to become good human beings. This view sees the state as the *guardian of virtue* charged with the responsibility of insuring that its citizens live good moral lives. In such a state any act that is immoral is a crime and can be punished by the state. According to this view, state laws against "private sins" (i.e. faults that have no impact on the common good) are legitimate because there are no victimless crimes. Every evil act has at least one victim: namely, the person who does the evil. As we shall see, Augustine seems to come close to this view, arguing that the state cannot be indifferent to private immorality any more than it can be to civil disruption.

In the description of the state outlined above, any society that seeks the temporal common good of its members and has sovereignty, can legitimately claim to be a state. This description thus answers the first question any political philosophy must answer: "What are the essential characteristics of a state?" The question is obviously important. To demand too much of a state is to eliminate many actually existing societies which can legitimately lay claim to statehood. This is a serious matter because if a political society is not in fact a true state, it loses the warrant for its claim that its laws must be obeyed. It has no basis for claiming a sovereignty which justifiably may be defended against outside attacks and which may serve as a foundation for establishing internal order. Such a "pseudo-state" cannot claim allegiance from inside or respect from outside. If, on the other hand, too little is demanded of the state, then it will not have the strength to work for its legitimate goals. If a people have *nothing in common*, it is difficult to see how they can achieve a temporal common good in any organized way.

These concerns were very much in Augustine's mind when he gave his own statement of the essential conditions that must be met before a state can exist.[8] His description is clearly minimalist, neither demanding nor excluding functions of the state in the promotion of virtue and/or the protection of the rights of God. For a state to exist only two things are necessary:

(1) there must be a group of beings who are capable of making a free choice, and
(2) they must in fact be bound together by agreement about common goals.[9]

Augustine would certainly agree that the nobility and perfection of a particular state depends on what its common goals are, but for a state to exist demands only that there be common goals. Thus he writes:

> A *people* is an assemblage of reasonable beings bound together by a common agreement as to the objects of their love. In order to discover the character of any people, we have only to observe what it loves. Yet whatever it loves, if it is at least a group of reasonable beings and not of beasts, and is bound together by an agreement as to the objects of love, it is reasonably called a *people*; and it will be a superior people in proportion as it is bound together by higher interests, an inferior people in proportion as it is bound together by lower interests. According to this definition of ours, the Roman people is a people, and its weal is without doubt a commonwealth or republic.[10]

8. For other examples of Augustine's attempt to define the state see *The City of God*, 15.8; 17.14; *Letter 138*, 2.10; *Letter 155*, 3.9; *Free Choice*, 1.7.16; *A Literal Commentary on Genesis*, 9.9. For commentary see Johannes van Oort, *Jerusalem and Babylon: A Study into Augustine's City of God* (Leiden: E. J. Brill, 1991), p. 103.

9. Augustine observes: "If there is unity, there is a people. Take away that point of unity and there is a mob. For what after all is a mob but a disorderly crowd?" (*Sermon 103*, 4).

10. *The City of God*, 19.24. Augustine uses an interesting analogy to explain how very different people can be brought together by a common object. "Our two eyes do not see each other and yet when the eyes are open the right eye cannot look at a particular object without the left eye looking also. They meet together in one object. The object of their attention is the same although their places are different" (*Commentary on*

Augustine does not demand "perfect" justice for a state to exist, only that degree of justice implied in the sacrifice of self-interest to common purpose. In the *City of God* (2.21), Augustine examines and rejects Scipio's opinion (reported and seconded by Cicero) that a state cannot exist unless it contains the perfection of justice. He rejects this demand for the very practical reason that there never has been (nor likely ever will be) any state that meets this criterion. Augustine's somewhat pessimistic view is based on his understanding of the nature of perfect justice and on his conviction that humans will always be imperfect.

Perfect justice is nothing less than "love serving God and therefore ruling well all things subject to humans."[11] The specific task of justice is to see

> . . . that all receive what belongs to them. It regulates the right order inside and outside the individual. It is therefore just for the soul to be subordinate to God, and the body to be subordinate to the soul, and for the body and soul taken together to be subject to God.[12]

Perfect justice is present in us only when we have control of ourselves, love others as they deserve to be loved, and love God unconditionally. If any of these aspects of justice are missing, the perfection of justice is missing. But, the only humans who are consistently capable of such perfection are those who are even now confirmed members of the city of God, those who are even now saints in heaven. Even the best of humans still living on earth are not secure in their virtue or the perfection of their love. Although they may rise to the heights of love from time to time, giving each the love due them, this is never a permanent condition. So-called earthly "saints" will sin from time to time and thus fail in the perfection of ordered love that is the essence of justice. No one in any state has ever practiced "perfect justice" for a very long time.

To demand perfect justice before one accepts a society as a state causes a problem. Perfect justice in a state demands that all of its members

---

the *Letter of John to the Parthians*, 6.10). Adam suggests that Augustine would conclude that most existing states are valid states even though they lack perfect justice. See Jeremy Adams, *The Populus of Augustine and Jerome: A Study in the Patristic Sense of Community* (New Haven: Yale University Press, 1971), pp. 131-35.

11. *The Morals of the Catholic Church and the Morals of the Manicheans*, 1.15.25. See *Commentary on Psalm 83*, 11.

12. *The City of God*, 19.4.

are perfectly just, giving to God his due by loving him above all and giving all others their due by loving them for the sake of God.[13] A state cannot be said to have perfect justice as long as there is one member (citizen or ruler) who is not perfectly just. This is so because "individual men are, as it were, the elements and seeds of the cities" and one cannot get good fruit from bad seeds.[14] It follows that if perfect justice is demanded before a human community can be said to be a true state, then none of the classical political societies of antiquity can be called states. But such an assertion is (in Augustine's view) simply absurd. In varying degrees all of the states of history, especially Rome in its days of glory, were concerned about the public good.[15] In preferring a more modest definition of the state, Augustine is able to admit as true states such disparate political societies as the truly Christian state (which he believed never existed), Israel, Rome, and many other secular civil societies. Though each varies greatly in the degree of its justice, each one exists under the direction of divine providence and therefore serves a purpose in God's grand plan for creation.[16]

Of course even the worst state must have some justice, at least the justice that is implied in having a unity of purpose and a rule of law directing all to the common good. If citizens are united in the social good that they love, there is some ground for respecting each other. Their concern for distributive and legal justice (each one receiving and giving their fair share to the society) can lead to the beginnings of commutative justice whereby they respect the rights of each other. Augustine describes justice as the preserver of the necessary order in society whereby the members love more that which is more important and love less that which is less important.[17] Such modest ordering of love can be the seed of that perfect justice which Augustine would wish for every individual and every society, the justice whereby every existing being (God included) receives that which is due.

---

13. Augustine's conviction that the worship of the true God must exist in a society before that society can be perfectly just is reflected in *The City of God*, 2.21; 19.21.

14. *Commentary on Psalm 9*, 8.

15. *The City of God*, 2.21. See D. J. MacQueen, "The Origin and Dynamics of Society and the State," *Augustinian Studies*, vol. 4 (1973), pp. 86-89.

16. *The City of God*, 5.26.

17. *On True Religion*, 48.93. Augustine remarks: "What musicians call harmony in music, in the state is known as concord. This is the closest and most secure bond in any commonwealth and it cannot exist without justice" (*The City of God*, 2.21). See also *ibid.*, 4.4.

2. The Purpose of the State

Augustine believed that the primary purpose of and present need for the state is to preserve peace: "the well-ordered concord of civil obedience and rule."[18] With this peace as a foundation, the state can then work to achieve the further goal of "combining men's wills to attain the things which are helpful to this life and the administration of those things necessary for the maintenance of this mortal life."[19] Such texts as the above suggest two distinct goals for a political society:

1. the preservation of the peace by seeking to insure the harmonious external conduct of the humans in it and to protect them from external attacks;
2. the administration and organization of those material goods necessary for the continuation of life this side of death.

Augustine does not seem to believe that the state has any special obligation to provide for the welfare of those who cannot provide for themselves. Charitable work is left to the church and private individuals. The state has little to do with the distribution of property. Its function is to organize that distribution through rules and regulations, for example by defining and determining the right of private property (including slaves). Thus Augustine writes that state laws

> . . . insure that men may possess the things which may be called "ours" for a season and which they eagerly covet, on condition that peace and

---

18. *The City of God*, 19.17. Augustine believed that temporal peace is a true good even when the means of attaining it is through a war for a just cause (*ibid.*, 15.4). It is indeed a gift of God himself (19.13), and it should not be looked down upon as being of little value (19.26). Deane writes: "For Augustine, the maintenance of earthly justice and temporal, external peace and order — the peace of Babylon, that is the maintenance of the combination of men's wills to attain a "common agreement among men regarding the acquisition of the necessities of life" (*The City of God*, 19.17), is always the basic and fundamental task that the state is expected to perform" (Deane, *op. cit.*, p. 133). Markus adds that the citizens of the two cities (the earthly city and the city of God) share a common interest in earthly peace which is composed of economic necessity, public order, and defense. R. A. Markus, "Two Conceptions of Political Authority: Augustine, *De civitate dei*, xix.14-15, and Some Thirteenth-Century Interpretations," *Journal of Theological Studies*, vol. 16, no. 1 (April 1965), p. 98.

19. *The City of God*, 19.17.

human society be preserved so far as they can be preserved in earthly things.[20]

In the real world (the world where most states are more "Babylon" than "Jerusalem") the means for achieving these purposes depend more on fear than love. In the real world the state can best achieve its goals through a coercive system based on laws telling people what they *should* do, a judicial system for determining whether or not they *did* what they should do, and a penal system for rewards and punishment on the basis of what they in fact *did do*. The state must take humans as it finds them, afraid for their own lives, their own property, their own good name, their own worldly success. In striving to control their unsociable passion for these earthly goods, the state accomplishes its goals most efficiently by threatening to take away those very goods which are so vehemently desired.

C. Is the State a Natural Society?

1. The Structure and the Importance of the Question

To assert that the state is a natural society is to claim the following:

1. There is a natural need for the state. Assuming a substantial growth in the human race, a society larger than and different from the family would be necessary and useful to promote the temporal common good.
2. The authority which would be required for the functioning of such a society could be acquired and exercised in a way that would not act against the essential equality of human beings or engage in a demeaning "domination" of those ruled by those who rule.[21]

This somewhat theoretical issue has important practical consequences. If the state is not *natural* to human beings, if it is necessary only

---

20. *Free Choice*, 1.15.32. See MacQueen *op. cit.*, p. 78.

21. I assume the truth of Simon's thesis that authority has two essential functions in every complex society and is therefore a property of all such societies. See Yves R. Simon, *A General Theory of Authority* (Notre Dame: University of Notre Dame Press, 1980), pp. 47-79. See also the earlier chapter of this book, "Friendship and Society," which contains a discussion of the functions of authority in society.

because of human perversity (or, even worse, if it is an *expression* of human perversity), then the only sensible course for those seeking virtue is to stay as far away from it as possible. Politics would not be a noble profession and no noble soul would think of participating in it. Being a politician or a king would be in the same category as being a slave-master, a line of work which, by definition, leads away from rather than towards the kingdom of God. If it is the creation of the devil, more of hell than of heaven, the argument that one should participate in it and try to make it better makes no more sense than trying to encourage a permanent resident in one of the circles of Dante's *Inferno* to try to improve the environment. If, on the other hand, the state is natural to humans, if it is a good thing sometimes used badly, then a socially conscious virtuous person should participate in affairs of the state and try to improve them. If the state is indeed good but wounded, there is hope for even the worst state. There is the chance that even the most abject "Babylon" could be moved to some degree towards becoming "Jerusalem." And even if the effort fails, at least it would perfect the person trying and be a service to the community. Put simply, if the state is a natural society, no one gets "dirty hands" through virtuous participation in its life.

2. The Need for the State

As we have seen in a previous chapter, Augustine was convinced that humans were social by nature even though they did not always act in a sociable way. He also believed that the family is a natural society which meets the two conditions outlined above. The union of Adam and Eve was needed for the continuation of the race. It was also a society of equals, a friendly society, in which necessary decision-making was achieved without unnatural domination. This natural and friendly exercise of authority typical of that first human family is quite different from the subordination of master over slave. Slavery is not "natural" to humanity. It is not demanded by human nature and indeed its very definition suggests the presence of a domination contrary to the natural equality of humans.[22] Even the most humane exercise of a slave-master's authority cannot make the social structure "natural" since the warrant of the institution rests on a condition contrary to moral fact: that one human can "own" another. It follows that

22. See *A Literal Commentary on Genesis,* 20.30; 22.34; *Questions on the Heptateuch,* 1.153.

though there is a natural need for the family, slavery is a matter of human choice and it comes from a will that has been twisted by sin.

The question here is whether the need for the state is to be traced to the same perverted source. Unfortunately Augustine never considered this question formally. He never wrote a specific treatise arguing for *innocent nature's need* for the state.[23] He wrote of the state as it actually exists, now tarnished by sin like every other temporal institution after Eden. Thus, he frequently emphasized that in humanity's present wounded condition the state is needed as a corrective for human perversity. Is it possible to argue that he would grant the need for the state even if humans had remained in a state of sinless innocence? I believe that it is possible to make such an argument, both for the *natural need* of the state and for the possibility that the rulers of the state could exercise their authority without causing an *unnatural subordination* of those ruled.

An outline of an argument from Augustine's writings for the *natural need* for the state is as follows:

1. It is natural for humans to desire peace.
2. Peace depends on order among disparate parts.
3. When the parts to be ordered are free beings, the order will be based on decisions of people who, because of different past experiences and different habits drawn from their unique past choices, will sometimes disagree.
4. In a complex society (composed of many families and many individuals), it is unlikely that consensus about means to achieve common goals will always be achieved.
5. Therefore, the ordering of such societies towards the common good of earthly peace can only be done efficiently through the exercise of authority.
6. But a society which seeks the temporal common good under the direction of authority is what is meant by the state.
7. There is therefore a "natural" need for the state.

Some of the important points in the argument will be explored in the section that follows.

23. See Markus, *op. cit.,* p. 81.

3. Development of the Argument

Augustine defines peace as the tranquility that comes out of order and defines order as the arrangement of like and unlike things in their proper places.[24] The human need for peace is just as natural as the thirst for happiness. Anyone who has studied human nature seriously must agree that there is no human heart that does not want and need peace.[25] The desire for peace is thus not the result of perversity but of nature. It existed in Eden and would have continued to exist if the human race had endured without sin. As we have seen, Augustine describes the first family as a society of ordered concord among persons living together where some were in positions of authority and others were subject to authority. Unfortunately humans did not remain long enough in innocence to see the development of the city or commonwealth, but if they did they would have certainly desired the extension of peace to the city, a peace which Augustine describes as "an ordered concord among the ruler and ruled in people joined in citizenship."[26]

Even without sin humans would have had a natural need for peace. They would also have had a natural need to "use" material things. They would have needed to eat and drink, to get from place to place, to dispose of the natural "effluvium" of living in community. Paradise was a pleasant earthly place but it was not heaven. Humans had more perfect bodies than we have now but they were not glorified bodies. Therefore, the orderly use of material things would have to be an element in the peace that they desired. The goods described by Augustine as the purposes of the state in our present condition would have been necessary goods in Eden also. Peace coming from an ordered daily life would be needed and so too would an organization of the material goods necessary for day by day living. Peace and temporal prosperity would have been a necessity of life common to a

---

24. *The City of God,* 19.13.

25. *Ibid.,* 19.12.

26. The Latin for these passages is instructive. It reads: "*Pax hominum, ordinata concordia. Pax domus, ordinata imperandi atque obediendi concordia cohabitantium. Pax civitatis, ordinata imperandi atque obediendi concordia civium*" (*The City of God,* 19.13). The same word, *concordia* (literally a "oneness of heart"), is used to designate the essential bond within the state, the family, and among humans generally. It is also used, as we have seen, to describe the essence of friendship. The only difference in these three uses here is that in the human race in general there is no ruler and ruled. All are equal as human beings. In the family and the state the *concordia* (friendship) exists between some who rule and others who are ruled.

multitude of humans even in a state of innocence. The only difference between then and now is that in humanity's state of innocence these goods would have been easier to achieve. As innocent humanity increased there may not have been "road rage," but there would still have been a need for traffic patterns and rules for traveling from here to there. Even the best of families would have needed to use material and temporal goods while they anticipated the greater goods of heaven.[27] Eden was not heaven. It was a way to heaven. It was not in eternity. It was in time. There would have been a need for the temporal peace and an orderly use of earthly things (the air, water, food, other bodily goods) on which such a temporal peace at least partially depends.[28]

Given an increase in the human race in a state of innocence, would such "orderly use of material goods" among many individuals and many families have resulted naturally from the bond of friendship among individuals or, if not, would the social structure of the family have been sufficient to bring it about? Certainly friendship and family existed in Eden. Would these have been sufficient to achieve temporal peace if humanity had not been wounded by sin? It seems unlikely. Since humans are beings of freedom and beings who learn by experience rather than by an infused knowledge common to all, it is reasonable to assume differences of opinion even in a state of innocence. The story of Adam and Eve proves that even two people who love each other can look at the same situation differently. Eve's experience with the tempter gave her new information concerning what should or should not be eaten. Adam had to be convinced of the new project before he made his fatal mistake.

The story of Adam and Eve shows that even in the best of conditions humans are likely to disagree on the best means even when they agree on the goals. They are *free* beings and they are also *different*. This difference can lead to conflicting choices; in order to achieve common action there is need for some peaceful resolution. It is certainly possible that such a resolution could come about without the exercise of authority saying: "Everyone has had their say and every position has its own value, but now we shall go *this* way." A community can agree on a common action by way of consensus if there is indeed clearly a *best* way. But

27. *The City of God*, 19.17.
28. *Ibid.*, 19.13. Augustine writes: "It is wrong to deny that the aims of human civilization are good because this is the highest end that humanity of itself can achieve. However lowly the goods of earth may seem, their aim is peace" (*ibid.*, 15.4).

in a complex society there will very often be no one "best" way to accomplish a desired goal. In such situations consensus on the basis of reasoned argument will become difficult, if not impossible. At the very least, trying to achieve such an improbable consensus will be inefficient. The only practical solution is to have someone in authority resolve the differences.

But would society have achieved such complexity in a state of innocence? If it did not, the natural authority residing in the father of the family would have been enough to resolve differences. There was no need for Adam and Eve to establish a state as long as their family was small and they were the only family. But there is no reason to suppose that the race would not have expanded if the innocence of Eden had been preserved. Certainly Augustine believed that procreation would have continued even if humans had never sinned. Even in Eden a complexity in human society would have arisen which would have been far beyond the ability of the family structure to settle. As the race expanded, there would have been a need to resolve differences of opinion among families and individuals who had fewer and fewer shared experiences.

To summarize, in the state of innocence it is very likely that society would become complex simply by increase in numbers and that such complexity would make it practically impossible to achieve consensus in or among families about the best means to achieve the temporal common good. This being the case, there would be a need for social organization of wider scope than the family, endowed with the authority and responsibility to seek the temporal common good of the individuals and the families that made it up. Such a society seems close to our understanding of the state. It also seems to be what Augustine means by a *people*, "an assemblage of reasonable beings bound together by common agreement as to the objects of their love," where what is loved is "earthly peace" and the order in temporal affairs necessary to achieve it.[29]

There is, then, a natural *need* for the state. The question remains whether the authority necessary to make the state work could be acquired and exercised without an unnatural subordination of one human to another. If there is no way for political authority to be used without causing an unnatural subordination of those ruled, then the state would be unnatural in its operation even though there is a natural need for it to exist. If the authority of the state is *unnatural*, then the institution itself must be

29. *Ibid.*, 19.24.

said to be unnatural. This raises again the question of the meaning of authority, and what the characteristics of natural authority might be.

4. The Meaning of Natural Authority

Authority may be said to be "natural" or "in accord with human nature" if the following conditions are verified:

(1) the *claim* that one has authority does not flow from some effect of human sinfulness;
(2) the *way* in which authority *is exercised* does not manifest a perversity coming from sinful human nature.

Authority will fail the first condition if the only reason for asserting that "a" is superior to "b" is because of a false assumption of inferiority resulting, for example, from conquest in war or enslavement or some similar event rooted in human sin. Authority will fail the second condition if in its exercise it does not seek to achieve the common good (as opposed to the selfish interests of the authority) and/or treats the subjects as though they were not free human beings equal before God.

As we have seen in our discussion of the family, there is a natural subordination of children to parents. Very young children are too deficient in knowledge and prudence to take care of themselves. One does not assume their inferiority; they are inferior in fact. The authority of parent over child becomes "unnatural" only if it is exercised beyond its due time or in an abusive manner. The subordination of slavery is quite different. The rule of master over the slave, even when exercised in a benign fashion, is essentially "unnatural" since it rests on the assumption that a human being can be the possession of another. Since even the most perversely "claimed" authority (i.e., master over slave) can be exercised in a way that is truly human, it is clear that the problem of the "naturalness" of political authority is a problem of *claim*. Is the very claim of a king to rule contrary to human nature? Does the claim itself rest on an assumed inequality among humans? Does the very claim to rule imply a demeaning of those to be ruled?

Markus suggests that the crucial question about the origin of political authority

> . . . is the question as to whether it is to be treated on the model of the authority of a master over his slave, or on that of a husband and father

over his wife and family. These are the paradigm cases which give us a clue to the senses in which the concept of nature is applied to particular social groupings.[30]

The structure of slavery clearly places it among those social institutions that flow from human sinfulness. The structure of the family places it among those that flow from nature. The issue is whether either is the best analogue for the state. If there are only these two choices, one must agree that the rule of the state is just a more sophisticated form of slavery. The state is obviously not the family "writ large." There is no natural inequality among its members. There is no assumption of greater experience or wisdom in the ruler as there is in the parent of a young child. But are these the only two choices?

I believe that there is a third possibility. It is the society described in Augustine's various writings on the rule and practices of religious communities. He himself created such a community and lived as a member for his last forty years on earth. The rule that he established for this group became the principle of organization for communities of men and women throughout North Africa and, eventually, throughout the world down to the present day. Because of humanity's present wounded condition, no one has ever consistently lived up to the ideals of this rule but even in its imperfect observance it gives both superior and subject a worthy goal, a norm by which they can measure the daily perfection or imperfection of their life together.

The religious community formed by Augustine was a *voluntary* society in that it was not one of those societies that a human *needed* in order to live a fully human life. All humans must begin life in a family and, given an increase in the human race, we have argued that eventually there would be a need for a larger society charged with the responsibility of maintaining peace and promoting prosperity among families. There is no similar need for a religious society like that created by Augustine. Participation is determined solely by the free choice of the members.

Like the family and the state, Augustine's religious community was composed of humans with all the strengths and weaknesses of ordinary people. Indeed, Augustine's famous description of humans as "cracked pots," people who have been wounded and tarnished by the fires of living, was directed first and foremost at members of his own commu-

30. Markus, *op. cit.,* p. 81.

137

nity.[31] Those who joined were commonplace Christians, *servi dei,* ordinary humans who happened to take their commitment to God and neighbor seriously. It was far from being a society of angels. It was not meant to be a haven for intellectuals or a club for those who thought themselves to be a religious elite. A noble social status was not required, only a willingness to be "one in heart with others and with God." As Augustine described it:

> Persons very often come to this service of God after a life of slavery. Some come from a life of manual labor in the fields. It would be terribly wrong to refuse to admit such people to the religious life. Indeed, many of them have given wonderful examples for our imitation.[32]

The religious community is like every other complex society in that there is a need for a ruler to perform those *essential* functions described in our discussion of authority in the earlier chapter on friendship. Furthermore, since no member of religious community is "perfect," authority's *substitutional* functions will also sometimes be needed. Augustine thus gives explicit instructions on how to take care of those not able at first to live up to the asceticism demanded. He also creates a procedure for correcting those who are unwilling to follow the rules. Although the one in authority is not *superior to* the others as a human being, he/she is truly the *Superior of* the group, "the person who is ultimately the one who has to bear the burden of the whole group, even though the whole is still more important than the one person at its head."[33]

Augustine believed that the authority of the Superior is necessary for the good of the community and that it should be exercised firmly but in a spirit of love. He gave Superiors the following directions:

31. *Commentary on Psalm 99,* 8.

32. *On the Work of Monks,* 22.25. On the "ordinary" nature of members of religious communities and on the democratic nature of such communities, see the following: J. McEvoy, "*Anima una et cor unum:* Friendship and Spiritual Unity in Augustine," *Recherches de Théologie Ancienne et Médiévale,* vol. 53 (1986), pp. 85-90; Tarsicius J. Van Bavel, O.S.A., *The Rule of St. Augustine with Introduction and Commentary,* trans. Raymond Canning, O.S.A. (London: Darton, Longman and Todd, 1984), p. 102; L. J. Van Der Lof, "The Threefold Meaning of *Servi Dei* in the Writings of Augustine," *Augustinian Studies,* vol. 12 (1981), pp. 43-59; Charles W. Brockwell, Jr., "Augustine's Ideal of Monastic Community: A Paradigm for His Doctrine of the Church," *Augustinian Studies,* vol. 8 (1977), pp. 91-109.

33. See Van Bavel, *op. cit.,* p. 103.

Let the Superior not deem himself happy in using his authority, but in serving the members of the community with love. In honor before them let him take the first place, but in fear before God, let him prefer the last place. Let him be for all an example of good works. Let him restrain the restless, comfort the discouraged, support the weak, with patience towards all. Let him willingly embrace regular discipline while imposing it cautiously upon others. Although both are necessary, let him seek to be loved more than feared, always remembering that he must account for you to God.[34]

Though one rules and another is ruled, Superior and subject must still be united in "oneness of heart." The subordination that results from the authority of the Superior is a subordination of friend to friend, where the one who rules is at the service of the one ruled and the one ruled obeys out of love for the Superior because of the service provided.

As described by Augustine, the moral authority of the Superior is clearly a true power to demand observance of the laws of the community. The *Rule of Augustine* is presented as a plan that *ought* to be followed by anyone who becomes a member of the religious society. Individuals are free to join or not join, but once they have joined they are *not* free to ignore the law without fault. Thus, Augustine stipulates that if members of the community fail in observance of the rule and do not correct themselves, they are to be brought to the Superior for judgment and punishment, a punishment that could even extend to expulsion from the society.[35]

The Superior also has more pedestrian functions, organizing the ordinary day by day activities of the members towards the common good in such mundane matters as determining who should take care of the library or storing the clothes.[36] The Superior may even determine what individuals should do in order to maintain their health. That Augustine meant these directives to be mandates and not recommendations is reflected in his warning to Superiors not to be too quick in apologizing for a harsh directive lest "by being too humble and submissive in your conduct towards

34. Adolar Zumkeller, O.S.A., *The Rule of St. Augustine*, trans. Julian C. Resch, O. Praem. (De Pere, WI: St. Norbert Abbey, 1961), pp. 57-9. See Augustine's *Letter 211*, 4. Van Bavel notes (*op. cit.*, pp. 102, 108) that Augustine calls the Superior in religious community the *"praepositus,"* "the one who is put forward," rather than "father" or "mother." This suggests that the leader is still one of many, a member of the group, the first among equals.

35. *The Rule of St. Augustine, op. cit.*, 4.11; Van Bavel, p. 18.

36. *Rule*, 5.10-11; Van Bavel, p. 21.

139

these young people, your authority, which they should be ready to accept, will be undermined."[37]

In Chapter 7 of his rule for religious communities, Augustine turns his attention to the duties of those who are ruled. He says to them:

> Obey your Superior as a father, but also give him due respect on account of his office, otherwise you offend God in him. . . . It is up to the Superior to see that all that has been said here is put into practice and that actions against the rule are not carelessly overlooked. It is his duty to point out abuses and correct them.[38]

Two important points are suggested in this passage. In the first place, although the Superior is *like a father,* his claim to respect is from his *office as Superior.* Through that office he has received God-given authority to rule. It is not an authority that he has taken upon himself but an authority that has been *given.* Secondly, the authority is specifically an executive authority to see to the accomplishment of the common good as this is described by the rule. The Superior must see to it that all the members of the society carry out the duties that they have taken upon themselves by becoming members. However, in the process the subjects retain their identity and their equality as free humans under God. All are bound to observe the rules set down by the one in charge, but not as slaves living under law but as free humans making their way with the help of God's grace towards their individual destinies.[39]

The example of the religious community gives no help in establishing the *need* for the state. It does help in establishing the *possibility* that it might exist as a society of friends. The religious community shows that it is possible for a group of equal, but imperfect, human beings to live in a society under authority where both the claim for and the exercise of that authority does not rest on the assumption of sin. Augustine's description of the religious community indicates his belief that authority within a society of equals could not only be acquired "naturally" but also exercised "naturally." In such a society authority could express itself through a loving domination by which the individuals are respected as equals before God while yet being directed towards a common goal.

If authority can be claimed and exercised in the society of the reli-

---

37. *Rule* 6.3; Van Bavel, p. 22.
38. *Rule,* 7.1-2; Van Bavel, p. 23.
39. *Rule,* 8.1; Van Bavel, p. 24.

gious community in ways that do not reflect human sin or perversity, there is no reason why the same thing could not happen in political society. The existence of political authority is therefore not a necessary obstacle to a state being a "natural" society, one that is an expression of what is good in human nature more than what is perverse. It is certainly true that in the real world the state is often more called upon to correct perversions than to promote good. It is also true that the state in this world will never reach its perfect form. It will always come up short because of the imperfection of its members. But the imperfections in political society (the selfishness of the ruled, the tyranny of rulers) do not make it less natural or necessary — any more than does divorce argue for the "unnaturalness" of the family. Humans are indeed imperfect but friendship, family, and the state remain natural and necessary ways of expressing their social nature.

5. Objection: "Shepherds, Not Kings"

An objection to the claim that Augustine believed the state to be a natural society is often based on texts where he seems to declare that any exercise of political authority is the expression of or is caused by humanity's sinful nature. One example is the following:

> God did not want rational beings, made in his own image, to dominate any being except the non-rational. He did not want a human to dominate another human; humans were meant to dominate only beasts.[40]

The obvious meaning of these sentences standing alone is that the relationship of king to subject is a relationship that comes only as a result of sin. However, when read in context, it is clear that Augustine is not speaking about the *ideal* relationship between ruler and citizen. He is speaking specifically about a dominion that comes from war where the losers are sometimes made, not citizens, but slaves of the conqueror. It is obvious that this situation comes about only because of sin. Without sin there would be no war and thus no conqueror. Without sin there would be no condition whereby a human treats another human as a lower order of being.

The argument that the state is *not* a natural society has been expanded by various scholars beyond this one text. Thus, for example, Gervase Corcoran, after quoting and dismissing four texts which are often

---

40. *The City of God*, 19.15.

cited to prove the naturalness of the state, goes on to argue that one who says that the state is natural must also hold that slavery is natural because they are equal in terms of the final destiny of their authority to rule. It is, of course, true that all human institutions will cease at the end of time and it is also true that any exercise of human *domination*, whether in the family or state or in voluntary associations such as various corporations, is no better than slavery. But these facts do not seem to address the central question of whether the state *by its very nature* is such an institution of unjust domination.[41]

One text cited by Corcoran to support his position is *Commentary on Psalm 124*, 7-8. However, in this passage Augustine seems to be speaking about slavery and why God allows unjust domination to occur in any human society and how good can come from it. There is no indication, as far as I can see, that he is saying that any exercise of authority other than that of master over slave is *in itself* unnatural. The distinction is important. It seems to me that the rule of master over slave is a bad institution that can be exercised well; the rule of parent over child or the rule of king over subject is a good and necessary institution that can be used badly. Barrow seems to support this analysis, saying, "St. Augustine attaches high value to the state and interpretations which make him disparage the state seem to be beside the mark."[42]

Corcoran, following Markus, further argues that the state cannot be a natural society since coercion is part of the essence of political authority and coercion entered into human experience only after sin. The passage from Markus that he cites is worth quoting in full:

> The parallel between society and the family is, indeed, important to Augustine. But it does not imply that political authority is grounded in the order of nature, as is paternal. A ruler or magistrate should behave like a

---

41. Gervase Corcoran, O.S.A., *St. Augustine on Slavery*, Studia Ephemeridis "Augustinianum," no. 22 (Rome: Patristic Institute "Augustinianum," 1985), p. 64. The texts he cites as being the basis for arguing that the state is a natural society are: *The Good of Marriage*, 1.1; *The City of God*, 19.16; *A Literal Commentary on Genesis*, 8.9.17; *Against Julian the Heretic*, 4.61.

42. R. H. Barrow, *Introduction to St. Augustine: "The City of God"* (London: Faber and Faber, 1950), pp. 235-36. Barrow goes on to say (p. 165) that "It is a mistake to attribute to St. Augustine the view that the Roman Empire was being justly extinguished, since the secular state was of the devil. On the contrary, the secular state is in his view based upon the ordinances of God and, therefore, is of Divine Institution." See *The City of God*, 5.1.

paterfamilias; but the analogy between the two men holds only in respect of family life in the fallen state of man. For the coercive power which is part of the very substance and meaning of political authority also exists in the family; it enters the family, as it enters society, through sin and disorder. But a family is a family without it — we may conceive, even in a sinful world, of a family in which paternal authority is an exercise of care and guidance without coercion. But coercive power is part of the essence of political authority. Without it the state is not a state, though we may imagine lesser societies without it. Political authority, coercive power and its apparatus are what transform society into a state. Society, so we may summarize Augustine's view, has its origins in the order of nature; the state is a dispensation rooted in sin.[43]

In order to respond to Markus's position, it is important to have a clear understanding of what is meant by coercion. Markus's argument clearly refers to a *harsh* coercion whereby rulers tyrannically impose their will on the subjects or have the authority to punish when the subjects do not obey the law. However, one can speak also about what we might call a *mild* coercive power whereby those in authority impose their will on others in exercising the two essential functions of authority: namely, looking out for the common good and making decisions about the best means of achieving the goals of society. These functions seem to be what Augustine means by the "administrative duties" of authority and what Markus seems to mean by the phrase "an exercise of care and guidance."[44] Markus admits that these functions are necessary even in a state of innocence for the orderly functioning of the family. Why then would they not be equally necessary in a state of innocence in some larger society needed to see to the order in the use of temporal goods among many families? The sometime need for *harsh coercion* now is an unfortunate fact of our sin-filled life, and is just as relevant in families and voluntary

---

43. See Markus, *op. cit.,* pp. 77-78; Corcoran, *op. cit.,* p. 65. Deane (*op. cit.,* pp. 138-39) argues in a similar fashion against the need for a state if sin had not occurred. He assumes that the entire apparatus of law, punishment, coercion, and repression constitute the *heart* of the state. We have argued that none of these make up the essence of the state or flow necessarily from that essence. A state is constituted by a union of wills looking to build an orderly, peaceful, prosperous society. Granted that in a state of innocence coercion would not be necessary, law would nevertheless be both useful and necessary since it is unlikely that a multitude of free beings will always come to a consensus on the best way of seeking the temporal good.

44. See *A Literal Commentary on Genesis,* 8.9.17.

societies as in political societies. There is no reason to say that harsh coercion defines the state any more than it defines the other societies
which now need it. Augustine, for one, did not make the authority to use
harsh coercion part of his own definition even though he readily admitted that no really existing state (or really existing family for that matter)
can get by without it.

The argument seems to assume that every law entails this *harsh coercion* and that there would have been no law if sin had not occurred. But
even in Eden all of creation and human beings in particular fell under the
mandate of God's eternal law commanding respect for the order of the
universe. This law was not the result of sin. It was given as a guideline to
enable human beings not to sin, to know what they should and should not
do. Their temptation to disobey came before the sin and it was a temptation to sin precisely because it was a temptation to break the law. The harsh
coercive aspect of the law (the punishment) occurred only after sin, but
the gentle coercive aspect of the law giving guidelines as to what should or
should not be done existed even before.

This would seem to answer Corcoran's question (p. 66) as to whether
in a state of innocence one can imagine a need for laws. In our discussion
of authority we have argued that even innocent humans are likely to have
different opinions about means to ends, about the organization of daily
life. The only way to resolve such differences is to have some authority,
some law which would give a guideline for action. In a state of innocence
such laws would indeed be "freely accepted," but their free acceptance does
not mean that they were not necessary in the first place. To follow traffic
laws freely does not prove that they are not needed.

The text where Augustine speaks about the operation of Divine
Providence through nature and through wills (angelic and human)
whereby, among other things, "societies are administered" is relevant
here.[45] The administrative function of authority in complex societies,
whether of sinners or saints, will always be necessary. The harsh coercive
function of imposing one's will on another as a person of lesser importance or the function of punishing those who break the law because they
believe that they are superior to others and to their laws, is the result of sin
and indeed has always been part of states as we know them. But this does
not prove that this harsh coercion is part of the essence of the state. True,
we have no record of a state that did not exercise this function but there

45. *Ibid.*

was no state until Cain established the first city after the fall of his parents from grace and his own murder of his brother.[46]

Finally, it is true that Augustine never speaks about whether and how the state would have existed in Eden.[47] But this is so because he was not particularly interested in such speculative matters. The fact that he never spoke about the possibility and even the necessity of the state eventually being formed is no proof that he would have denied that possibility and necessity. It is clear that Augustine believed that the race would have increased even without sin. If this had happened, the problem of administration of temporal affairs would have gone far beyond the capabilities of any family to provide. This need would have been present not because individuals and families were tainted with sin; it would have been needed because individuals and the families they form are never the same and have different views on how goals should be accomplished.

6. "Dreaming of Jerusalem": The Ideal State

Augustine believed that the first political society was created by a murderer, Cain, and was composed of all those who had dedicated themselves to the goals of the earthly city. It thus reflected the worst elements in fallen humanity. But Augustine also believed that many humans then and now were not consumed by such perversity. These were the pilgrim people who lived virtuously in this life dreaming of their permanent home in the heavenly Jerusalem. They spent their lives dreaming of heaven and doing their best to make life on earth a bit more heavenly. These were symbolized by the descendants of Cain's second brother, Seth, and especially by Enos,

---

46. As Corcoran has noted (p. 67), it is true that in speaking about the "administration of societies" (*A Literal Commentary on Genesis*, 8.9.17) Augustine is speaking about societies as they actually exist in a sinning world, all of which societies are "terrestrial and mortal." But I would suggest that this need for "administration of society" would have applied just as well to the state in Eden as in fact it did to the family. That Augustine does not list political authority among his examples of natural subordination, does not seem as significant as it is made out to be. The authority of parent over child is not mentioned either but this authority is clearly natural. Moreover, some of the supposedly "natural" subordinations that *are* mentioned seem off the mark. The subordination of woman to man comes up only in Augustine's discussion of the family and it is clear that there will be no such subordination of woman to man in heaven since the family will no longer exist. The subordination of poor to rich is even more questionable, unless it is taken as a sad fact of our sinful existence.

47. Corcoran, *op. cit.*, p. 66.

Seth's son, who represented those gatherings of humans who would live following the will of God and hoping for eternal joy.[48] While living in earthly societies (families, states, religious communities), these would try to instill in them the values and virtues of the heavenly society. While dreaming of the heavenly Jerusalem, they would also dream of making earthly societies imitate that ideal society of friends.

These "Jerusalem dreamers" would try to bring into their relationships on earth the love of friendship that is characteristic of citizens of the city of God. In all their societies they would aim at creating the elements crucial for friendship: a knowledge that could be the basis for mutual understanding and trust, a concern for the good of the other, a unity of heart with each other and with God that would truly make their society to be "one out of many." Of course, the size of the society would be an obstacle to true friendship with everyone. But they would try to love others, if not as actual friends, at least in order that they might become friends. They would be so open to others that they would consider no one to be a stranger, realizing that all people are members of the one human family.[49]

It is clear that when Augustine spoke about friendship as the foundation of society, he did not mean to restrict its application to the family or to communities of religious. Zumkeller observes that when Augustine spoke of authority to rule as a "love that serves," he was not speaking only about the authority that should exist in the religious community. It was a description of every society that is ruled by the ideals of the city of God, the eternal society where all "serve one another in love: superiors with a loyal care: subjects by their obedience."[50]

---

48. *The City of God,* 15.18. For a more extensive discussion of the creation of the first city see Donald X. Burt, "Cain's City: Augustine's Reflections on the Origins of the Civil Society (Book XV 1-8)," *Augustinus: De civitate dei,* ed. Christoph Horn (Berlin: Akademie Verlag, 1997), pp. 195-210.

49. *83 Diverse Questions,* 71.6; *Letter 130,* 13. Speaking about the two commandments to love God and neighbor (Matt 22:37-39), Augustine says: "Here is laudable security for the commonwealth. For a state is neither founded nor preserved perfectly save in the foundation and by the bond of faith and of firm concord when the highest common good is loved by all, and this highest and truest thing is God; when, too, men love one another in God with absolute sincerity since they love one another for his sake from whom they cannot hide the real character of their love" (*Letter 137,* 5.17).

50. *The City of God,* 14.28. Adolar Zumkeller, O.S.A., *Augustine's Ideal of the Religious Life,* trans. Edmund Colledge, O.S.A. (New York: Fordham University Press, 1986), p. 236. Barrow (*op. cit.,* p. 235) comments that for Augustine the difference between a legitimate command of authority and domination of the subject is that in the

The true descendants of the holy Seth, those who one day will be permanent citizens of the city of God, share the weakness in knowledge and will that afflicts all humans now. Therefore, their efforts to establish the perfect state, the earthly "Jerusalem," will never be perfect or permanent. But, despite the imperfection of its achievement, it remains a worthwhile goal and justifies "future saints" becoming involved in matters of state.[51] Indeed, Augustine says that the virtuous have an *obligation* to serve, accepting willingly whatever position divine providence allots to them and exercising their responsibilities diligently. If they are subjects, they should be so willing to obey that the ruler becomes almost embarrassed to give commands. None should seek positions of authority unless they are truly qualified for them, but they should not be reluctant to become qualified and thereafter seek out a position whereby they can use their talents for the benefit of the common good.[52] If, at some later time, they should become the supreme rulers of their community, they should rule with such grace that it is a pleasure to obey them. Whether ruler or ruled in the political society, they should seek to make others their friends and be guided in all their actions by the great golden rule of friendship: "Don't do to others what you would not want done to yourself."[53]

In a state trying to become an earthly Jerusalem, rulers would rule with a healthy humility, ever conscious that they too are human and share with their subjects all the frailty of the species. Their greater freedom to satisfy personal desires would make them more reluctant to give in to them. Their power to be vicious without penalty would prompt them to even greater virtue. They would remember their past failures and rejoice more in controlling their own passions than ruling the community. Their regime would be characterized by justice tempered by mercy but their kindness would not prevent them from passing laws when necessary and punishing those who ignore such laws. They would take action against the criminal out of love for the common good, not out of revenge. They would allow mercy to override justice only when it became clear that such mercy

---

former case the motivation of the command is the promotion of each individual regarded as a neighbor in the Christian sense. It is thus the exercise of an authority in an atmosphere of friendship.

51. See *Commentary on Psalm 61*, 8.

52. Augustine remarks that the virtuous can be most useful in the function of the state (*Letter 151*, 14) and have an obligation to participate in government (*Against Faustus the Manichean*, 22.58). See Deane, *op. cit.*, pp. 300-301.

53. *On Order*, 2.8.25.

would bring about desired reform in the criminal while not encouraging others to take the law lightly. In the ideal state, rulers would consider their office as a sacred calling, an opportunity to make the fullness of love for God and fellow-citizen a reality in the land.[54]

How the ruler should be chosen depends on the society and the circumstances. All authority ultimately comes from God but how that authority comes to humans varies. In the family context, Augustine believed that the ruler is determined by nature. In a voluntary society, the members properly decide who should be in charge. In the state, there is no one best way to determine the ruler, but Augustine gives two guidelines. First, no person or group of persons has an innate right to rule. Human beings are equal by nature and remain so until some accidental event occurs which separates those who should rule and those to be ruled. No one is born to be a political leader; leaders must be selected either directly by God (for example, as David was in the Old Testament) or indirectly through some human agency. Secondly, the one who is given the authority to rule should be that one who is best able to promote and protect the common good.

In society dominated by friendship and ideals of the heavenly city, Augustine believed that it is proper for the community to be involved in the selection of its leader. In such an ideal political society the community will be well-ordered and serious, composed of citizens who place public good over private interests and who are willing to spend time as watchful guardians of the common good. If such an extraordinary community can be found it is reasonable to give citizens the power to select the rulers who will guard the public welfare.[55] When the state is less than ideal, Augustine recommends a method other than selection by the group. He knew from his own experience that democracy does not work when citizens are ignorant or depraved. In a political community where everyone favors private desires over public good, where votes are bought and sold, where power is likely to be handed over to an evil element by people who do not care or do not know any better, it makes sense for a few truly good people to wrest the power of conferring offices from the people and set up a monarchy or oli-

---

54. *The City of God*, 5.24. Commenting on *The City of God*, 19.16, Barrow (*op. cit.*, p. 233) finds in Augustine the idea of government as service, emphasizing care for the interests of the subjects (*consulere*) and compassionate forethought (*providendi misericordiae*). Even when it is necessary to correct others, they should be corrected with love (*Admonition and Grace*, 15.46). See Barrow, *op. cit.*, p. 163.

55. *Free Choice*, 1.6.14.

garchy of the best.[56] When the people are the "worst" they can be hardly expected to choose the "best" to rule them. Whatever right such perverse citizens had to participate in the selection of leaders is rightly overridden by the law of reason, which stipulates that a fickle people should be denied that privilege.

7. Conclusion

The strength of a truly ordered society comes from the virtue which makes unity possible even between those who are greater and those who are less. It is something like a living jigsaw puzzle where the dissimilar pieces fit easily together, the smaller rounding off the rough edges of the greater and each one's fullness filling in the other's gaps. In Augustine's dream of a state that is a society of friends there may be radical differences in accidentals but still all are able to come together as a whole, united by the common desire to create a harmonious and beautiful reality in the midst of the sometime chaos and ugliness of life.

Augustine recognized that every state (indeed every human society) will have some of the characteristics of the dark city of Cain, but from his advice to those who wished to be good kings and good citizens it is evident that he believed that no state needed to be dominated by such tendencies. It is possible for a state to take care of the legitimate temporal needs of its citizens while not neglecting or ignoring the fact that all are still pilgrims on this earth making their way to an eternal city where finally and forever a perfect peace will be found. Even the worst of states can be improved if ruler and ruled can come to love in the right way, loving God above all and each other as friends. It is a goal worth striving for even if seldom realized perfectly. The reality of political life is that every state is afflicted with the troubles of Henoch, the city of Cain. Incompetent or malicious leaders, indifferent or self-serving citizens, violent criminals, war, poverty, and slavery are found in every state. How one should deal with such problems will be discussed in the chapter that follows.

56. *Ibid.*

CHAPTER 8

Law and Violence

A. Introduction: Coping with Babylon

In the previous chapter we have argued that Augustine considered the state to be a good society, one which was needed by human beings during their life on earth. When driven by the force of friendly love with God and neighbor, it could even be a prophetic image of what life in the city of God would be, that heavenly Jerusalem in which God is the only king and in which humans and angels are united in a true unity of heart [*concordia*]. This vision of the best state is a hope-filled dream for both citizen and ruler, a goal worthy of pursuit; unfortunately the reality of political society is always something less. Though good people might "dream of Jerusalem," their day by day life is spent "coping with Babylon" — dealing with the imperfections in themselves and others which cause the societies they form to be likewise imperfect. As Augustine remarked one day, it truly would be a wonderful world if

> . . . the rule and government of human affairs were in the hands of the wise and those who realized that they were subject to God. But, since this is not now the case, we must spend our days patiently and meekly enduring government which rules through force.[1]

1. *The Trinity*, 3.4.9. John Rist writes: ". . . the bleak and brutal hierarchies of Roman North Africa are the setting for Augustine's pessimistic estimation of the edifying power of the state. Augustine's Africa is deformed by misery (*A Literal Commentary on Genesis*, 11.35.48), madness (*The City of God*, 22.22), and the sufferings of children

It is important to stress that the misuses of political power that sometimes occur cannot be blamed on the nature of the state, anymore than abuse of one's spouse or one's child can be blamed on the nature of the family. The perversions of those in power would not exist if there were no perversions in the people themselves, the individual human beings who are the elements and, as it were, the seeds of the state.[2] Individual citizens are related to the state in something like the way a letter is related to a word. They are integral parts of the whole and their defects are causative of the imperfections of the whole. The greed of a political society for more and more wealth through war and deception is merely the greed of individuals *"writ large,"* those few who have the power of wealth but who are yet haunted by fear, who are heavy with care, never secure, always restless, breathless from endless quarrels with enemies, adding possessions beyond measure as they increase the mountain of anxiety that distresses them.[3]

In the previous chapter we have argued that even if the state were an earthly Jerusalem composed only of God-centered saints some minimal *organizing law* would have been necessary to bring order to the day by day activity of the complex society. In the imperfect "Babylon" that is the reality of political life, there is a need for *directive and coercive law.* Humans weakened in intellect and will now need law as a guide for the perplexed and as a restraint for the malicious. Although it may be true that some are still motivated to obey out of love, the majority are moved only by fear. Now peace in society can be insured only through punishment of the criminal within and war against the enemy without.[4]

(*Against Julian the Heretic,* 5.1.4). Yet few beyond the sufferers are concerned. In Augustine's rather Hobbesian universe, the stronger will impose some kind of rule and some kind of peace, and willy-nilly that 'peace' will somewhat restrain the hand of other malefactors" (John Rist, *Augustine: Ancient Thought Baptized* [Cambridge: Cambridge University Press, 1994], p. 225). For the historical background of the North African Christianity faced by Augustine, see J. E. Merdinger, *Rome and the African Church in the Time of Augustine* (New Haven: Yale University Press, 1997), pp. 3-27.

2. *Commentary on Psalm 9,* 8.

3. *The City of God,* 4.3.

4. *Letter 185,* 6.21. Deane summarizes Augustine's position as follows: "Only a small minority of men are, during their earthly lives converted by God's grace and changed from sinful to redeemed men and this handful of saints cannot in this world be certainly distinguished from the crowd of sinners among whom they live, work, and die. It is therefore absolutely impossible to establish on earth a society or state made up of saints or true Christians. Thus, if we wish to understand how social, economic, and political life operate, and how, indeed, they *must* operate, we have to start with the as-

Considering the imperfections of the citizens and leaders of every political society, it is only to be expected that some legislation will be bad law, that some punishment will go too far, that some wars waged will be unjust. As a result, there are many questions for a person trying to lead a virtuous life in the midst of an imperfect political society. How should one act when constrained by bad laws? How far can one go in protecting oneself and society against the violent attacks of others? When is punishment for a crime warranted and when does it go too far? What rules should be observed in waging war? How should one dedicated to the ideals of the heavenly Jerusalem live in a political society infected with the habits of Babylon? These are the questions to be considered in this chapter and the chapters that follow. We begin with an examination of the nature and limits of civil law.

B. The Nature and Limits of Civil Law

A widely accepted definition of law is as follows: *Law is a reasonable command promulgated by one in authority for the common good.* Law is said to be a *command* to differentiate it from a mere voiced opinion or suggestion regarding how one should act in a particular circumstance. Law involves a true imposition of will by the one who makes the law upon the one who is expected to obey, such that, if the law is disobeyed, one may legitimately describe the subject as a "law-breaker" and therefore liable to be punished. Such power to impose one's will implies a *superiority* of ruler over ruled which is the basis for a claim of an *authority* over the ruled. To say that the law must be *reasonable* implies (1) that it does not violate any higher law; (2) that it is a necessary or useful means of serving the common good; (3) that one bound by the law is able to observe it and the one who creates the law is able to enforce it.

Since one cannot be bound by a law that is unknown, the law must be adequately *promulgated* to those who are to be bound by it. Finally, the law must serve the *common good* of the society. For the political society this would include both the *temporal* peace and the prosperity of its citi-

---

sumption that we are dealing, for the most part, with fallen, sinful men" (Herbert A. Deane, *The Political and Social Ideas of St. Augustine* [New York: Columbia University Press, 1963], p. 40). "Thus (he adds), every earthly state will be composed primarily of sinners with perhaps a scattering of saints living in their midst" (*ibid.*, p. 116).

zens. As we shall see, this limitation of the state to purely temporal affairs (leaving to the church matters dealing with eternal salvation) was not as firmly observed in Augustine's day as it is now, in the age of the secular state.[5]

Each aspect of this definition of law imposes restrictions on its extent. Added to these is the requirement that any temporal law must be *in accord with eternal law,* the law whereby God commands that the order of the universe be preserved. As applied to the human race, eternal law requires that humans act in accord with their nature and with their particular position and responsibilities in life — for example, as parents, spouses, employees, and members of various societies.[6]

A further restriction on civil law is that it must be enacted by one with the *authority* to do so. Even though a supposed law commands a great and good action, it is not a law if the one who gives the command has no authority to do so. Such authority must ultimately come from God since God is the only person who is by nature superior to human beings. Augustine agreed completely with the sentiment expressed by St. Paul:

> There is no authority except from God, and those authorities who exist have been instituted by God. Therefore he who resists these authorities resists what God has appointed, and those who resist will incur judgment.[7]

Augustine did not believe in any "divine right" of kings, but he did believe that divine power was reflected in every legitimate exercise of civil rule. It is for this reason that one who has authority in the state has the right to

---

5. In his *Free Choice* (1.15), Augustine gives a list of some of the areas where temporal law legitimately legislates so that "peace and human society" may be preserved. Included are matters relating to the health of the body, personal freedom, and ownership of personal possessions.

6. Augustine writes: "In temporal law there is nothing just and lawful which men have not derived from eternal law" (*Free Choice,* 1.6). "The good and wise person who creates temporal law should consult that eternal law so that he might discern what should be commanded and what should be forbidden in time" (*On True Religion,* 31.58). In the same vein, he writes to Marcellinus that settling with one's enemies through agreement rather than revenge is the source of the state's strength and such a process is commanded by divine authority (*Letter 130,* 1.10-11). See also *Sermon 62,* 8.13; *Commentary on Psalm 145,* 15; *Letter 185,* 2.8. For commentary, see R. A. Markus, *Saeculum* (Cambridge: Cambridge University Press, 1970), pp. 88-89.

7. Romans 13:1-5. See 1 Peter 2:13-14.

. . . command something which neither he nor anyone else has ever commanded before. Obedience to such authority is not against the common interest, but disobedience would be. In human society there is general agreement that kings should be obeyed [and] that in the government of human society the lesser authority must be subject to the greater.[8]

C. Dealing with the Imperfect State

Unfortunately, not every political society will be a comfortable home for those dedicated to the ideals of the city of God. Though dreaming and desiring the peace of the heavenly Jerusalem, good people are sometimes called upon to live in political societies dominated by thirst for power and the other vices of an earthly Babylon. There will be good and bad states and, while hoping for the best, the virtuous person must sometimes put up with the worst. The best political society would contain citizens and rulers who have the true faith and who lead a virtuous life based on that faith, and where the leaders have the practical art of governing.[9] Augustine had some doubts about whether such an ideal state could ever exist, given the defects in human beings, and therefore something less is the best that can realistically be hoped for. This "less good but not too bad" state is one in which the leaders have some skill in governing and do live a somewhat noble life but for less than virtuous reasons. They are concerned about living well and doing well and governing well not so much out of love for God or neighbor as out of love for a good reputation. Augustine found examples of these "noble pagan politicians" in the best days of the Roman Empire when the emperors, though not believing in God and not totally committed to basic principles of morality, at least tried to lead somewhat decent

8. *Confessions,* 3.8.15. See *Exposition of Some Propositions from the Epistle to the Romans,* 72; *Commentary on Psalm 124,* #7. See R. H. Barrow, *Introduction to St. Augustine: City of God* (London: Faber & Faber, 1950), p. 235. Speaking specifically against the Donatist complaints about the intervention of civil society in church matters, Augustine responds that anyone who resists duly constituted authority resists the command of God (*Against Writings of Petelian the Donatist,* 2.20.45). See *Sermon 358,* 6, where Augustine implores the people to avoid a civil disturbance, if not out of love for their bishops, at least out of respect for the civil authority which acts with the authority of God in trying to keep the peace.

9. *The City of God,* 5.19.

lives and to rule justly for the sake of their own personal glory. It would, of course, have been better if their nobility of rule was prompted by love of God and neighbor rather than concern about how history would remember them, but at least their rule was enlightened. Such limited goodness was certainly far better than those very worst of states (exemplified historically in the city of Cain) where rulers and ruled alike were motivated by self-interest — protecting themselves at all costs and dominating those who were weaker. Still, even in these worst case scenarios, assuming that citizens and rulers had at least enough unity of purpose to justify calling their gathering a "society," such true authority as existed had its source in God.[10]

There is no question that life is difficult for a virtuous person living in the domain of an evil ruler, but the vices of the ruler do not excuse the subject from obeying the law of the land as long as it does not violate the law of God.[11] Augustine believed that a Christian could not justify disobedience to the law because the ruler was not a saint. Christians should give obedience even to the worst of earthly rulers because in their obedience they are really obeying God who, in his Providence, determines that certain individuals should rule and others should be subject. Even in a tyrannical state, the obligations to pay taxes and show respect for public authority are just. However, this respect for the ruler does not mean that a believer should relinquish to the ruler control over his or her belief in God.[12]

Augustine cites the example of Shadrach, Meshach, and Abednego to show how good people should act if commanded to act against their conscience. When King Nebuchadnezzar ordered the three men to offer sacrifice to his idols, they responded with passive resistance. Refusing to obey the law, they submitted themselves quietly to the penalty, neither offering violent resistance to the law nor rebelling against the lawgiver. They thus

10. *Ibid.*, 5.21.

11. *Ibid.*, 5.17. Augustine instructed the people of Hippo: "If your parents are bringing you up for Christ, they are to be heard in all things. They must be obeyed in every command, but let them not command anything against one above themselves. . . . Your country again should be above your very parents. Thus, if they command anything against your country, they are not to be listened to. And if your country should command something against the laws of God, it should not be listened to" (*Sermon 62*, 8).

12. *Exposition of some Propositions from the Epistle to the Romans*, 72. See *Sermon 302*, 19. See Deane, *op. cit.*, pp. 148-49.

demonstrated the good that can come out of bad laws, laws which favored untruth over truth. Through such oppressive laws "staunch believers are tested and faithful champions are crowned."[13]

Another example Augustine offers is that of the Christian soldiers who served the wicked emperor Julian. They refused his commands to offer incense to the pagan gods, but at the same time when commanded to march against this or that enemy of the state, they obeyed immediately. They did not revolt because of the emperor's paganism but neither did they bow to his orders to act against the true God. They obeyed in other matters because Julian's pagan belief did not change the fact that he was a ruler and, as such, participated in the divine authority to rule his subjects for the sake of the common good.[14]

Deane is correct in his observation that Augustine favored passive resistance to bad rulers over violent revolution. After an unfortunate situation in which his own parishioners participated in the lynching of an unpopular public official, Augustine showed his abhorrence of such mob violence in his harsh words to the participants. He told them:

> Judges exist who have the power to deal with evil men. When you as an ordinary person take the law into your own hands, you are substituting one evil for another. By venting your rage against the violent, you join them in their violence. It is no excuse to say that you were only a passive bystander if you could have controlled those who did participate but did nothing to stop them.[15]

Augustine's resistance to violent response against bad rulers was based on a number of factors. First, such violence showed too much attachment to this life.[16] Secondly, internal unrest is the worst affliction of society. Once a mob is unleashed there is no holding them back. It is better by far to preserve some semblance of peace while suffering cruel rule and unjust punishment than to "unleash the hounds" and foment anarchy. Finally, a revolution, even if it is successful, is a short-term solution. This life is but a "mist that passes."[17] The real focus of the Christian should be on the life that is to come. One should not let passing events disturb one's

13. See *Letter 185*, 2.8; *Letter 105*, 7.
14. *Commentary on Psalm 124*, 7.
15. *Sermon 302*, 10-11. See Deane, *op. cit.*, p. 149.
16. *Sermon 302*, 3-7.
17. *Ibid.*, 7.

spiritual quest for the eternal home. Even the worst of states is not forever. Thus, it is more sensible to take a stance of "social quietism," refusing to obey only those laws which command immoral action. Time will soon do away with all bad rulers or, at least, will release subjects from their tyranny. As Augustine once remarked:

> As far as this life of mortals is concerned, a life which is spent and finished in a few days, what does it matter under whose government a dying human lives as long as those who govern do not command impiety and iniquity?[18]

A good law is a blessing because it can correct the malicious but even the worst law and most perverse ruler cannot destroy our freedom to choose God.[19] A civil ruler cannot control our thoughts and thus, though we are enslaved by state power, we need not fear that they can control our eternal destiny. To enslave the body is one thing; to enslave the soul is quite another.[20] Therefore, all the evils imposed on the good person by unjust rulers are but a test of their virtue. As Augustine observes:

> The good person, even though a slave, is truly free. The evil person who is in charge is still a slave, a slave not to some king but even more disastrously to the many vices infecting the soul.[21]

D. The Moral Response to Violence

1. Introduction

Violence is a fact of human history and it must be considered by any political theory that claims to be realistic. Since Eden, every age has been tinged with violence. Humans die in wars. Criminals perform deadly deeds that seem to cry out for severe punishment, even death. Terrorists use random destruction to promote a cause. Innocents perish at the hands of unjust aggressors. It seems that in every age the truth expressed by Augustine to a

18. *The City of God*, 5.17.
19. *Against Cresconius the Donatist*, 3.51.56.
20. *On True Religion*, 55.3.
21. *The City of God*, 4.3.

friend remains true: "We exist in peace only through the sworn oaths of barbarians."[22]

The reason peace this side of death is so hard to achieve is because of the "cracks" in each individual. At one and the same time we humans desire to be more than we can be while being tempted to be less than we are. We are dusty angels, looking to the heavens as we fight for the goods of this earth. We want everything and are jealous of those who have anything that is not ours. As Augustine says:

> Each individual in this earthly community is driven by his passion to pursue his self-interest. Unfortunately, there are not enough existing goods to satisfy everyone completely [and] as a result this earthly city suffers a chronic condition of war in which those who win oppress those who lose.[23]

As a result:

> Because of the instability found in every human, no nation has ever been so safe as to do away with all fear of hostile attacks on its life.[24]

The practical problem is not how to do away with all threat of violence — because that is impossible — but how to deal with violence when it occurs. What methods to control violence are both realistic and consistent with moral principle? How can we humans live a rational (noble) life in a violent world? Must we stay passive in the face of every attack on our rights or the rights of those we care about? Indeed, if I am in a position of authority, am I morally at fault if I do *not* respond to violent attacks on those for whom I am responsible? Specifically, how far may a state go in protecting itself from alien nations and alienated citizens? How far does the moral law allow one to go in preserving order?

2. The Causes of Violence

In order to deal with violence in society one must first reach some conclusion about its causes. There are at least three possible explanations. The

22. *Letter 47*, 2. See P. R. L. Brown, "Political Society," in R. A. Markus, ed., *Augustine* (Garden City, NY: Doubleday & Company, 1972), p. 324.
23. *The City of God*, 18.2. See Deane, *op. cit.*, pp. 46-47.
24. *The City of God*, 17.13.

first maintains that violent actions derive their energy from human nature itself. Humans are *by nature* aggressive animals and the only way to control their violent tendencies is by confinement and control. Like wild animals, humans must be caged by laws, if not by bars, to protect them from themselves and others. Humans cannot be changed, only controlled. A second approach argues that human action, good or bad, is completely determined *by environment*. Given the right conditions, any one of us can be made into peaceful creatures. In the wrong environment even a saint can be turned into a violent beast. Violence, therefore, *can* be cured. The only problem is to find and create the environment that will cure it.

A final view is that we are neither made to be violent by our nature nor are we predetermined by our environment to be aggressive. Humans are *free*. Granted that in some cases humans are driven by uncontrollable compulsions and granted that it is often extremely difficult to overcome the wounds inflicted by a poor environment, most humans in most cases become what they are because they choose to. Thus, it is at least theoretically possible to convince humans that they should freely choose to reject all violence. The cure for violence is to appeal to the rational free nature of human beings and, at least in some cases, this approach will work.[25]

Augustine's view of the primary cause of human violence comes closest to this third view, but he would disagree with those who claim that any human being can be truly good without any outside help from divine grace. Certainly humans have the power of free choice but it is a

25. Examples of each view can be found throughout ancient and modern philosophy. For example, Hobbes and Nietzsche hold that the human animal is fundamentally anti-social and must be corralled and controlled by strong laws and strong leaders. Schopenhauer writes: "Man is at bottom a savage, horrible beast. We know it if only in the business of taming and restraining him which we call civilization" (*The Pessimist's Handbook*, ed. Hazel E. Barnes [Lincoln, Nebraska: University of Nebraska Press, 1964], pp. 338-39). The influence of environment has been stressed by Behaviorism and such philosophers as Marx and Rousseau. The view that "virtue is knowledge" comes close to the position that freedom is the determining factor in that it does point to an internal cause that is in the control of the individual. However, when it maintains that knowledge *predetermines* choice, it can be interpreted as a form of environmentalism. In its purest form, the theory that emphasizes freedom maintains that even with the most complete knowledge of the best alternative, humans could still choose the opposite. An example of how these approaches are reflected in current debate about social issues can be found in an interesting article by Andrew Hacker, "On Original Sin and Conservatives," in *The New York Times Magazine*, February 25, 1973, pp. 13ff. A comparison of the views of Augustine and Hobbes is given by Deane, *op. cit.*, pp. 50, 234-35.

wounded power. In ordinary matters humans are responsible for their history. They choose to be what they are and to do what they do. However they are also flawed and their flaws often result in disorderly choice and perverse action.

This disorder in human choice can manifest itself in any of three ways. First, it sometimes causes humans to prefer earthly things to higher values. Humans are caught in the middle of reality. They are less than God but are better than the rest of creation. They tend by nature to need both God and the everyday world of material goods. An unwounded humanity would have been able resolve these conflicting needs, but in their wounded state humans often find themselves at odds with themselves.

The second expression of disordered choice relates to the manner in which we choose. We humans have become so self-centered that now we tend to choose even truly good things in selfish ways. Our selfish attitudes endanger even our most noble actions. When we fall in love with another human we must strain to make our love truly dedicated to the loved one and not to ourselves. When we enjoy the good things of this life (for example, earthly life itself), we find it difficult to avoid making them the "be all and end all" of our existence. Sometimes we reach for the things we enjoy with no thought of the needs of others. We are choosing true goods but in a selfish way.

Finally, disordered choice may be found sometimes in its selection of means for acquiring true goods. For example, while it is certainly good to preserve one's life, this does not justify any and all means to that end. I may not save myself by committing an injustice against another human. I may not save my life by blaspheming God. A just war may become immoral because of the way in which it is waged. Even our most noble purpose in doing something will not justify perverse means in doing it.

Augustine was convinced that disordered choice was the chief cause of violence in this life. Wounded will and darkened intellect are the culprits, not environment and not human nature. Neither king nor citizen, neither pope nor peasant, is exempt from these flaws. All humans share a common disability and without the grace of God all would succumb to the sometimes evil that it suggests. Perhaps remembering his own wild and confused youth, Augustine became convinced that the tendency towards abject stupidity and uncontrolled passion is found in every one of us. Every one of us is born in ignorance and as soon as we become conscious all sorts of crazy desires begin to surface. As Augustine somberly observes, without God's grace we would engage in every evil ever recorded in human history and probably invent a few of our own along the way.[26]

3. The Morality of Violent Acts

The disorder that causes the immorality of human actions can come from three possible sources:

(1) the act itself;
(2) the lack of authority to perform the act in this particular circumstance;
(3) the intention and/or attitude of the person performing the action.[27]

Each of these deserves some further explanation.

First of all, an act may be immoral because it is in conflict with the order of the universe by its very nature. Thus, blasphemy contradicts the factual subordination of the creature to the Creator. It is impossible for the Creator to be subordinate to the creature, but blasphemy (the cursing of God) by its very nature asserts such subordination. It must therefore be *always and everywhere* forbidden. Even God could not make it to be moral. In like manner, adultery is *always* immoral because its practice denies the existence of the contract that its definition asserts. No authorization, divine or human, no noble intention, no set of circumstances can make blasphemy or adultery or other "naturally disordered acts" to be morally good. Perhaps they can be understood and even forgiven, but they can never be justified.

A second source of immorality in a human act is the lack of proper authority to perform the act in a particular case. For example, taking the goods of another becomes stealing only when it is against the reasonable will of the owner. A morally indifferent medical procedure can become immoral if done without the consent of a competent patient. Unlike those acts which are disordered by nature, the disorder of these acts can be remedied. If proper authorization is present, the taking of the goods of another

26. *The City of God*, 22.22. For an extended and well-documented presentation of Augustine's views on the human condition see Deane, *op. cit.*, pp. 39-77. See also G. R. Evans, *Augustine on Evil* (Cambridge: Cambridge University Press, 1982), pp. 29ff.

27. *Against Faustus the Manichean*, 22.73.

ceases to be evil. If appropriate patient consent is present, a medical procedure can become an expression of professional virtue.

The third cause of immorality in the human act is in the intention and/or attitude of the person performing the act. A bad intention can vitiate even the most noble action. There is no merit in "doing" good if we are choosing badly, if we are loving in a disordered way. Augustine makes this point clearly when he writes against Faustus:

> Injustice occurs in every case where a person loves as a goal something which should be desired only as means to an end, or seeks for the sake of something else things which ought to be loved for themselves. By such disordered desire humans disturb the natural order which the eternal law requires all of us to respect.[28]

It is important to have a clear understanding of the meaning of violence before trying to apply moral principles to particular violent actions. Two different kinds of violence can be distinguished. A violent act can be described as any act which *contravenes the rights* of another. It can also be described as an act which *causes injury* to the life, property, or person of a human being, oneself, or others. In Augustine's moral system, it is evident that the first type of violent actions (those which violate rights) are always immoral. They are *out of order* precisely because they are contrary to fact. Reality proclaims that rights exist; the unjust action pretends that they do not. In choosing injustice the agent is guilty of disordered love, effectively desiring a reordering of fact whereby the victim of the injustice becomes subordinate to the perpetrator.

The moral status of violence which simply inflicts "injury" on another is not as clear. The word "injury" covers a multitude of hurts. Any lessening of a good contributing to human flourishing falls under this concept. A diminishing of life or health or freedom is always injurious to the one who suffers the loss even when it is voluntarily accepted. It seems unreasonable to assert that such "injuring" is either always moral or always immoral. Intuitively, it is more sensible to maintain that some cases of injuring are moral and that other cases are not and therefore that some "violent" actions are justified and others are not. Having granted this, the problem becomes one of identifying the norm which will differentiate between the two.

For Augustine, the norm is the general norm of morality discussed in

28. *Ibid.*, 22.78.

the chapter on ethics, namely: *An act is morally good if it is an act of ordered love: that is, if it is a choice which fosters the order of the universe.* An act that is "violent" because it causes injury will be immoral if it is disordered in any one of the three ways specified by Augustine in his debate with Faustus, that is:

1. if it is disordered by *its very nature;*
2. if it is done *without proper authority;*
3. if it is done *with bad intention.*

Though no act that causes injury will be immoral in and of itself, any injurious act can be said to be immoral if it is done without proper authority or with bad intention. Spanking a child causes pain but it is not for that reason immoral. It becomes immoral if the one who disciplines has no authority to do so or does it with an improper attitude or in an immoderate way. Though Augustine lamented mightily about the beatings he received during his early school years, he did not question the authority of his teachers to discipline their students. He complained only about their hypocrisy in punishing the young for the very same games that they (the teachers) played as adults. The disorder in their acts came not from a lack of *right* but from a lack of *right attitude.* The imposition of unwanted discipline is not disorderly in itself; it becomes so from the disordered intention and attitude of those who impose it. Indeed, Augustine came to realize that a bit of discipline is good for most human beings, though most of us are unwilling to accept it when it affects ourselves. Those charged with the care of others must be ready to punish as well as reward. It could even be a virtuous act for a father to give a beating to his son if it were truly necessary for the son's own good.[29]

This last example suggests that sometimes a violent action is *morally required.* This would happen when the violence fostered order rather than disorder. The rationale for this possibility rests on the following assumptions:

1. Violence (in the sense of doing injury) is not in and of itself disorderly. Violence, to be moral, needs justification but such justification is possible.
2. The order of the universe is served by the lessening of violence and therefore those charged with keeping the peace or with the care and

---

29. *Confessions,* 1.9.14-15; *Commentary on the Letter of John to the Parthians,* 7.8.

training of others cannot be indifferent to its existence. Ordered love must act when it can to lessen the injury coming from violent acts whether these flow from blind forces of nature or perverse choices of humans.

3. In some cases the use of violence can quantitatively lessen the amount of violence in the universe. For example, mandatory vaccination against small pox ("injurious" in the sense of being an invasion of bodily integrity and a lessening of individual freedom) may prevent a much greater quantity of "injury" coming from a deadly plague.

4. In some cases the use of violence can lessen disorder in the universe by preventing violence which is both injurious and unjust. Thus a police officer charged with protection of the common good may actually lessen the disorder in the universe by killing an aggressor who threatens to kill an innocent civilian. Though a human life will be lost, it seems intuitively to be less disordered to have an unjust aggressor die than an innocent victim.

In sum, a typical Augustinian analysis of violence will admit that violence is *morally permitted* if it is an act of ordered love; that is, if it is a choice which does not disturb the order of the universe. One may be *morally obliged* to perform a violent act if it is clear that such an act is necessary or useful for the preservation or promotion of order. The sad fact of our present condition is that we live in a world of violence and sometimes justified violence may be the only way of lessening the disorder coming from unjust violence. To be sure, it is not a perfect solution, but in an imperfect world it may just be the only way to work for that order and peace which God originally intended and now desires for the human race.

4. Killing Humans: General Principles

The question here is whether the violent act of killing a human being is ever morally permitted. Augustine approaches this question from a worldview which has come to be described as the *sanctity of life* position. Its fundamental principle is:

> Human life is sacred and should always be respected and, as far as reasonably possible, preserved.

This principle rests on three assumptions about the real world:

1. God exists and loves each and every human being from the first moment of the person's existence. The sanctity of the individual is based on the fact of this infinite love. It does not depend on a particular level of development or achievement.
2. Life is loaned to each individual in trust. Because the individual is given life to accomplish a purpose determined by God, the individual never acquires that perfect dominion over life which permits its destruction without asking whether it is in accord with God's will. Acts of preserving or destroying life, fighting to continue life or allowing to die, must be able to be interpreted as being in accord with the will of God, that one who has ultimate dominion over every human life.
3. Human beings are called to be cooperators in implementing God's intentions in a universe in which all things do not automatically work out for the good. God wills the order of the universe and the peace and happiness that flows from such perfect order. Humans have the responsibility of working for and with this divine will in their daily life. Humans cannot be spectators in the war between good and evil. When they can, they must use their intelligence and free will to lessen the amount of suffering and injustice in the world.[30]

Working from these assumptions about the nature of reality, Augustine comes to the conclusion that the killing of a human being is not always and everywhere wrong. It is not like blasphemy, an act which is always disordered. If killing is a disorderly act and therefore immoral, it will be so because it is done without proper authority and/or because it is done

---

30. On these points see James M. Gustafson, *The Contribution of Theology to Medical Ethics* (Chicago: Marquette University Press, 1975), pp. 22-23. Paul Ramsey reflected the sanctity of life position clearly when he wrote: "No one is ever much more than a fellow fetus; and in order not to become confused about life's primary value, it is best not to concentrate on degrees of relative worth we may later acquire" (Paul Ramsey, "The Morality of Abortion," in *Moral Problems*, ed. James Rachels [New York: Harper & Row, 1975], p. 45). Augustine said much the same thing when he wrote: "In view of the encompassing network of the universe and the whole creation . . . a network that is perfectly ordered in time and place, where not even one leaf of a tree is superfluous . . . it is not possible to create a superfluous human being" (*Free Choice*, 3.23).

with a bad intention. Augustine expresses these conclusions in various ways and in various places. For example:

> Everyone who kills a human being without authorization of lawful power is a murderer.[31]

> Even though it is said "you shall not kill!" it should not be thought to be a violation of this precept when the law itself permits killing or when God commands that someone be killed. When he who makes the law orders a course of action, the subject of the law is not allowed to refuse.[32]

> The divine law which forbids the killing of human beings does allow for some exceptions: (1) when God authorizes killing by means of a general law that can apply to a number of cases and (2) when God authorizes the killing in an individual instance at a particular time. The human being who kills in such cases is only the sword in the hand of God and is thus not acting on his own nor does he violate the commandment: "You should not kill!" Thus, it does not go against God's will to wage war at God's bidding, or for those authorized by the state to execute criminals under the guidance of law and the reasonable demands of justice. Thus, Abraham was not only innocent of criminal viciousness but was even praised for his virtue when he consented to sacrifice his son out of obedience to God. However, anyone who kills himself or another is guilty of murder except in the two circumstances mentioned above: (1) someone acting directly under the orders of God in an special case or (2) someone acting under a general principle that can be reasonably argued to be in accord with God's will.[33]

This last quotation indicates the two possible ways in which (in Augustine's opinion) divine authorization for killing can be given. First of all, it may be given by a *just law or rule which has general application to a wide range of similar cases.* When civil rulers wage just wars or execute criminals for cause, they need not wait for explicit authorization from God in each individual case. The law imposing upon them the obligation to protect the common good gives them the authority to initiate killing acts which seem (on the basis of a prayerful rational analysis of the situation) necessary to fulfill that obligation. The divine authorization may also be given by an *ex-*

---

31. *Letter 204*, 5.
32. *Questions on the Heptateuch*, 2.17.
33. *The City of God*, 1.21.

plicit permission or command in a particular case. It is possible that God will command a king to begin a war or to execute a criminal. It is even possible that God will command an ordinary individual to kill. Augustine points to the story of Samson's suicide and Abraham's sacrifice of Isaac as instances where this latter extraordinary event occurred. Both cases involve the directly willed death of an innocent person and both were justified because God either permitted the killing act (Samson) or commanded it (Isaac).

There are important differences in the two modes of authorization. Authorization by general law (for example, in the just war or capital punishment) allows the state authority to act within broad parameters in deciding when to wage war or to execute criminals. The ruler of a civil society is permitted to allow killing for just cause but is not usually explicitly commanded to do so. Discretion is given to the proper authority to decide in an individual case whether to kill or let live. In coming to a decision there is the possibility of arguing from precedents. Decisions made in one instance will have moral implications for future cases of the same kind. One can argue from what has been to what should be. When the authorization comes through some special revelation in an individual case, no such argument can be constructed. Thus, the cases of Samson's suicide and Abraham's intended sacrifice of his son are unique cases and no general rule can be inferred from them except that "One may kill a human being if there is certitude that God has commanded it."[34] There is no question that God could make a similar command again, but the event would be truly extraordinary. Augustine does not exclude this possibility but he does warn those who believe that God is giving them such a terrible charge: "Make certain that there is no doubt that the command is divine."[35] In matters of human life and human death one must be sure that the supposed "divine connection" is not a wrong number.

Augustine's general position on the killing of human beings may be summarized in the following statements:

1. It is possible that the choice to kill a human being is a moral act. To be so, the act must be commanded or permitted by the authority of God. As Augustine insists: "No private individual has the personal

34. *Ibid.,* 1.26.
35. *Ibid.*

right to kill another human being even in circumstances where the person killed is guilty of some crime."[36]

2. Historically, such authorization has been given in two different ways:

   a. *by general law giving rational guidelines to be applied by those with authority over human communities in situations where the killing act is necessary for the protection of the community.* This mode of authorization assumes that the one killed is not an innocent person, but one who is or has been involved in some materially unjust action against the community. Also the authorization in these cases gives *permission to kill* if in the prudent judgment of the human authority this is seen to be absolutely necessary for the protection of the community. Only in extraordinary circumstances will there be an *obligation to kill* and the burden of proof is on the one who asserts such an obligation.

   b. *by a special revelation from God commanding the killing act.* Such commands may be directed to civil authorities to wage a particular war or to execute a particular individual. Such commands may even be given to private individuals to kill an innocent human being, one neither perpetrating nor guilty of a crime.

3. Even though authorization to kill has been received, the action may still become immoral if intention is disordered (for example, if a soldier takes fiendish glee in injuring the enemy) or if the God-given authority is exercised for self-serving reasons.

These are the general principles which provide the foundation for Augustine's conclusions concerning war and capital punishment, the topics for the two chapters to follow.[37]

---

36. *Ibid.*, 1.17.

37. The moral principles guiding the taking of human life also apply on the individual level in matters such as suicide (Samson), killing the innocent (Abraham and Isaac), and killing in defense of one's own life. Since we are examining only the state's power to kill, these issues will not be discussed here. I have examined such issues in the following two articles: "To Live or Let Die: Augustine on Killing the Innocent," *Proceedings of the American Catholic Philosophical Association* (1984), pp. 112-19; "Augustine on the Morality of Violence: Theoretical Issues and Applications," *Studia Ephemeridis "Augustinianum,"* no. 26 (1987), vol. 3, pp. 25-54.

CHAPTER 9

War and Peace

A. The Nature of Peace

The importance of peace in Augustine's thought is suggested by the fact that the word *pax* in one of its various forms appears more than 2500 times in his writings. The reasons for his emphasis are evident. The driving force of all human action is the desire for happiness and no one can be happy without peace. As he observes, there is nothing so much talked about, so fervently desired, so welcomed when achieved, in a word, so good for us as peace.[1] Every human thirsts for peace but it is hard to come by. An individual's peace depends on a good will, a will that is driven by an ordered love, and in the present circumstances of life humans find such love hard to maintain.[2] In his 30s Augustine had confidence in his unaided ability to choose the good if he so desired but in his later years he became more and more convinced that his ability to choose rightly and love well was dependent on the grace of God. Peace was therefore more a gift of God than a human accomplishment.[3] Accepting the gift of God's grace (and doing so requires the grace of acceptance), humans are strengthened in the midst of the pressures of life before death and are insured that their life after death will be free of all strife.[4] Through the grace to love peace above

1. *The City of God,* 19.11.
2. *Exposition of Some Propositions from the Epistle to the Romans,* 13-18; *Commentary on Psalm 121,* 12.
3. *The City of God,* 15.4.
4. *Commentary on the Gospel of John,* 104.1.

169

all, greed is conquered and jealousy disappears.[5] This is so because it makes no sense to clutch greedily at peace or to be envious of the peace that others have. The wonderful characteristic of peace is that it can be shared freely with others without lessening one's portion.[6]

Peace, like health, can be defined only negatively, as the *absence* of dissention and strife. Its perfect realization, therefore, is in that theoretical world of absolute unity, a world in which there is "One" and not "many." In the really existing world of multiplicity peace is found in an ordered tranquility, an arrangement of like and unlike things whereby each of them has its proper place.[7]

The beginning of peace for the individual comes when love is well-ordered and the objects of such love are possessed.[8] For a person to have perfect peace there must be internal and external harmony. The body must have an ordered balance among its parts; the soul, an ordered satisfaction of its appetites. The sensitive appetites must seek neither too much nor too little of those material things necessary for sustaining physical life. The intellectual appetites must reflect a correspondence between desire and moral values. A person's internal peace depends on good order between body and soul and health in the living whole. As we have seen, peace between humans comes with an orderly friendship or "oneness of heart" *(concordia)*. Peace in the family comes when such friendship is reflected in a harmonious arrangement of authority and obedience among those who live together. Peace among citizens living in political community rests on a harmony between rulers and those ruled. Finally, the peace of the heavenly city, that most ordered and harmonious society, will be realized at the end of time when humans and angels will rejoice in God and rejoice in each other because of God.[9]

The effort to achieve peace must begin within oneself. One cannot hope to draw others to peace unless one possesses it within, and at least here, in the realm of the interior man, there is some truth in saying "to love peace is to have it."[10] We may not be always able to control our times, but we have some control over our reaction to our times. Living a good life, we

---

5. *Exposition of the Epistle to the Galatians,* 52.

6. *Sermon 357,* 1.

7. *The City of God,* 19.13.1.

8. *Commentary on Psalm 84,* 10; *Sermon 357,* 2; *The Morals of the Catholic Church and the Morals of the Manicheans,* 1.3.4.

9. *The City of God,* 19.13.1.

10. *Sermon 357,* 2-3.

make our times good, at least with respect to their impact on our eternal destiny. A good life gives a basis for hope and in that hope we can find interior peace.[11]

Creating such peace will always be a difficult task. As long as we live in our disintegrating body we must cope with our unruly flesh and weakened spirit. Only a person with no temptation, only a person who is finally free of hunger, thirst, illness, and tiredness can find a complete peace within the self. Lacking that, there will always be a daily battle to be fought, a threat or obstacle to be overcome.[12] We are thus never free of anxiety. In the best of times the good and beauty of this world tempts us. In the worst of times we are in danger of despairing because of the evil we see around us and in us.[13] Even the most advanced in virtue, one who is here and now at peace with himself and the world, must carry on the battle to retain that peace, conscious always of the God who will assist him as he toils and will crown him when he finally succeeds.[14]

Having achieved a modicum of internal peace, the individual can then seek peace with other human beings. There are two basic rules for peaceful relations with others. First, one must do them no harm; second, one must try as far as possible to benefit them.[15] Ideally, peace with others rests on a quiet mutual trust such as one might find between inseparable friends.[16] Realistically, it often can only be found in a fragile hope resting on the trustworthiness of sworn oaths of unknown barbarians.[17] Peace with strangers is always fragile and uncertain and even peace with those we know may not survive whatever changes in them (or in us) tomorrow may bring.[18]

Some peace can be found in the present life but perfect peace can be achieved only after death by those destined to reach heaven. There are at least three reasons for this. First and foremost, the perfection of peace comes when it is permanent, but this is not secured until after death when the person enjoys that direct vision and perfect love of God which removes even the possibility of sinning. Secondly, even though we may have every-

11. *Sermon 80*, 8.
12. *Commentary on Psalm 84*, 10.
13. *Sermon 20a*, 1.
14. *Sermon 61a*, 7.
15. *The City of God*, 19.14.
16. *Sermon 357*, 1.
17. *Letter 47*, 2.
18. *The City of God*, 19.5.

thing anyone could wish for in this life (Augustine lists such things as money, a large family, blameless sons, pretty daughters, full cupboards, plenty of cattle, no ruined walls or broken fences, no tumult or quarreling in the streets, nothing but quiet and peace, an abundance of wealth in the home and in the state), the best that comes from this is a temporary and incomplete sort of peace. It does not fulfill all our desires because it is temporal, tied to material things, and therefore destined someday to perish.[19] Even though we are satisfied with what we have at the present moment, the prospect of death causes fear that all the goods we possess here and now will eventually be lost.[20] There is still something more needed for our peace and happiness to become perfect: that they be never-ending.[21] Finally, as long as there is life this side of death there will be conflict: internal conflict with a body slowly falling apart and a soul constantly besieged by temptations.

Peace in this life is difficult even for saintly people who earnestly strive for the goods of the eternal city. It is even more of a problem for those who are dedicated only to the values and goods of this world. They too form a community, an earthly city, since they are united by the things that they love, namely, the goods of this earth.[22] Such peace, resting as it does on temporal values and material goods, can be nothing better than incomplete and fragile. It is incomplete because it does not take into account the eternal values that should dominate every aspect of human life. In a society committed to temporal values, communities are formed by individuals acting for selfish reasons, more concerned for their own welfare than the welfare of others. The peace that results is fragile because there is no true "oneness of heart." Such justice as exists is based on self-interest more than respect for the rights of others.[23]

In the earthly city humans seek happiness but it is happiness mixed with fear because the community in which it exists is constantly torn by conflicting opinions and desires which frequently explode into domestic quarrels and wars with foreigners. All societies seek to be lord of the world. They want peace but only on their own terms.[24] Their victories are hollow because in their very success the victors become fearful of future failure.

19. *Commentary on Psalm 143*, 18; *Commentary on Psalm 89*, 9.
20. *The Happy Life*, 2.11.
21. *The Morals of the Catholic Church and the Morals of the Manicheans*, 1.3.5.
22. *The City of God*, 19.24.
23. *Commentary on the Gospel of John*, 77.5.
24. *The City of God*, 19.12.

They learn the bitter lesson that the power to win a war is not nearly enough power to keep a peace.

Still, the temporal peace that one can achieve while living on earth is not a negligible good. It can bring with it a health, security, and human fellowship that are true gifts of God. Indeed, it is God who gives the strength to preserve such peace when achieved and the fortitude to restore it when lost.[25] Avoiding war and seeking the material goods necessary for a pleasant earthly life are not unworthy goals even for citizens of the heavenly city. Tragedy in life does not come from the human desire for temporal goods. Rather it comes from loving such temporal goods so fervently and exclusively that the eternal goods of heaven are forgotten, that vision of God and eternal fellowship which brings the ultimate victory of an eternal, supreme, and untroubled peace.[26]

The difference between citizens of the earthly city and citizens of the heavenly city is not that one group seeks peace and the other does not. The difference lies in the quality of peace they seek and how they use the peace of this world. Whereas the citizens of this world are intent upon acquiring only the temporal peace that they can get from earthly possessions and comforts, citizens of the heavenly city look beyond these goods to the heaven promised them, using the material and temporal goods of this life as pilgrims use the advantages of the territory they pass through. For them such goods are not snares and obstructions hindering their journey home; they are ways to ease or at least not increase the burdens of the corruptible body they are dragging down their pilgrim path. Citizens of the earthly city seek an earthly peace, a harmony between authority and obedience in a society driven by a collective will to achieve those things necessary for existence this side of death. Members of the heavenly city, on the other hand, make use of such earthly peace only as long as their mortality demands it. They are not reluctant to follow the laws and customs that guarantee an orderly life on earth. In this they have common purpose with those who see such peaceful temporal life as the only goal and who believe that the limited peace it achieves is the highest peace attainable.[27]

For citizens of the earthly city, the perfection of peace, if it is to be achieved at all, can be achieved only in time; for citizens of the heavenly

---

25. *Ibid.*, 19.13.2.
26. *Ibid.*, 15.4.
27. *Ibid.*, 19.17.

city, peace now comes from hope.[28] This hope is a secure hope for those who have faith in Christ. His resurrection and his promise of eternal life gives assurance that perfect peace is attainable. As a result, believers in Christ can be happy in this life and certain of their destiny in the next, looking forward to the fulfillment of his promise of eternal peace for those who love well.[29]

Even for saints the best peace that can be achieved in this life is through hope based on the promises of Christ and faithful obedience to the eternal law. The peace of heaven will begin with the face to face vision of God and will be fully realized in a union between creature and Creator.[30] Augustine hints at how a union of such disparate beings can take place when he notes that, just as now humans live through an embodiment of a rational soul, in heaven they shall be enlivened by the fullness of the Holy Spirit, that same Spirit who now supports them by grace as they continue their earthly journey.[31] In heaven it will be God loving his now-perfected image in the creature.

Attempting to describe how humans shall feel when they are bathed by this flood of infinite love, Augustine uses an analogy of drunkards who seem to lose their minds by over-indulging in good wine. When in heaven humans see God and are joined to him in love, they shall experience such unspeakable joy that in a certain way they will "lose their human minds as they are made divine and are intoxicated with the sweetness of God's house."[32] They shall be joined to that one who alone can satisfy all their desires, "glued to God" by love and never more to be separated.[33] Then will be experienced the final peace of resting in God. There is no adequate analogy for such peace in this life. Indeed, compared to that peace, all earthly joy will seem like misery.

This union with God will carry with it a peace with ourselves and peace with neighbors. We shall be "friends with our body."[34] There will be a harmony between resurrected body and soul. No longer will we be at war with ourselves.[35] There will be no more obstacles to overcome, no longer any uncontrollable desires for domination. Once death is passed we shall

---

28. *Commentary on Psalm 147*, 20.
29. *Commentary on Psalm 122*, 9; *Sermon 229H*, 3; *Sermon 242A*, 1.
30. *The City of God*, 19.24.
31. *Sermon 256*, 3.
32. *Commentary on Psalm 35*, 14.
33. *Commentary on Psalm 62*, 17.
34. *Sermon 155*, 14.15; *The City of God*, 22.30.1.
35. *Enchiridion on Faith, Hope, and Charity*, 23.91.

have perfect health in body and soul. Whereas now we love even those closest to us with a trust based on faith (because none of us knows completely the mystery of "the other"), in heaven God will bring to light the things hidden in darkness and will reveal the secrets of the heart. Then our love for our human loves will come from the vision of how lovely they indeed are.[36] In some way our life in heaven will be like the life enjoyed by Adam and Eve in Eden before their sin. Like them we shall walk together hand in hand with God as our friend, but with an important difference. In heaven we shall know that our peaceful joy will never end.[37]

Just now such wonderful, unending peace is impossible. In our present condition sometimes peace between individuals can be achieved only through conflict; just now peace between nations often must be won through war. It is to this dark necessity of human life that we must now direct our attention.

B. The Nature and Morality of War[38]

The *American Heritage Dictionary of the English Language* defines war as "a state of open, armed, often prolonged conflict carried on between nations,

---

36. *Ibid.*, 32.121.

37. *Letter 55*, 9.17.

38. For an overview of attitudes towards war see F. S. Northedge, "Peace, War, and Philosophy," in *The Encyclopedia of Philosophy*, ed. Paul Edwards (New York: Macmillan Publishing Company, 1967), vol. 6, pp. 63-67; Mortimer Adler, "War and Peace," in *The Great Ideas* (originally published as volumes 1 and 2 of *The Great Books of the Western World*) (New York: Macmillan Publishing, 1992), pp. 901-11. For more discussion of Augustine's position on war see Gustave Combès, *La doctrine politique de saint Augustin* (Paris: Librairie Plon, 1927), pp. 255-300; Herbert Deane, *op. cit.*, pp. 154ff.; Louis J. Swift, *The Early Fathers on War and Military Service* (Wilmington: Michael Glazier, Inc., 1983), pp. 110-48; John Helgeland, Robert J. Daly, and J. Patout Burns, *Christians and the Military* (Philadelphia: Fortress Press, 1985), pp. 73-86; John Langan, "The Elements of St. Augustine's Just War Theory," *Journal of Religious Ethics*, vol. 12, no. 1 (Spring 1984), pp. 19-38; Richard S. Hartigan, "St. Augustine on War and Killing: The Problem of the Innocent," *Journal of the History of Ideas*, vol. 27 (1966), pp. 195-204. Louis Swift responds to Hartigan in "Augustine on War and Killing: Another View," *Harvard Theological Review*, vol. 66 (1973), pp. 369-83. See also R. A. Markus, "Saint Augustine's Views on the Just War," in *The Church and War*, ed. W. J. Sheils (London: Basil Blackwell, 1983); David A. Lenihan, "The Just War Theory in the Works of Saint Augustine," *Augustinian Studies*, vol. 19 (1988), pp. 37-70; *idem*, "The Influence of Augustine's Just War: The Early Middle Ages," *Augustinian Studies*, vol. 27, no. 1 (1996), pp. 55-94.

states, or parties." As defined, war is obviously an activity which involves violence, an action which brings harm to persons and property. The overriding principles measuring the morality of war are the same two which govern all human actions relating to others: the principle of justice and the principle of "Do no harm." Justice, in its aspect of commutative justice, demands that the existing rights of other human beings be respected. The principle of "Do no harm" commands that, unless reasonably excused, we must not harm others in pursuit of our own good and that we must rescue others from harm that comes from any source. Justice admits of no exceptions. We must *always* respect the rights of others. For a war to be moral it must therefore be just and must avoid all unnecessary harm.

A presumably just war must be just in its goal, its authorization, and in the means whereby it is waged. There first of all must be a *just reason for going to war (jus belli)* and the decision to wage the war must be made by one who has the *proper authority* to make that decision. Given the fulfillment of these conditions, the war can be *begun* morally but it still can become immoral because of the *way in which it is carried on*. There must be *jus in bello* also whereby no rights are violated and no unnecessary harm is done in waging the war.

Augustine subscribed to the common sense conviction that war should be avoided whenever possible and that every war needs individual justification to be morally acceptable. He was not an absolute pacifist. Obviously the best world would be a world in which peace is guaranteed, but this is not the world in which we live just now. As Augustine sadly observes:

> Human society is a single community despite the width of its expansion to all parts of the world and the extreme differences one finds in this place or that. The human race is one because of the common nature shared by its members. However, each individual is driven by his passion to pursue private goals. Unfortunately the objects of these purposes are such that no one person (much less all in the community) can be perfectly satisfied. Only God, the good without limits, can satisfy the human thirst. As a result the earthly community in which humans live just now is in a permanent state of civil war where those who fail are oppressed by those who succeed.[39]

---

39. *The City of God*, 18.2; 5.22. See P. R. L. Brown, "Political Society," in *Augustine: A Collection of Critical Essays*, ed. R. A. Markus, *op. cit.*, p. 324.

The painful truth about human society is that, though God determined that humans should have their origin in common parents, "so that they might be united not only by a likeness of nature but even by family ties," the wars they wage against their own kind are more vicious than any fought by any species of supposedly anti-social animals.[40]

How should good people respond to such violence? Here Augustine makes an important distinction between acting to defend oneself and acting to defend others, especially when one is charged with governance of a human community such as the family and the state. Augustine believed that killing in defense of one's own life was immoral, not so much because the attacker's life was worth more than one's own, but rather because when you kill another to save your own life you show an inordinate attachment to the temporal and temporary good that is your life this side of death. According to his way of thinking, it is simply not sensible to kill another in defense of a good that can (and eventually will) be taken away even against your will. It is for this reason Augustine says:

> I do not approve of killing another person in order to avoid being killed yourself. The only exception would be if you are a soldier or a public official and thus are not acting on your own behalf but for the sake of others or for the sake of the society in which you live.[41]

---

40. *The City of God*, 12.22-23. David Lenihan ("The Just War Theory in the Works of St. Augustine" [1988], *op. cit.*, pp. 41-42) comments: "It is not militarism that Augustine venerates but order. Order is essential to the Augustinian world-view. Without order the world would be prey to chaos and the unbridled passions inherent in sinful man. Accordingly Augustine accepts military service for the purpose of order, all as part of God's plan which includes the wars of the Roman empire." He goes on to note that all the wars Augustine experienced were civil wars (even the barbarians were part of the Roman Empire) and thus the disruption of order was from within rather than from without. Even the Donatist movement and, to a lesser extent, the Arian barbarian wars were civil as well as theological disturbances, since Rome identified itself with the Catholic Church. "Thus, when Augustine condoned the wars of Boniface and praised the actions of Darius and advised Marcellinus on the moral acceptability of military service, he was referring to internal police actions of the empire and not external adventures" (*ibid.*, p. 53).

41. *Letter 47*, 5. For a more extensive discussion of this point see *Free Choice*, 1.4-5. See also Donald X. Burt, "The Moral Uses Of Violence: An Augustinian View," *op. cit.*, pp. 45-48; Louis J. Swift, *The Early Fathers on War and Military Service, op. cit.*, pp. 136-37. Swift cites a passage from *The City of God* (22.6) where Augustine (following Cicero) suggests that whereas death is natural for humans, it is not natural for the state.

Earthly peace is certainly a worthwhile good. It is worth preserving and protecting, and those in charge of a community cannot be indifferent to its absence. The good ruler should indeed wage war with tears in his eyes, but sadness about the necessity does not do away with the necessity. Indeed, the *injustice of the hostile nation's attack* creates the *duty* to wage war in defense of the community.[42] Unprincipled nations may rejoice in wars and conquest, but it is an unfortunate last resort for nations of principle. The war is always unfortunate but it would be even more unfortunate to allow evil nations to dominate those who are good.[43] As Augustine says:

> Even in war the goal is to achieve peace . . . [and] when victory goes to the combatant with the more just cause surely this is a reason for rejoicing and the peace that results is welcome.[44]

Of course, it would be better to negotiate peace than to win it through violent conflict, to "destroy war with a word" rather than end it with a sword.[45] Apart from the disruption caused by a war in progress, the peace and happiness achieved through the spilling of blood is as fragile as glittering glass. "One can never shake off the horrible dread that such peace may suddenly shatter into fragments."[46]

Pacifism may be an option, indeed even an obligation, when it comes to defending one's own life, but for the civil ruler it is not a condition that he can impose upon the community he rules. Of course if the whole community elects pacifism in the face of an unjust attack by a violent and cruel enemy, then the ruler would need to bow to its wishes. Just as one must honor the wishes of competent persons who do not wish you to defend their lives by killing the attacker, so too a community's refusal to defend itself violently must be respected. However, there is no *obligation* on a Christian community to refuse self-defense. Against those who argued that Christ's message was to "turn the other cheek" when attacked, Augustine argues that Christ was referring to an inward disposition rather than a bodily action.[47] Even Christ became somewhat violent against the incur-

---

42. *The City of God,* 19.7.
43. *Ibid.,* 4.14.
44. *Ibid.,* 15.4; 19.17.
45. *Letter 239,* 1.
46. *The City of God,* 4.3.
47. *Against Faustus the Manichean,* 22.76; *Letter 138,* 13; *Commentary on the Lord's Sermon on the Mount,* 1.19.57-58. Augustine writes: "Christ's command not to

sions of the money-lenders in the Temple, and he seemed to believe that it was good that the disciples had a sword in Gethsemane, though he condemned the way they used it. As Augustine instructed the imperial official Marcellinus:

> The precepts of patience are always to be preserved in the heart in order to keep it in readiness, and those kindly feelings which keep us from returning evil for evil are always to be nourished by the will. But it remains true that we often must act with a kind harshness when we are trying to make recalcitrant souls change their ways. We must so act because we must consider their welfare rather than their inclination. . . . Thus if the earthly state observes the teachings of Christ, even war will be waged with kindness. And if the peace that follows is based on piety and justice, it will be that much easier to take into account the needs of the conquered.[48]

Every decision to go to war is a momentous event and it must be left in the hands of those who act with the authority and guidance of God. Augustine believed that the only person with such authority is that one who is the officially designated leader of the nation.[49] As we have seen, he believed that God is the source of all true authority of human over human. It is by divine providence that any particular civil society exists. Along with its existence comes the bestowal of authority to rule and this is centered in the official designated to lead. Whether bad or good, the temporal ruler has authority ultimately from God and should be obeyed in all matters that do not conflict with faith and morals. Once a person is designated leader in a society, whether it be the family or the state, there is an obligation to rule. Every person has an obligation to serve God in his or her particular capacity in life and no exception is made for one who has been legitimately chosen to rule the state. Thus, as Augustine remarked to Petelian:

---

resist evil was intended to forestall our taking the kind of delight in revenge which feeds on another's misfortune. It was not meant to encourage us to neglect the correction of others" (*Letter 47*, 5). I believe that Lenihan ("The Just War . . ." [1988], p. 56) goes too far in saying that the "evil in war is subjective and depends on the interior attitude of the soul." Certainly interior dispositions are important but they will not substitute for the absence of authority or just cause for war. Attitude cannot give what you do not have; it can only vitiate what you do have.

48. *Letter 138*, 2.14.
49. *Against Faustus the Manichean*, 22.75.

When we consider humanity's condition living in society, it is clear that kings by the very fact that they are kings have a service to give to the Lord . . . a service that cannot be given by anyone who is not a king.[50]

Since there is a special obligation to use the authority to rule, it is safe to assume that with the authority comes a divine grace to use the authority well, to make wise decisions in the service of the common good. Certainly Augustine had no misconceptions about the king being any better a human being than the rest of the human race. Rulers are as wounded by sin as those they rule. Like the rest of the human race, kings are sometimes blinded by stupidity and dominated by passion. It is for this reason that while Augustine maintains that kings may never morally kill in defense of their own personal good, he insists that they have a moral obligation to defend the community against the attack of an aggressor nation. The reasons for this paradox rest on two crucial differences between defending oneself and defending others:

1. The ruler has an obligation to protect the common good and the well-being of the citizens; the individual is under no equivalent obligation to protect her/his life, especially if this demands the use of violent force against the attacker.
2. Because the authority to rule comes from God, it can be assumed that the civil ruler receives special help in fulfilling the obligations of leadership. These obligations include the responsibility for making prudent decisions in time of crisis and carrying out those decisions without untoward passion. The individual, acting in her/his own behalf, has no claim to such special help.

In sum, the civil ruler has the authority and the special obligation to combat the injustices that touch or threaten the society. Since the authority to rule has been bestowed by the providence of God, that same providence must grant special help so that the authority may be used well. It is still possible for a particular ruler to choose to use violence stupidly or with uncontrolled passion, but by the grace of God such immoral exercise of violence is

50. *Against the Writings of Petelian the Donatist*, 9.92.210. See *Commentary on Psalm 124*, 7; *Exposition of some Propositions from the Epistle to the Romans*, 72. Lenihan argues that Augustine was at heart a pacifist. He saw nothing wrong with Peter carrying a sword, he didn't want him to use it (Lenihan, "The Just War . . . ," pp. 38 and 45).

less likely for a king than for a subject. It is for this reason that Augustine seems to leave no room for *conscientious objection*. Once war is declared, it is the responsibility of the soldier to obey. Even if the king has acquired his throne in some unjust way, all commands that are not clearly unjust should be obeyed. Doubts about the justice of any war should be resolved in favor of the ruler since Augustine believed that analysis of the justice or injustice of going to war or waging war are beyond the competence of the ordinary soldier. Only the king has the information and the divine guidance to decide such matters. If the war is in fact unjust then the king is culpable; the soldier following commands remains innocent. Thus, the soldier should obey if the command is clearly moral or if he has some unresolvable doubt about the morality of the command. Of course, if the command is *clearly* contrary to the eternal law, then the soldier *must* disobey.[51]

Augustine believed that the right to repel aggression was written into the very law of nature. Although he had reservations about individuals killing in order to save their own lives or goods, he had no hesitation in allowing individuals to repel aggression against the lives of others or in having public officials act to save the state from unjust attack. The first consideration when analyzing a particular war is (assuming that war is declared by one with the proper authority) whether the *reasons for going to war* are just, whether there is present *jus belli*. Augustine writes:

> A great deal depends on the reasons why humans undertake wars and on their authority to begin a war. The natural order of the universe which seeks peace among humans must allow the king the power to enter into a war if he thinks it necessary. That same natural order commands that the soldiers should then perform their duty, protecting the peace and safety of the political community. When war is undertaken in accord with the will of God (the God who wishes to rebuke, humble, and crush malicious human beings), it must be just to wage it.[52]

51. *Letter 185*, 2.8. See *Against Faustus the Manichean*, 22.75. G. Combès, *op. cit.*, p. 290. See also Hartigan, "Saint Augustine on War and Killing," pp. 195-204; Louis J. Swift, "Augustine on War and Killing: Another View," *op. cit.*, vol. 66 (1973), pp. 369-83. Also his *The Early Fathers on War . . .* , *op. cit.*, pp. 139-40. As Swift notes in this latter work (p. 138), Augustine had little sympathy for any attempt to overthrow an established government. "It is incumbent on men to resist temporal power when it commands something that is contrary to God's will (*Letter 185*, 2.8), but an individual's only recourse in such circumstances appears to be passive resistance." See *Letter 189*, 4; *Letter 138*, 15.

52. *Against Faustus the Manichean*, 22.75.

A just war is thus one that is a reaction to possible/actual injuries or in response to a direct command of God. Augustine believed that just wars could be either defensive or offensive. A just defensive war is one that is waged to protect the security of the state. Just offensive wars may be one of two kinds: (1) wars seeking reparations for damage done or goods stolen; (2) wars commanded by God to punish a criminal state.[53]

If wars are declared for good reason by one with the authority to do so, they are just at least in their initiation. Unfortunately, the lesson of history is that many if not most wars are begun for the wrong reasons. As Augustine comments:

> What else can we call it but crime on a grand scale when a nation wages war solely from a desire to dominate others and goes on to crush and grind down neighboring nations that have caused no one any harm?[54]

Sometimes a spirit of extreme nationalism makes a people believe that they are predestined for greatness and makes them wish that the whole world should bow before their greatness. Sometimes wars are begun to distract the citizens from internal troubles by creating an external enemy. Sometimes wars happen simply as a means of satisfying the personal ambition of the ruler. Indeed, every war that is unjust starts with some sort of disordered love for the goods of this world.[55] And, though Augustine never makes the application to nations specifically, I suspect that he would agree that some wars are started out of the same passion that prompted him to steal the pears in his youth just for the sake of doing something evil. He would likely admit that after humanity's fall from grace humans sometimes kill, injure, destroy, and vandalize for no other reason than that they find it pleasurable.

53. For defensive war, see *The City of God*, 22.6. Augustine writes: "As a rule just wars are those which avenge injuries, as for example when some nation or state has neglected to punish a wrong committed by its citizens or which has retained something that was wrongfully taken" (*Questions on the Heptateuch*, 6.10). Augustine cites Israel's war against the Amorites as an example of a justified offensive war. The Amorites denial of free passage through their territory to the wandering Israelites was equivalent to a denial of a quasi-natural right, "a right that should have been granted in accord with the most reasonable standards governing human society," and therefore war was justified in pursuit of the denied right. See *Questions on the Heptateuch*, 4.44.

54. *The City of God*, 4.6.

55. For wars waged for the wrong reasons see *ibid.*, 3.14; 3.21; 4.15; 5.12; 15.4; 18.2.

Even a war begun for the best of reasons by one who clearly has the authority to make the decision can become unjust through the way in which it is waged. A *jus belli* can become immoral because there is no *jus in bello*. The injustice comes not from the killing; it comes from the attitude and methods of those who kill. As Augustine remarks:

> The real evils in war are the love of violence, the cruel passion for revenge, the blind hatred of the enemy, the sometimes insane uncontrolled resistance to attack, the lust for power, and other things of this sort.[56]

For a war to be waged justly, Augustine insists that alliances must be honored, the rights of noncombatants must be preserved. Wars must not be waged by nations intoxicated by the thrill of violence. Every war should be waged reluctantly, and with sadness. Though there is a certain glory in battlefield bravery, it is always more glorious to achieve one's goals by negotiation than by combat. War should always be waged as a last resort and should never be waged if there is no reasonable hope of success. The only justification for war is to restore order and peace to civil society and anything, such as useless victories, that hinders the quick accomplishment of that peace should be rejected. In sum, every war should be waged modestly and ended graciously out of prudence if for no other reason. The victor should realize that the vanquished will not always be a subjugated people and that memories of harsh treatment last forever.[57]

Augustine uses the community's legitimate desire for peace and order to justify its wars against external disruption. How he used this same desire for peace and order to justify punishment of the community's own criminal citizens is the topic to be examined in the chapter than follows.

---

56. *Against Faustus the Manichean*, 22.74.
57. See *The City of God*, 1.4-5; 18.2; 15.4; 5.17. See also *Letter 229*, 2; *Letter 189*, 6; *Letter 220*, 12.

CHAPTER 10

Crime and Punishment

A. Introduction[1]

In our present human condition, wherever there are laws there is the possibility of crime and wherever there is crime there is the possibility of punishment. The terms "crime" and "punishment" warrant some clarification. For our purposes here a *crime* may be described as an action which violates any moral law or any valid human law. The response to crime, *punishment*, is an act which, in response to the commission of crimes, inflicts on the criminals a condition that is displeasing to them. Such displeasing conditions may include anything that could cause pain or stress — such as execution, whipping, imprisonment, fines, loss of reputation. Punishment is thus a form of violence as defined in the previous chapter. It takes away a right of the criminal (for example, prison limiting the natural right to freedom) and/or does them injury in some way (for example, by forcing them to pay a fine, by taking away their life, etc).

Punishment differs from other sorts of violence in two ways. First, the person who is punished knowingly and willingly acted in contravention of a just law and is thus *guilty* of a criminal act. Insane persons who perform the same physical act and are then imprisoned in a mental hospital are not, strictly speaking, suffering punishment. They are undergoing

---

1. Helpful discussions of punishment in general can be found in Mortimer Adler, *The Great Ideas* (formerly volumes 1-2 of the Great Books Series) and the article on "Punishment" in the *Encyclopedia of Philosophy,* vol. 7.

therapy for their disruptive mental condition. Secondly, punishment occurs after the criminal act is perpetrated. It thus cannot be interpreted as an act of self-defense. The particular action which merited punishment is now finished and the "attack" has ceased to be. Punishment, if it is to be justified, cannot be justified on the principles regulating moral defense against an unjust aggressor.

Historically four reasons that justify punishment have been suggested:

1. *Prevention:* The punishment is aimed at preventing *this criminal* from committing the crime again. It is not necessarily aimed at changing the criminal's perverse tendencies. Its sole concern is to prevent the criminal from ever again exercising those perverse tendencies.

2. *Rehabilitation:* The punishment is aimed specifically at *curing this particular criminal,* changing him so that he will never again want to commit this crime. Its aim is not only to protect society but also to return the criminal to society as a productive member.

3. *Deterrence:* This purpose of punishment is directed towards *others,* influencing them by the example made of the criminal so that they will never commit the crime themselves.

4. *Retribution:* This purpose of punishment has as its focus *restoring the balance of justice* that was disrupted by the crime. When justice exists among members of a society it is something like a perfectly balanced seesaw. Neither end is lower or higher than the other. When a crime is committed, the criminal's end gets an advantage. It has greater weight in that it has taken to itself a right that properly belongs to another individual or to society itself. Something has been gained that should not have been gained. The only way to restore the balance of justice is to take from the criminal something equivalent to what was taken from society. If the criminal has attacked the rights of others, this injustice can be remedied only by an equal limitation on the rights of the criminal.

The first three purposes of punishment in some way or other have the effect of protecting society. Even though the rehabilitative purpose is primarily focused on the cure of the criminal, it also indirectly benefits society since, if the criminal is truly cured, society will not be attacked again. The retributive purpose of punishment is aimed at something greater than society, justice itself, and thus is independent of the good (or, for that matter, the evil) that is brought to others by the execution of the punishment. If it is assumed that the only requirement for a moral punishment is that it fulfills one of these four purposes (an assumption I would be unwilling to grant), it would follow that in the case of the first three purposes, any punishment that works is moral. There is no need to "have the punishment fit the crime." It need only prevent the crime from occurring again. Only when punishment is justified as retribution must the punishment be no more or less severe than the crime done.

Since punishment is a form of violence, it needs to be justified. It is not a morally neutral action such as brushing your teeth or going to the store — actions which in and of themselves carry no moral character. As in the case of war, there are three questions that must be considered in evaluating the state's punishment of criminals:

1. Is there present *jus ad poenam,* a reason that would justify the imposition of this particular punishment in this particular case? Is this particular punishment necessary or at least useful in achieving the legitimate purposes of punishment? Could these purposes be achieved in other less intrusive ways, ways which minimize the violence imposed upon the criminal?.

2. Does the state have the *authority* to impose this punishment on this person? For example, it may be granted that the state can punish in general, but does this include the authority to use capital punishment? Has the state been given the *authority to kill* in order to punish a criminal? Again, granted that the state can punish those who commit crimes against the civil society, can it (and indeed *must it*) also punish crimes against God? Does the state have the authority to punish those who act against or simply disagree with the established religion? Granted that the state can punish violent acts, can it also punish religious beliefs, demanding not only that one *not practice* divergent religions but also that one *be converted* to the state-sanctioned religion?

3. Finally, is there present *jus in poena?* Is the method used in punishing the criminal a moral method? For example, a reasonable moral law entails that the punishment imposed must respect their humanity. A so-called "cruel and unusual" punishment would be immoral since the implication of the words suggests that the punishment no longer sees the criminal as a human being. A punishment could also fail this

requirement of being *just in its implementation* if it is not, or cannot be, imposed fairly. Thus, in our day, one of the arguments against the use of capital punishment is that it is more likely to be imposed on the poor or minorities than on the more affluent members of the society.

In examining Augustine's views on punishment two questions will be addressed. The first of these is: "What, if any, limits are there on the way in which the state punishes criminals?" The second question is: "Does the state ever have the right to take a criminal's life? Is capital punishment ever justified?" The further question of the state's right and obligation to make divergent belief a criminal act will be considered in the chapter that follows.

B. Augustine's Views on Punishment[2]

Augustine firmly believed that punishment is sometimes necessary in this life. Indeed, in certain circumstances it would be a denial of love not to punish, as when an excessively kind parent neglects to punish a disobedient and destructive child. It is certainly not unchristian to punish a disobedient child who has put himself in danger. Augustine makes this point in a comment on Christ's command to Peter to forgive "seventy times seven" (Luke 17:3-4):

> There must be a spirit where law and order keep wide awake and where large-hearted kindness does not go to sleep. Do you suppose that you are doing evil to repay evil when you discipline the sinner? In fact sometimes you are giving good for evil and you would not be doing good if you did not punish. Certainly a deserved punishment should always be imposed as gently as possible, but it still should be imposed. In order to explain my point, consider these two adults. Here is a careless little boy who insists on sitting in a place where it is known that snakes lurk. If the boy sits there he would certainly be bitten and die. The two adults know this, but they act differently. One says "Don't sit there!" But the boy ig-

---

2. For an examination of Augustine's views on capital punishment see Gustave Combès, *La doctrine politique de saint Augustin* (Paris: Librairie Plon, 1927), pp. 188ff. See also Fernández Blázquez, *La pena de muerte según San Agustin* (Madrid: Ediciones Augustinus Revista, 1975).

nores the command. He sits there and perishes. The other adult says, "The boy will not listen to us. We must speak severely to him, drag him away and give him a good smack if this is necessary to save his life!" The first adult says, "No! Leave him alone! Don't hit him! Don't harm him!" Which of these two is really kind? The one who spares him to die of snake-bite or the one who is stern with him in order to save his life? If you can see the obvious answer, you will not hesitate to correct those under your care for their welfare.[3]

Even though Augustine would agree that the ideal punishment should be in the form of a *friendly persuasion,* it still must sometimes include a *kind harshness* against the present evil inclinations of unwilling souls. To refuse to limit the freedom of criminals by some useful form of restraint allows a greater evil to occur as they become bold and their evil will is strengthened in its self-destructive resolve.[4] Even though Augustine frequently pleaded with civil authority to mitigate their punishments (especially if the death penalty was to be imposed), he never asked that every criminal be pardoned. He had too much respect for a human's capacity for evil to believe that every pardoned criminal would suddenly become a paragon of virtue. There was always the danger that the one pardoned would not only be ungrateful but would even go on with unchecked boldness to commit greater crimes. Having been saved himself from death once, he would go on to cause a multitude of deaths. And, even if this did not happen, his pardon could tempt others to commit even worse crimes. The paradox is that there is both a good that comes from severe punishment and a good that comes from trying to restrain such severity as much as possible.[5]

---

3. *Sermon 114A,* 5-6. See *Sermon 13,* 9.

4. *Letter 138,* 2.14.

5. *Letter 153,* 6, 16-19. "For us to be truly virtuous, we must not only do no harm to any person but we must also restrain them from wrongdoing and punish the evil that they in fact do. We must do this in order that the person punished may profit from the experience or at least others will be warned not to do the same thing themselves" (*The City of God,* 19.16). Augustine outlines the dilemma of whether to punish or pardon in a letter to Paulinus and Therasia, two of his friends. He writes: "In setting the limit of punishment, are we to proportion it to the kind and degree of the offenses as well as the endurance of the individual soul? It is a deep and difficult matter to estimate what each one can endure and what his limit of endurance is, so as to help him without doing any harm. I personally doubt that many are saved from worse conduct by fear of impending punishment, at least of such penalties as are inflicted by men. And here is a dilemma which often occurs: If you punish a man, you may ruin him; if you leave him

Augustine recognized that determining a proportionate punishment for a particular crime is always a difficult task. It is even more difficult to decide how much punishment is effective in having a truly positive effect on the rehabilitation of the criminal. Augustine had some doubts whether many were saved from committing a crime simply because of fear of punishment. Sometimes a criminal can be hardened in viciousness by punishment. If the punishment is death, it could bring about the worst of all punishments: eternal condemnation of one who in bitterness has rejected God. How much to punish and whether to pardon are questions never easily answered and Augustine frankly admits that as a bishop he made mistakes every day in passing judgment on those subject to his authority. The only advice that Augustine gives to those in authority is to try to maintain a humble and kindly spirit:

> In correcting others you should not come to think too highly of yourself. Even though externally you may seem harsh, inside you must maintain a spirit of love and gentleness.[6]

Granted that punishment is sometimes necessary, various questions still need to be answered. Certainly God as the Lord of all has the right to punish humans who sin, but through what authority can the state punish? I as an individual may not like what you have done, but to "punish" you for it is not my right. To attempt to do so without the authority to do so is tantamount to revenge. How is it, then, that when I gather together with others in civil society, that state which we form gains the right to punish in our behalf? Logically, the answer to this question depends on factors analogous to those justifying war. There must be *proper authority,* a *jus ad poenam* (a just cause for punishing), and *jus in poena* (justice in the method of punishing).

It is clear that Augustine had no doubts about the state's *authority* to punish criminals, even execute them, for just cause. Thus he says:

---

unpunished, you may ruin another. I admit that I make mistakes in this matter every day, and that I do not know when and how to follow what is written: 'Them that sin, reprove before all, that the rest may also have fear'" (*Letter 95,* 3). The passage also brings out Augustine's view that the primary purpose of punishment is to help the criminal and to prevent others from making the same mistake. See Herbert Deane, *Political and Social Ideas of St. Augustine* (New York: Columbia University Press, 1963), pp. 134-43.

6. *Sermon 88,* 19-20; *Letter 95,* 3. See Deane, *op. cit.,* pp. 134-43.

There is no violation of the commandment "You shall not kill!" for a state to wage war at God's bidding or for authorized representatives of the state to put criminals to death for a reason justified under God's law.[7]

It is also clear that he believed that individual persons do not have this right. As mentioned in a previous chapter, the difference between the state punishing and citizens "taking the law into their own hands" is stated with vigor in his sermon to the people in his parish who participated in the lynching of an unpopular public official. He said to them, no doubt with some passion:

> My people, I will say this as clearly as I can. Only evil people do violence against evil people. But this is quite different from those who must act because of their position in society. A judge must often condemn some to be executed even though he is not pleased with the necessity. As far as he can he avoids the shedding of blood, but at the same time he must protect the public order. To use violence in such instances is part of the duties of his profession.[8]

The source of this authority to punish is the same as the authority to rule. It comes directly from God, the source of all authority of human over human. As we have argued in the previous chapters on the nature of the state and on war and peace, the state, like the family, is a *natural society*, a society that is necessary and useful for the development of the human race. God's will to create humans as free social beings must also logically include those elements required for a multitude of individuals to live with one another in organized communities. In the state this implies someone "in charge" who has the responsibility for overseeing the pursuit of the common good. Unfortunately, in the present condition of humanity, this must include the right to make laws and to punish those who attack society by disobeying those laws.

It is clear from the passages quoted above that Augustine believed that the state sometimes has a *justifying reason* for punishing some of its citizens even to the point of execution, if this was necessary to protect the community. Though he himself does not make the distinction in the passages cited, this reason would seem to embrace both *prevention* (prevent-

7. *The City of God*, 1.21.
8. *Sermon 302*, 16.

ing this criminal from repeating the crime) and *deterrence* of others through fear of like punishment. In other places Augustine also defends the legitimacy of punishment for pure *retribution* — that is, aiming at balancing the scales of justice independent of any desire to stop others from committing the same crime, at least when God is the one punishing.

Thus, in his debate with Faustus about the morality of some of the violent acts reported in the Old Testament, he insists that there was nothing morally wrong in Moses executing those who had worshipped idols while he was on the mountain conversing with the one true God (Exodus 32). The reason for the execution was retribution pure and simple but it was justified because it was explicitly commanded by God to make amends for the terrible insult offered to him.[9] Although there is some suggestion that the punishment was also aimed at deterring others from the same blasphemy, the main purpose was to punish the insult. Of course, Moses was on firm ground here because he was acting under the direct command of God who has the authority to balance the scales of justice. There is a truth in the harsh statement "Revenge is mine, says the Lord" (Romans 12:19) but for God what we call "revenge" is clearly retribution. The problem for human individuals and human societies is to determine with certainty when (if ever) that retributive power is communicated to human beings. Augustine's frequent warnings against revenge are a sign that he did not think it happened very often and that when the claim is made the authorization must be beyond doubt.

---

9. *Against Faustus the Manichean*, 22.79. Another example of God using death as a means of punishing those who broke his laws is the sad case of Ananias and Sapphira in the New Testament (Acts 5:4), who lied about the extent of their goods available to the Christian community and who died on the spot. Augustine reads into the execution an aspect of rehabilitation, suggesting that God may have called for their physical death in order to save them for eternity. In his discussion of the incident in this light, he said to his listeners: "We should not think of physical death as being a severe punishment. If only, indeed, punishment stopped there! After all, did anything very dreadful happen by calling for the death of mortal creatures who were going to die anyway at sometime or other?" (*Sermon 148*, 1). This approach to death explains why it seems that Augustine would approve of the use of capital punishment if it could be proven in a particular case that it was a means of saving the criminal's soul. I believe that he thought it unlikely that this ever happened, especially in those cases where the criminality involved heresy or schism. For another suggestion of the retributive use of punishment see *Letter 185*, 8, where Augustine speaks (against the Donatists) about laws (and consequently punishments) imposed primarily to defend the truth, a reason which does not imply preventing humans or dissuading humans from doing the criminal act again.

For example, in the debate about the use of civil authority against the Donatists there was a two-fold question. Even if the state has the authority to pass laws regulating religious belief, does it also have the right to punish by execution the heretics and schismatics as a form of retribution for the "injury" they have done, not against the state nor even against the church, but rather against God himself? Where and when did God call earthly kings "up the mountain" as he did with Moses to give explicit authorization to kill the "idol-worshippers"?

The state thus has the *authority* to punish for cause and there are situations where there is *just cause (jus ad poenam)* for punishment. But for the imposition of punishment to be moral there must also be justice in the process *(jus in poena)* and this depends in part on the attitude of the one who punishes. As with all other human actions, punishment must be exercised in a spirit of love. The crime must be hated and not the criminal. The punishment must not be imposed with a spirit of revenge. This internal attitude must be present even in those cases where the punishment is imposed for reasons of deterrence and retribution. Augustine admits that it is legitimate to punish to deter further crime and even (on rare occasions) simply for the sake of retribution, but he clearly believed that the main purpose for any punishment, whether done by a parent in the family or a bishop in the church or a king in the state, is *therapeutic and rehabilitative.* The primary intent must be to cure the one punished of the evil tendencies which prompted the crime. The overriding concern must be to get the malefactor to repent, and any form of punishment that stands in the way of the possible repentance must be suspect. Augustine's attitude toward punishment is that it is, or at least should be, another expression of friendship done out of love and with the aim of "curing" the criminal and potential criminals from the tendency towards a behavior that could stand in the way of their eternal happiness. Put simply, punishment is a good thing if it is a form of *"friendly persuasion"* — a gentle (and sometimes not so gentle) effort to bring a loved one back to the straight and narrow path to eternal happiness. And even when (because of the madness and "evil that sometimes rests in the hearts of men") cure and rehabilitation is impossible, when all that can be done is to prevent the criminal from doing harm to others, even then the punishment should be imposed in a spirit of love, not out of anger or revenge.

In this life the model for such loving action is found in the parent who punishes a wayward child. The following lengthy passage well expresses what seems to me to be Augustine's view on the conditions for a moral use of punishment when there is a just cause for punishing — that is, when there is present one of the four reasons for punishing anyone:

> Any punishment which aims at correcting the one who does wrong is in fact a form of mercy. The only person who is fit to punish anyone is the one whose love has overcome the hatred which often rages in us when we desire revenge. For instance it is unlikely that parents hate their young son when he does wrong and they "box his ears" to prevent him from doing it again. When it comes to punishing someone, two things must be considered. First, does the one who imposes the punishment have a right to do so? Second, does the one punishing impose the punishment with the same kind of feelings that a father has toward a son who is still so young that he cannot possibly be hated? This example is a good illustration of how one can love and punish another at the same time rather than let the object of love go undisciplined. The goal in such ideal cases is not to make the wrongdoers miserable through punishment but to bring them happiness through correction.[10]

C. The Morality of Capital Punishment

In the practical order, can capital punishment ever meet these conditions? In one his earliest works Augustine expresses a sentiment which is a fair statement of his attitude towards capital punishment through the rest of his long life. In trying to make the point that the divine order expresses itself even in the most foul aspects of life, he writes:

> What is more hideous than a hangman? What is more cruel and ferocious than his character? And yet he holds a necessary post in the very

10. *Commentary on the Lord's Sermon on the Mount,* 1.20.63. Augustine describes how the ideal ruler will impose punishment in the following words: "We call those Christian emperors happy when they are slow to punish, quick to forgive; when they punish, not out of private revenge, but only when forced by the order and security of the republic, and when they pardon, not to encourage impunity, but with the hope of reform; when they temper with mercy and generosity the inevitable harshness of their decrees" (*The City of God,* 5.24). It is admittedly difficult to administer justice in this wise way. Augustine believed that only God can rule without arrogance; humans have a constant temptation to rule others simply for the joy of ruling (*Confessions,* 10.36), a temptation which he believed manifests itself even in infancy (*Confessions,* 1.6.8). See John M. Rist, *Augustine: Ancient Thought Baptized* (Cambridge: Cambridge University Press, 1994), p. 230.

midst of laws, and he is incorporated into the order of a well-regulated state; himself criminal in character, he is nevertheless, by others' arrangement, the penalty of evildoers.[11]

The analogy that follows, comparing the necessary functions in an imperfect world of the hangman who punishes criminals and the pimp and prostitute who channel otherwise destructive lusts away from injury to the innocent, suggests that Augustine considered capital punishment at its best to be the lesser of two evils. Punishment in general and perhaps even capital punishment, if required at all, is required only because we live in a fallen world, a world in which peace will be disturbed by humans acting maliciously against the rights of others. Crime exists: this is the reason for punishment. The question remains whether there are any circumstances where execution should be the punishment of choice and, if so, why.

One clear example where execution is the only alternative is when God specifically commands it as retribution for a crime. Augustine cites the example of the holy men in the Old Testament who, acting under God's direct inspiration, used execution as a means of therapy — either for the criminal himself, by preventing him from further sins, or for those who in witnessing the execution were filled with a "salutary fear" lest they suffer the same fate for doing the same thing. Thus, Elias killed the priests of Baal by his own hand, acting under direction from God (1 Kings 18:40) and later killed over 100 men by calling down on them fire from heaven (2 Kings 1:10). He did not act rashly in either case but with an intent to demonstrate that the God of Israel was the one true God. Other prophets who did similar things also acted in individual cases with clear authority from God when it served the best interests of human beings. Augustine notes that such violent incidents, where wrongdoers were punished with death, were not uncommon during Old Testament times when humans were ruled mostly by fear. He believed that they should be less common now under the New Testament law where humans are ruled by love. But

---

11. *On Order*, 2.4.12. Herbert Deane comments (*op. cit.*, p. 329, fn. 133) that it is incorrect to maintain that Augustine was *absolutely* against *all* uses of capital punishment. He did believe that it is sometimes necessary, certainly when commanded by God, and also when it is truly necessary to insure the peace and order in society. The righteous judge might prefer not to pass a sentence of execution but at times it seems to him necessary to prevent law and order from being undermined (*Sermon 302*, 16). But in this latter case Augustine insists that there be no other way of preserving the order in society.

this does not mean that such incidents could not happen, that the spirit of love excludes even the possibility of execution for crime. The case of Ananias and Sapphira (see note 9) proves this. Though they lived in the age of love, they were not returned to earthly life immediately after and forgiven on appeal. They were buried.[12]

Augustine does admit the authority of the state to execute the criminal if this is necessary to preserve public order but he emphasizes that this must truly be the last and only resort to achieve that purpose; indeed, he seems to have doubts that this is ever the case. An example of his hesitancy on this issue can be found in his letter to Marcellinus, the special delegate of the Emperor Honorious designated as the civil authority to settle the dispute between Catholics and Donatists. The occasion for Augustine's letter was an incident in which members of the radical Donatist faction (the Circumcellions) were convicted of having murdered one Catholic priest and seriously mutilated another. Although their actions were prompted by a religious dispute, the actions themselves were obviously civil crimes where, if the "eye for an eye" doctrine of retribution were applied, the punishment should have been execution. Despite this horrendous crime, Augustine pleads for mercy. He writes:

> I have been a prey to the deepest anxiety for fear your Highness might perhaps decree that they be sentenced to the utmost penalty of the law, by suffering a punishment in proportion to their deeds. Therefore, in this letter, I *beg* you by the faith which you have in Christ and by the mercy of the same Lord Christ, not to do this, not to let it be done under any circumstance. For although we [bishops] can refuse to be held responsible for the death of men who were not manifestly presented for trial on charge of ours, but on the indictment of officers whose duty it is

---

12. *Commentary on the Lord's Sermon on the Mount*, 1.20.64. Augustine clearly justifies execution as retributive punishment when the injustice is against God — that is, when the human being does not give God what is due. It is not clear to me that Augustine ever justifies in practice the use of execution as retribution for crimes against the state or against other individuals. In the latter case, retribution comes close to being revenge; in the former case, the civil society, though sometimes justified in *balancing the scales of justice* for crimes against God, has no clear authority to execute as retribution for crimes against itself. Of course it may punish to protect itself from further crime and even more it may punish to "cure" its citizens of their tendency to commit crimes but its right to punish simply because injury has been done to society or to individual humans (not taking into consideration the supposed "injury" done to God by every willful sin) is not clear in Augustine's writings.

to safeguard the public peace, we yet do not wish that the martyrdom of the servants of God should be avenged by similar suffering, as if by way of retaliation.

Augustine continues, emphasizing that he is not adverse to *punishment per se*, only *capital punishment*:

> However, we do not object to wicked men being deprived of their freedom to do wrong, but we wish it to go just that far, so that, *without losing their life or being maimed in any part of their body*, they may be restrained by the law from their mad frenzy, guided into the way of peace and sanity, and assigned to some useful work to replace their criminal activities. It is true, this is called a penalty, but who can fail to see that *it should be called a benefit rather than a chastisement when violence and cruelty are held in check, but the remedy of repentance is not withheld?* (emphasis added)[13]

Augustine goes on to tell Marcellinus that, as a Christian judge he must play the part of a loving father, showing anger against the crime but making allowance for the human weakness of the criminal. He applauds Marcellinus in that during the interrogation he did not use extreme torture but only "beat them with rods," a corporal punishment which in the day seems to have been accepted as being a form of *friendly persuasion* used by schoolmasters, parents, and even bishops in the correction of those they cared about. Augustine (continuing his instructions to Marcellinus) notes that "it is generally necessary to carry out an inquiry ruthlessly, so that, when the guilt has been uncovered, there may be scope for moderation." Perhaps his reason for making this distinction between "ruthless inquiry" and "moderation in punishment" is that for purposes of correction and "curing" the criminal of the crime, the first step is admission of guilt. Punishment as therapy is useless if the person will not even admit the sickness, and the infliction of modest pain on the body is certainly better than the eternal pain resulting from unrepented crimes. Therefore, his final advice to Marcellinus is:

> Do not seek out the executioner now that you have established the guilt when you refuse the services of the torturer in order to discover the guilt.[14]

13. *Letter 133*, 1.
14. *Ibid.*, 2.

Augustine writes in a similar vein in an earlier letter (408-409) to Donatus, the then proconsul of Africa:

I should prefer that the Church of Africa, beset as it is with trials, should not have to depend on the help of any temporal power (even though the help that does come from Christian authorities is given in the name of the Lord). However, there is one thing only about which I have grave misgivings in your administration of justice: namely that you decide to apply the penalty with more regard for the gravity of the crime than for the exercise of Christian clemency, for it is certainly true that of *all crimes committed by impious men, devoid of all feeling, those against a Christian commonwealth are more monstrous and more revolting than acts committed against any other group.* But even so, we beg you by Christ Himself not to act too rigidly. We are not looking for vengeance on earth over our enemies and our suffering should not reduce us to such anguish of soul that we forget the teachings of Him for whose name and truth we suffer. We do love our enemies, and we do pray for them. *Hence, in applying the deterring effect of judges and laws, we wish them to be restrained, but not put to death; otherwise, they might incur the punishment of everlasting judgment. At the same time we do want public authority to act against them, but not to make use of the extreme punishment which they deserve.* In hearing these Church cases, then, even when you discover that the Church has been outrageously attacked and injured, we ask you to forget that you have the power of life and death, but not to forget our request. Do not consider what we ask as something of little importance, my honorable and beloved son. What we ask *is that those whose conversions we pray for should not be put to death.* Passing over the fact that we ought never to depart from the rule of overcoming evil by good, let your Prudence also consider that only churchmen have the duty of bringing these Church cases before you. Consequently, if you think the death penalty should be inflicted on these men, you will frighten us off, and no such cases would come to your court by our agency. (Emphasis added)[15]

15. *Letter 100,* 1-2. Augustine repeats the same theme in an emotional outburst (obviously aimed at public officials) in one of his sermons: "So do not condemn people to death, or while you are attacking the sin you will destroy the man. Do not condemn to death, and there will be someone there who can repent. Do not have a person put to death and you will have someone who can be reformed. As a man having this kind of love for men in your heart, be a judge of the earth. Love terrifying them if you like, but still go on loving. I don't deny that penalties must be applied. I don't forbid it. But let it be done in a spirit of love, a spirit of caring, a spirit of reforming" (*Sermon 13,* 8-9).

In a follow-up letter on the same case, written to Apringius the pro-consul of Africa in 412, Augustine repeats his plea for mercy. He appeals to Apringius specifically as a Christian but notes that if the civil authority were non-Christian he would make the same argument against the death penalty even though he could no longer argue from Christian love. He also admits that if there were no other punishment decreed for curbing the wickedness of desperate men, extreme necessity might require that such men be put to death. But even here Augustine remarks that if the crime in question was the killing of two Christians because of their faith (thereby making them martyrs) and the execution of the murderers was considered to be the creation of two new martyrs, he would prefer that the guilty be freed rather than that they besmirch the blood of their martyred victims with their own criminal blood. Instead of executing and thus maiming their bodies as they had maimed their victims, he advises that their bodies be used for useful work so that they could use their bodies for the good. Finally, he pleads, even though these criminals have cut short the life-span of a minister of the church, their span of years should be lengthened so that they might possibly repent of their crimes.[16]

Augustine's conclusions about punishment in general and capital punishment in particular can be summarized as follows:

1. punishment is sometimes necessary;
2. the state has the authority to punish for cause;
3. the primary (but not only) purpose of punishment is to cure the criminal and others from the tendency to repeat the crime;
4. punishment must be imposed in a spirit of love;
5. capital punishment may be justified in rare cases when God directly commands it or when it is the *only* way to preserve the peace and order of the society;
6. apart from such rare situations, capital punishment should not be used because it takes away the criminal's chance to repent.

---

16. *Letter 134*, 3-4. In a letter sent in 414, Augustine says to Macedonius: "We do not in any way approve the faults which we wish to see corrected, nor do we wish wrongdoing to go unpunished because we take pleasure in it. We pity the man while detesting the deed or crime, and the more the vice displeases us, the less do we want the culprit to die unrepentant. We are forced by our love for humanity to intercede for the guilty lest they end this life by punishment only to find that punishment does not end with this life" (*Letter 153*, 1.3).

Whether capital punishment or any punishment should be imposed upon heretics and others who differ in belief and practice from the established church protected and fostered by the state is the question to be addressed in the chapter that follows.

CHAPTER 11

Church and State

A. Introduction

The question of the proper relation between church and state raises a number of issues. The central problem may be stated as follows. Given that there exists a society (the state) with primary responsibility for the temporal common good and that there is another society (the church) with primary responsibility for the spiritual growth and salvation of individual human beings, what is the appropriate relationship between them? There are three possibilities:

a. the two societies should be independent entities with no interference or intervention in each other's life;
b. the church should be subordinate to the state, existing as an agency of civil authority and serving its goals;
c. the state should be subordinate to the church in the sense of supporting the church in its work and protecting it by laws aimed at furthering its purposes.

As we shall see, Augustine subscribed to the last option, believing that the authorities in the state were agents of God with the responsibility of promoting God's interests on earth and that those interests included the protection of that religious body that was the instrument of his grace and revelation in time.

But how far is church or state obliged to go in protection and promotion of God's truth? Can error be tolerated? On an individual level should we passively tolerate those who disagree with us? How should we deal with another person whose ideas are contrary to ours? Should we treat them with understanding? Should we forcefully try to convince them of the "error" of their way of thinking? Or, if they refuse to agree with us should we then shun them as being unworthy of our attention and perhaps dangerous to our well-being?

When the issue of toleration is applied to a society (be it social, religious, or civil), the question becomes to what extent the society can tolerate views contrary to the accepted belief. Can those who believe differently be punished for their contrary ideas? The state has the primary duty to protect the peace and temporal prosperity of its members. When does a difference in ideas become dangerous to these goals? The church must be concerned with the eternal welfare of its members and perhaps of every human being. Does this obligation give the church the right and obligation to demand orthodoxy of its members? Does it give it the right to in some way "force" those outside to become members? Can it use state power to pursue this goal?

These are some of the questions Augustine addressed in dealing with the pagans, Jews, heretics, and schismatics of his day. The heretics and schismatics were members of the church who had separated themselves from the main body by a serious difference in belief or practice. The pagans, Jews, and others, like the Manicheans (who were never baptized), were not part of the institutional church and thus never subject to its law. Does the church have a set of responsibilities and rights over them different from its obligations to those of its own members who have wandered from the "sheepfold?" In dealing with any case of those who believed differently the practical question facing church authorities was: "To what extent can we use the state's power to accomplish church goals?"

In order to unravel this last problem, the questions previously raised in the discussion of the state's general right to punish must be addressed:

1. Does the state have the *authority* to legislate with respect to religion, for example by favoring one religion and proscribing all others?
2. Assuming that the state has such authority, what are the *reasons justifying the exercise* of that authority in a particular case?
3. Assuming that there are good reasons for exercising the authority (for example, by outlawing a particular religion), what are *the limits on how the state may implement* its authority? What is the *proper atti-*

tude or motivation that should be present in those who make and enforce such laws?

Most of Augustine's thought justifying civil intervention in matters of religion was developed within the context of the Donatist controversy and was based on his convictions about the nature of the true church of Christ, that church which had its roots in the apostolic community of believers who walked with Christ and which (in Augustine's opinion) was continued in the Catholic Church as it existed throughout the world. Consequently, in order to understand his conclusions on state intervention in matters of religion, it will be helpful to begin with an examination of his views on the nature of the church and with a brief history of the Donatist controversy.

1. The Nature of the Church

Augustine believed that the Catholic Church as it existed in the fifth century was the direct descendant of the church created by Jesus Christ. It was composed of the community of those humans spread over many places through time who were united in the one mystical body of which Christ was the head. He expressed this idea in many places but a typical example is the following excerpt from a sermon delivered to his congregation in Hippo:

> You heard when the Psalm [Ps. 73.21] was read that a poor and needy man cries out to God in this world. As you ought to remember, this is the voice of one person and yet not of one person. It is not the voice of one person because the faithful are many, many people scattered throughout the whole world like so many pieces of grain groaning in the midst of the chaff. And yet it is the voice of one person because all of these faithful are members of Christ and thus form with him one body.[1]

It is obvious that when Augustine speaks about *THE Church* he is not thinking about the various bureaucratic structures necessary to enable a religious society to operate efficiently. Much less is he referring to the

---

1. *Commentary on the Gospel of John,* 7.1.2. For a commentary on Augustine's view of the church, see R. A. Markus, *Saeculum: History and Society in the Theology of St. Augustine* (Cambridge: Cambridge University Press, 1970), pp. 105-32.

physical structures of cathedral, monastery, and convent erected by the faithful over the years to house their worship. For him "Church" meant one thing only: the community of humans who were united in some way with Christ in faith and hope and love, those especially who entered the community through baptism and who thereafter were faithful to the baptismal promises made.

Although baptism into the Catholic Church was the ordinary way of being a member of the Body of Christ, Augustine recognized that there were other ways of becoming a member. Martyrdom for the sake of Christ certainly merited membership in his Mystical Body even though the martyr was not yet baptized. Augustine also recognized that some who lived before Christ, the great prophets and other pious people who perhaps had learned of Christ through a private revelation, could not be excluded. As he said to the people of Hippo one morning:

> From the beginning of the human race, whoever knew Christ in some way and believed in him and led a pious and just life according to his commandments, was undoubtedly saved by him. We now believe in Christ both as dwelling with the Father and as having come on earth in the flesh. In like manner some of old believed in him both as dwelling with the Father and as destined to come as Messiah in the flesh. The nature of this faith has not changed, nor is salvation any different now from the way it was then. The only difference is that those events which in the past were foretold as future events in our present time are now proclaimed as having actually occurred in the past. With regard to the way in which salvation comes to believers and to other pious persons, let us leave that in the hands of God and accept his will. The religion practiced under other names and through other rites and more obscurely revealed and perhaps known by fewer persons than is the case now is one and the same faith. The salvation provided by this faith, which alone is the path to promised salvation, was never lacking to those who were worthy of it.[2]

Even though the phrase "salvation provided by faith is never lacking to those worthy of it" seems to suggest that salvation is possible for those of different faiths and perhaps even of no faith, this was not Augustine's view. Outside of those who were martyred because they knew and believed

---

2. *Letter 102*, 11-12, 15. See also *Commentary on Psalm 90/2*, 1; *Commentary on Psalm 36/3*, 4.

in Christ and those who received the sacrament of baptism and who (when they reached maturity) were committed believers in Christ, there were relatively few who could be members of Christ's Mystical Body and most of these were the "saints" of the Old Testament. Although Augustine may have left open the door to the possibility of what was later to be called the "baptism of desire," he never went through that door himself. He believed that it was not enough simply to lead a good life; in some way or other one also had to have some sort of faith in Christ, and though he admitted that this could come through a private revelation, he insisted that the only secure way to the faith that saves was through martyrdom or valid baptism. This belief left him in an uncomfortable position of having to assume that salvation was denied to unbaptized infants and adults who were without faith but were otherwise fine people who lived according to the principles of Christianity without believing in or even knowing about the teaching of Christ. His position is stated clearly in the following passage:

> No one achieves eternal salvation who does not have Christ as his head. No one can have Christ as head if he is not a part of Christ's body which is the church.[3]

One must belong to "Christ's church" in order to be saved and the ordinary entrance to the church is through Catholic baptism.

Believing in Jesus Christ and being baptized into his church is the beginning of the path to salvation, but it is only the beginning. Being a baptized member of the church is not enough, one must be a *good* member, loving God above all and other humans as oneself, tasks that would be only imperfectly accomplished by most.[4] Part of the basis for Augustine's complaint against the Donatists came from their insistence that only the perfect could be members of the true church. Augustine countered that the true church existing in time would always be a mixture of the good and the bad. When Augustine speaks about the faithful as "groaning amid the chaff," he is not speaking only about "unbelievers." A good bit of the chaff is to be found in the church itself. Indeed, all believers (with the exception

---

3. *Letter to Catholics on the Unity of the Church*, 19.49.

4. Augustine believed that the true Church is composed of "that fixed number of the saints predestined (for salvation) before the foundation of the world" (*On Baptism Against the Donatists*, 5.27.38). Just now one can not be sure who is a member because "many who seem to be on the outside are in fact on the inside and many who seem to be on the inside are in fact on the outside" (*Admonition and Grace*, 7.16).

of Mary, the mother of Christ) have their days of "being chaff" when they do not live fully the life that is expected of a member of Christ's Body. All humans are "cracked" and being baptized does not change that. Just as Augustine once said that to baptize a drunk gets only a baptized drunk, so he would contend that baptizing a cracked pot yields only a baptized cracked pot.

From Augustine's point of view, the happy part of this need to be a member of the Body of Christ to be saved was that one did not need to be perfect to be a member. Being a member and staying a member of the Body of Christ was more dependent on God's grace than human will-power. Contrary to what the Donatists claimed, baptism and all other sacraments "worked" not because of the perfection of the minister and/or recipient but because of the power of God. Discovery of the way to heaven and the strength to follow that path comes from faithful listening to the Word of God as preserved by and preached by the community of Christ's Body and accepting the life and strength that comes from remaining a participating member of that Body. But to do any of these great things one needs the grace of God.

The institutional church was important in this only as an external sign whereby one could trace one's roots back to the apostolic community united with Christ, that community that had been explicitly and directly given the commission to preach the teaching of Christ to the whole world, to administer Christ's sacraments and to celebrate as community that great act of sacrifice, performed first by Christ on Calvary and repeated now in the unbloody sacrifice of the mass. Augustine was convinced that it was only by continuity with that first small externally visible version of the Body of Christ found in the original Christian community at Jerusalem that one now could be sure that one was indeed a member (though unworthy) of that community of Christ which was the special vehicle for reaching the vision of God and the perfect happiness caused by that vision.

Augustine believed that being a member of the community of Christ was the most important thing in this life for any human because it gave the possibility of eternal joy. It is for this reason that Augustine will counsel "putting up with" someone (e.g., an unruly husband) who disrupts the peace of the family, and patiently enduring a tyrannical king who disrupts the peace of the state, while he is adamantly intolerant of anyone who threatens to disrupt the unity and peace of the Body of Christ, the historic Christian community. Augustine saw Donatism as such a disruptive force.[5] It split the Christian community into two groups: the "pure" [the Donatist Christian] and the "impure" [the Roman Catholic Christian] and claimed that only the former were truly united with Christ and on the way to salvation.

For Augustine, the community of good and bad which was in union with the apostolic community headed by Peter and his successors had the only valid claim to be the church of Christ. It was this church that was the Body of Christ on earth. It was this church who was the mother who nourished and guided humanity on its pilgrimage to the Heavenly City. It is no wonder that Augustine was so upset by the Donatist attack. He saw it as an attack on his mother.

2. History of Donatism

Donatism was a movement within North African Christianity which had its origin in the disputes that followed the persecution of Diocletian (303-305).[6] In 303 Diocletian ordered that all the Sacred Scriptures of the Christians be handed over to civil authorities and that all church property be registered. This was followed by a demand that every citizen perform a ritual act signifying loyalty to the Emperor and the gods of the Empire. The penalty for non-compliance was death. Many Christians, bishops included, obeyed the edict. These came to be known as the *traditores*, the "traitors" who had "handed over" the Sacred Scriptures to civil authority. They were universally condemned by those who had maintained a steadfast commitment to the faith by refusing to give up any of the sacred books. Frend describes the position of those who had remained faithful as follows:

5. Augustine viewed any heresy as a serious matter since it endangered the eternal life of souls. He was also convinced that there was always a moral fault in the position of the heretic and, in the case of the Donatists, the moral fault was a lack of charity. This is reflected in his definition of heretics as "those who entertain in Christ's Church unsound and distorted ideas and who stubbornly refuse, even after warnings, to correct their contagious and death-dealing doctrines, but go on defending them" (*The City of God*, 18.51).

6. For a complete discussion of Donatism and Augustine's reaction to it, see W. H. C. Frend, *The Donatist Church* (Oxford: Clarendon Press, 1952). See also Gerald Bonner, *St. Augustine of Hippo: Life and Controversies* (Philadelphia: Westminster Press, 1963), pp. 237-311; Geoffrey Grimshaw Willis, *St. Augustine and the Donatist Controversy* (London: S.P.C.K., 1950).

Even to alter a single letter of the scriptures was a crime, but contemptuously to destroy the whole at the command of pagan magistrates was to merit eternal punishment in hell. Whoever, therefore, maintained communion with the *traditores* would not participate in the joys of heaven.[7]

Pardon for such miscreants could only come after long and hard penance. Until then they were condemned, and any sacrament attempted by an unrepentant priest or bishop was invalid.

The end of the persecution in 305 did not end the turmoil in North Africa. Too many highly placed Christians had failed in their responsibility to remain faithful and there were persistent clashes between those who had fallen and those who had stood their ground. The dispute came to a head in 311-312 with the consecration of Caecilian as Primate of Africa at Carthage by three bishops, one of whom was suspected of being a *traditor.* Seventy bishops from Numidia (the place where the major concentration of those who rejected the *traditores* existed), traveled to Carthage under the lead of Secundus of Tigisis. Upon arriving he declared Caecilian's consecration suspect and called a council of bishops to resolve the matter. Caecilian was condemned and the Numidian bishops (with the support of the Carthaginian lower classes) elected Majorinus in his place. The split (schism) in the North African Christian community was now complete. Upon the death of Majorinus in 313, Donatus of Casae Nigrae was chosen to replace him, reigning for 40 years. Thereafter the *anti-traditores* party he represented came to be known by his name: the church of the Donatists.

The Donatists believed that since the Christian church was meant by Christ to be holy, only those who were holy could be part of it. All sinners were excluded and any rituals or prayers they performed were ineffective. The validity of all sacraments depended on the holiness of the administrator and the recipient. To be baptized by one who was not a member of this "church of holiness" was invalid and to receive the grace of the sacrament it was necessary to be rebaptized. The dispute was disturbing to both church and state in the western world. North Africa was a very powerful part of the western empire. Carthage was the second largest city and the North African church rivaled the church at Rome in influence and strength. Donatism was especially powerful in North Africa because the

---

7. W. H. C. Frend, *op. cit.,* p. 10. See Peter Brown, *Augustine of Hippo* (Berkeley: University of California Press, 1967), p. 213.

native people saw it as an "African Christianity" that bravely confronted the alien "Roman" Christianity of Catholicism.

In fact, there was little to choose between the two groups when it came to doctrine. Their main dispute was about which group had continuity with the apostolic church created by Jesus and what degree of perfection was required of individuals to be upstanding members of that church. Both agreed that the state had a legitimate interest in religious disputes and both freely called upon the state to intervene to support their cause.[8]

This mixture of religious and civil interests in Augustine's day is not surprising. The Roman Empire had a long history of using religion as a means of preserving civil order. In earlier years the emperors were defenders of the pagan gods, going so far as to declare themselves as gods too. Christianity and other religions were tolerated as long as they lived in peaceful co-existence with the official religion of the empire. When adherents of other religions were seen to be antagonistic, refusing to perform the rituals honoring the gods of the empire, they were persecuted. With the conversion of Constantine in 312, this general attitude towards religion did not change, only the official religion. Now Christianity became the official state religion and, as before, unity in religion was seen to be a way of preserving unity in the empire. Thus Constantine was not deviating from the policy of his predecessors when he took an active part in the North African dispute between Donatist and Catholic. As a Christian emperor he was as much concerned (though perhaps for different reasons) about maintaining unity in the church as were the bishops.

The Emperor's concern for maintaining civil peace was sharpened by the fact that the religious dispute was not a quiet debate between a few people in a library. A majority of the population was affected, sometimes violently. In the fourth and fifth century most of the North African educated classes were still pagan and thus disinterested in the dispute among christians. Christianity was a religion of the lower classes in the province of Numidia where Augustine lived and worked. There were those who went to church and the churches that they attended were usually Donatist. When Augustine became bishop of Hippo, the majority of the town was Donatist, the local Donatist church attracting many more Sunday wor-

8. See Brown, *op. cit.*, p. 228. Merdinger notes that the Donatists were the first to call for imperial intervention to resolve the religious dispute with the Catholics. Eventually the Catholics beat them at this game. See J. E. Merdinger, *Rome and the African Church in the Time of Augustine* (New Haven: Yale University Press, 1997), p. 104.

shippers than Augustine's church. If one added in the healthy sprinkling of Manicheans, Jews, and pagans living in Hippo, the Catholics were obviously a solid minority.[9] Given the passionate nature of the North African, it is no wonder that disputes about ownership of church property and about belief were as likely to be settled by weapons as by argument. A fanatic fringe of the Donatists, the *Circumcellions,* were especially troublesome. They considered violence to be the best means of conversion. Clergy were killed, Catholic churches were vandalized and desecrated, rebaptism of peasants on Catholic estates was imposed by force.[10] It was a frightening time and the secular authorities needed to intervene to preserve some semblance of order.

Constantine tried to resolve the North African dispute through a church council first at Rome and then at Arles where the decision of the assembled delegates in 314 was against the Donatists, but this did little to stop the conflict. After seven more years of fruitless effort, Constantine gave up trying for a peaceful resolution and washed his hands of the matter. From that time until the end of the fourth century the Donatist fortunes swung between violent suppression under Macarius (the imperial commissioner in 347) through toleration under the emperor Julian in 361-63. Such grudging tolerance ended when Honorious became emperor in 398. He favored the Catholic position and there was a gradual hardening of regulations, limiting all other religious practice. Finally in 405 he issued an Edict of Unity which declared that the Donatists were indeed heretics and were therefore forbidden to own property or have public celebrations of their belief.

The final act in the state suppression of Donatism took place in 411-412. Under the command of the emperor Honorius a council was called at Carthage, presided over by the imperial delegate, Marcellinus, a good friend of Augustine. Its purpose was to provide a final chance for Donatist and Catholic to make their case, to confirm the Catholic position, and to decide whether Donatism was to be tolerated in the future. The continuing strength of the disputing parties was reflected in the number of bishops who attended: 286 Catholic and 284 Donatist. The decision of the conference was that Donatism should be officially proscribed. The decision was appealed directly to Honorius but without success. In January 30, 412, he issued a final command that Donatism should be outlawed. Donatist

---

9. See Merdinger, *op. cit.,* pp. 68-69.
10. *Letter 185,* 4.15. See Frend, *op. cit.,* pp. 72-73, 172-78, 257-58.

property was confiscated, Donatist clergy were condemned to exile, and Donatist membership became a crime to be punished by fine.[11]

Implementation of the edict proved more difficult than its issuance. Donatism was still a force in North Africa long after Augustine died in 430 and, as Frend suggests,

> Donatism may have remained the religion of a large proportion of the African villagers in the fifth century as well as the fourth. Perhaps, after all, the Circumcellions had the last word.[12]

In fact, Donatism in North Africa outlasted the first emperor to condemn it (Constantine) by 400 years and there is some hint that its passionate conviction that the true Church is only for the pure has lasted in various forms down to the present day.[13]

B. Augustine on the Justification of State Intervention in Religious Disputes

There is no question that Augustine believed that the state had the authority to legislate in matters of religion. At the very beginning of his debate with the Donatists, he writes to Parmenian defending the right and duty of the Christian ruler to act in defense of God's interests in matters of religious dispute. He argues that just as civil authority can punish the murderer and the thief, so it can punish heresy and schism.[14] At about the same time (400-02), in response to a letter of the Donatist Petelian, Augustine carries forward the argument by insisting that Christian kings cannot make a neat separation between their Christianity and their position as a ruler of the state. Kings are bound to serve God not simply as private individuals but precisely as kings. He writes:

> When we take into consideration the nature of human society, we find that kings, by the very fact that they are kings, have a service which they

---

11. See Emilien Lamirande, *Church, State and Toleration: An Intriguing Change of Mind in St. Augustine,* The Saint Augustine Lecture: 1974 (Villanova, PA: Villanova University Press, 1975), p. 11.

12. Frend, *op. cit.,* p. 299.

13. Merdinger, *op. cit.,* p. 89.

14. See *Against the Letter of Parmenian,* 1.16.

can render to God, a service which cannot be supplied by those who do not have the authority of kings.[15]

The source of this regal obligation is found in the fact that every king receives his authority ultimately from God. With that authority comes the responsibility to care for the welfare of the ordinary citizens. But, Augustine asks, if kings are representatives of God, how can they be excused when they take violations of human rights like adultery seriously but ignore violations of divine rights such as sacrilege?[16] A king serves God by commanding what is right and forbidding what is wrong both in moral law and in religious observance. If there is no violation of individual freedom in forbidding crimes attacking individuals such as adultery, theft, or murder — why claim that it violates freedom when a ruler forbids heresy, an attack on the true church and on God?[17] Crimes against true religion deserve punishment as much as any other crime. Augustine argues that in punishing heretics and schismatics

> . . . kings serve God, as they are divinely commanded because of their position as kings, if they command the good and prohibit evil in their kingdom not only with regard to those things which pertain to human society but also as regards things pertaining to divine religion. And indeed it does not make sense to complain: "But you should respect my freedom!" Indeed, why do you not proclaim that you should allow free will to have its way in questions of murder and debauchery and other evil deeds and crimes? God did indeed give humans free will, but he neither wished that the good should go unrewarded nor that the evil should go unpunished.[18]

The crime of the Donatists and others who break away from the church is that they are revolting against Christ and the church. If they use violence to promote their cause, they are even more in the wrong, but the essential element in their crime is in their revolution against God in the person of his church.[19] Augustine believed that heretics and schismatics, far from being honest but confused seekers of truth, are those who "for the sake of some temporal advantage, especially for the sake of glory and pre-

---

15. *Against the Writings of Petelian the Donatist*, 2.210.
16. *Letter 185*, 5.20.
17. *Letter 204*, 4. See *Against Gaudentius the Donatist*, 1.19.
18. *Against Cresconius the Donatist*, 3.51.
19. *Letter 89*, 2.

eminence," originate or follow false and new opinions.[20] With such a negative view of heresy and schism, it is no wonder that he considered them to be innately dangerous, disreputable, and worthy of eradication even if it meant using civil power to accomplish their elimination.

C. Justifying Reasons for State Intervention

Augustine believed that there were at least three possible justifications for civil intervention to resolve religious disputes, especially those between the Catholic Church and schismatic churches such as the Donatists.

First, as we have seen above, he was firmly convinced that the Roman Catholic Church had the divinely appointed mission to save the world. Consequently, he considered any movement which endangered this mission as dangerous in the extreme and deserving of the most severe penalties. By their attack on the sacramental system (tying in the efficacy of the sacrament to the "purity" of the minister and demanding rebaptism for one baptized as a Catholic) and their claim to be the true church founded by Christ, the Donatists disrupted the unity of the church. Their attack on Catholicism amounted to an attack on the Body of Christ, ripping from it confused souls who, once separated, were cut off from the only source of saving grace. Such an attack on "God's Body" was in a way an insult to God himself and the civil rulers were bound to use their office to prevent such insults. Civil intervention was thus justified to *restore unity to the Catholic church* and thereby *defend the honor due to God*.

Secondly, the more violent fringes of Donatism were interfering with the day by day life of the church. Some civil intervention was therefore needed, not only to protect the Christian community, but also to protect *innocent individuals* who were being threatened by the violence of the terrorist factions on both sides of the dispute.[21]

Finally, the Donatists, by their divisive stance and by the violence that they sometimes used to further their cause, endangered the peace, order, and unity of the empire itself. Donatism was attractive to many in North Africa because it was seen as an expression of the local culture, an ideology that confronted the "foreign" intrusions of Roman empire and

20. *The Usefulness of Believing*, 1.1.
21. See Geoffrey Willis, *op. cit.*, p. 129.

the Roman church. Thus, state action against the Donatists was justified to *protect the life of the empire itself.*

Such reasoning justified civil intervention, but the question remained: "How far should this intervention go?" Over the more than thirty years of Augustine's conflict with Donatism, his position on the degree and reasons for civil intervention clearly changed. From initial reluctance to call in civil power to support the Catholic case, he gradually accepted its use as a defensive measure against the violence of the Donatists, and finally came to accept it as an offensive weapon for destroying the movement and providing a forceful suasion for individual conversions.[22]

Up to the year 400 Augustine seems firmly opposed to any use of civil intervention against the Donatists. Thus, in a letter written in 392 to the Donatist bishop Maximinus proposing a discussion of their differences, Augustine says:

> I shall not take any action while the army is present lest anyone of yours should think that I wanted to use force rather than a peaceful method. After the departure of the army I shall see to it that all who hear us may know that it was no part of my plan that men should be forced into communion against their will, but that truth should be manifest to those seeking it in quietness.[23]

Although Augustine rejects the use of civil power to influence the debate during these years, he did not believe that its use for good cause was always out of place.[24] At that particular time he simply did not deem it advisable. He did not mean to imply either that the church never has the right to call for the use of such power or that the state did not have the duty to respond to that call when it comes.

In the first decade of the fifth century, Augustine began to see the need for civil power to offset the increasing violence against church people and property. At this stage it seems that he favors such intervention reluctantly and only as a *defensive* measure against the attacks of the Donatists, attacks which prevented many from making up their own minds free from

22. This change in view is reflected in comments that Augustine made at the end of his life in the review of earlier writings. See *Retractions*, 2.31.

23. *Letter 23*, 7. See *Against the So-called Fundamental Letter of Mani*, 1.1. See Bonner, *op. cit.*, p. 301.

24. See *Letter 51*, 3, written in 399/400, where Augustine suggests to the Donatist Crispinus that it is only "Christian mildness" that restrains him from asking for the civil action that their "monstrous sacrilege" deserves.

threats. He was still convinced of the power of truth to sway the mind if only it could be given a chance. Though justifying civil intervention, he still hoped that it would not be necessary as an *offensive* weapon that would pressure Donatists back to Catholicism. Thus, when Augustine learned that the Donatist bishop Crispinus had used force to rebaptize eighty tenant farmers on his estate, he did not call in civil authority to remedy the situation. Instead he proposed a free discussion of the Catholic and Donatist position in the presence of the rebaptized farmers so that

> . . . when they are free from the fear of coercion, they may choose according to their own free will. And, if there are some people who have come over to us, under the compulsion of their own masters, let the same thing be done there as here. Let them hear us both and choose what pleases them.[25]

Unfortunately, the environment was not conducive to such a fair and free discussion; the violence of the Circumcellions was increasing. As a consequence, Augustine and his fellow Catholic bishops came more and more to the view that civil power had to be called in, not to persuade the indifferent, but to protect the terrified. Consequently, at the ninth Council of Carthage (16 June 404), a majority of the Catholic bishops favored an imperial decree of union that would end the heresy. Augustine at first cautioned prudence, saying that such a decree should be aimed at defense, not suppression. However, a new incident occurred which brought about a quick imperial intervention. The Catholic bishop of Bagai was attacked by a band of Donatists and this incident was brought directly to the attention of the Emperor Honorius. He issued an edict (12 February 405) forcing union of the Donatists with the Catholics. The good effects that seemed to flow from the enforcement of this imperial edict prompted Augustine to reconsider his reluctance to use civil force to resolve church division. In 408 he wrote to Vincent, the Rogatist (Rogatism was a sect within Donatism) bishop of Cartenna, explaining his change of mind:

> I have, then, yielded to the facts suggested to me by my colleagues, although my first feeling about it was that no one was to be forced into the unity of Christ. But this opinion of mine has been set aside, not because of opposing arguments, but by reason of proven facts.[26]

25. *Letter 66*, 2.
26. *Letter 93*, 17. See *Letter 185*, 29.

Although there is some dispute whether or not the repressive civil laws really decreased the Donatist numbers, Augustine was much impressed by the good effects of the enforcement of the imperial edict. The mass conversions which resulted convinced Augustine that civil action might possibly bring about the Church unity that he so desperately desired. He thus entered the final stage of his thought about the justification of civil intervention. He began to argue for the use of civil force as an *offensive* weapon against schism and heresy, a weapon which would use civil penalties to persuade heretics and schismatics to leave their wandering ways and rejoin the Catholic church. The reason for this change was Augustine's deeply felt conviction that as a shepherd of souls he had the responsibility to save as many as he could from the destructive doctrines of those attacking the church. As he told his people in a sermon delivered in 406, his fear of his own eternal damnation forced him to pursue the Donatists. With some emotion he proclaimed:

> I shall call back the erring. I shall seek out the lost. Whether they are willing or not, I shall *do* it![27]

The death knell for Donatism as an organized, public body was sounded at the Council of Carthage in 411. The whole controversy was aired out with both sides permitted to make their strongest arguments. The judgment of Marcellinus, the imperial representative, favored the Catholics and this decision was upheld by an imperial edict of unity on 30 January 412. In essence, the decision of the emperor forbade the Donatists to meet and directed that all their property be turned over to the Catholics. With that edict Donatism was deprived of any semblance of official state recognition. To profess Donatism even privately was now a crime punishable by civil law.

Augustine justified such civil legislation by arguing that its purpose was not to force conversion but only to make the unconverted consider their position more seriously. Civil penalties forced the ordinary Donatists to ask the question: "Am I so committed to my belief that I am willing to suffer civil penalties in order to maintain it?"[28] In threatening punishment,

---

27. *Sermon 46*, 7.14. Augustine commented to his parishioners that while in the beginning the apostles were fishers of men, now Christians must be hunters, beating the thickets and driving the wandering sheep into the nets that will save them. See *Sermon 400*, 11.

28. *Against the Writings of Petelian*, 2.186.

the state was acting like a father who uses discipline so that his beloved son might *freely choose* to give up that activity which threatens his welfare. Augustine believed that it was this message of love that should be read into the actions of Christian kings who were trying to use the power given them by God to protect their subjects from eternal disaster.[29]

Augustine remained convinced that if the law removed external obstacles to conversion and made the heretic or schismatic think seriously about their situation, they would freely and sincerely choose to return to the church. The first step in conversion was to give people an opportunity to hear the truth and to motivate them to pay attention to the truth. Like freshmen in a required philosophy course, the audience had to be *forced to come in* and then motivated to think about ultimate questions. This reasoning was at the root of Augustine's most forceful argument justifying civil intervention, the so-called *Compelle intrare* ("Compel them to enter") argument.

The first complete presentation of this approach occurred in a letter written in 416 to Donatus, a Donatist priest. Augustine draws a parallel between the wedding feast described in Scripture (Luke 14:15-24) and the action of the state forcing Donatists into union with Catholics. Just as the lord of the banquet not only invites guests but even compels them to attend, so the church, acting in the name of God, sends out its servant (the civil powers) to bring the indifferent and unwilling to the eternal banquet of faith and glory.[30]

Augustine agreed that faith cannot be forced; but, continuing the analogy with the banquet, he makes the point that even though the guests were forced to attend, once they were there they enjoyed the feast willingly.[31] In the same way, Augustine believed, once the heretics have been brought to the "gates of faith" they would take the final step through conviction. Augustine admitted that this method of getting the indifferent into the banquet hall and at the feet of the Master was not the ideal method, but it seemed to work and certainly seemed preferable to abandoning those who would only come to believe through a friendly severity. In Augustine's words:

29. *Ibid.*, 2.217.

30. Augustine believed that identifying the civil authorities as the servants who were sent out by the lord of the banquet to gather the recalcitrant guests was at least suggested in the words of the psalm (81:11): "And all the kings of the earth shall adore Him; all nations shall serve Him." See *Letter 163*, 10.

31. *Sermon 112*, 7.8. See *Against Gaudentius the Donatist*, 1.25.

It is indeed better (as no one ever could deny) that men should be led to worship God by teaching, than that they should be driven to it by fear of punishment or pain. But it does not follow that because the former course produces the better men, those who do not yield to it should be neglected. For many have found advantage (as we have proven, and are daily proving by experience) in being first compelled by fear or pain, so that they might afterwards be influenced by teaching and follow by action what they had learned through words.[32]

As was the case for punishment in general, Augustine insisted that any punishment imposed on heretics or schismatics had to be done out of love. It should be like that of a loving father disciplining a disruptive boy for his own good or like that of a concerned doctor cauterizing a deadly wound in order to cure the patient. It would be wonderful if all children could be trained through meaningful dialogue and all the sick could be cured by conversation, but this is not realistic. Sometimes painful methods must be used to get the good effect. So too it would be ideal if all heretics and schismatics could be persuaded by rational debate to return to the church, but this too was not realistic. In Augustine's experience, many of these dissenters were like seriously sick people in irrational frenzy and many others were infected with a lassitude which made teaching impossible without some incentive to listen. And as far as the use of civil power is concerned, Augustine argues that if it is cruel for a Christian king committed to the welfare of his people to be indifferent to their attempted suicide, it is no less cruel for him to stand back and watch while they suffer eternal death by continuing to adhere to a heretical doctrine.[33]

The aim of laws regulating religion certainly includes the protection of the church and preservation of the peace of the state, but in Augustine's opinion the primary justification for such laws is to *cure* individual heretics/schismatics of the confusion and perversity that leads to eternal pun-

---

32. *Letter 185*, 6.21. See John M. Rist, *Augustine: Ancient Thought Baptized* (Cambridge: Cambridge University Press, 1994), p. 274.

33. *Letter 173*, 4. Markus observes (*op. cit.*, pp. 141-43) that Augustine saw a wall of hardened habit separating the schismatic communities (such as the Donatists) from the unity of the one fold (see *Letter 89*, 7). A discipline that induced fear was not contrary to freedom. It was a way of enabling freedom by breaking down the walls of such restricting habit. In recommending discipline, Augustine was thus motivated by pastoral concerns. He likens coercion to a medicine administered to an unwilling patient for his own good (*Letter 93*, 1.3). It is thus a work of love, for it is "better to love with discipline than to deceive with indulgence" (*Letter 93*, 2.4).

ishment. It is for this reason that although Augustine seems to accept (though reluctantly) capital punishment in special cases, he never accepts it as a punishment for heresy or schism. The reason is simple. Other punishments leave a lifetime for conversion; capital punishment cuts short a life that might otherwise have been corrected.[34]

It was impossible for Augustine to remain indifferent to the people affected and infected by the scourge of Donatism. Although he was generally sympathetic towards those who had ideas different from his own, he could not remain indifferent to a movement which actively proselytized its views and thereby endangered the salvation of individual souls, the unity of the church, and the civil peace. In all of Augustine's actions against the Donatists, charity was the motive and peace the goal. The paradox is that Augustine pursued the heretics because he loved them so much. He was concerned with their eternal welfare. He believed with all the sincerity of his heart that humans could most surely attain salvation only within the Catholic church. His words and actions against heresy and schism were but logical conclusions from those convictions. Is this persecution? Augustine rather considered it to be a form of *friendly persuasion* motivated by love.

D. Toleration of Pagans, Jews, and Manicheans

Augustine's defense of civil power to subdue the Donatists was quite vigorous and the use of such power was sometimes quite harsh. His treatment of pagans, Jews, Manicheans, and other non-Catholic groups was mild by comparison. In Augustine's day the *pagan* population of Hippo was a minority.[35] The town was mainly Christian, though some pagans still held positions of authority. In Rome and in North Africa the pagans were mostly freethinkers, committed more to the ideals of the old empire than the gods of the old religion. As a consequence, and unlike the Donatists,

---

34. Augustine admittedly had a second reason for his reluctance to put heretics or schismatics to death for their belief. He did not want to create "martyrs" that might create an emotional attachment to a false faith. However it seems true that his primary reason remained an aversion to creating a practice that could result in the eternal damnation of the one executed.

35. For a description of pagan life in Augustine's North Africa, see F. Van der Meer, *Augustine the Bishop* (London: Sheed & Ward, 1961), pp. 29ff. See also Emilien Lamirande, *op. cit.*, pp. 26ff.

these intellectuals seldom if ever became especially violent or fanatic specifically in defense of the pagan gods.[36]

The debate between Christianity and paganism was usually carried on at a highly rational level. For example, the communication between Augustine and such pagan correspondents as Maximus *(Letter 17)*, Dioscorus *(Letters 117, 118)*, Longinianus *(Letters 233, 234, 235)*, Volusianus *(Letter 132)*, and his response to the questions posed by a group of Carthaginian thinkers *(Letter 37)*, were always polite and courteous. As Combès observes:

> To convert by force of honesty, devotion, and tenderness, to seek occasions for making contact with their minds, to accumulate proofs which might convince them, to make appeal to sentiments which might move them, to lead those still hesitating to become Christians by appeal to their reason and their heart: such was the method of Saint Augustine with regard to the faithful of the ancient religion. Their persons and their goods were sacred to him.[37]

Augustine was tolerant of the *person* of the individual pagan and he also had a high regard for the classic culture of the Greeks and Romans. He believed that the study of the liberal arts taught by the great pagan thinkers of antiquity could be a step in the understanding of the Christian faith. At the same time, he fully supported the imperial edicts of Valentian II and Theodosius that outlawed both public and private practice of pagan rites. Their use of magic, their superstitions, their celebrations seemed to Augustine to be works of the devil. Their representations of the gods in theater productions were provocative if not positively obscene. Augustine

---

36. An exception to the pagan commitment to non-violence occurred in 408 in the town of Calama where Possidius was bishop. The latter tried to stop a traditional pagan procession and rioting followed. Pagan ruffians (aided and abetted now by Donatist confreres) stoned the Catholic church in the town and tried to burn it down. Clergy and monks were sought out for beating and one was killed. Possidius himself was saved only by hiding. See Van der Meer, *op. cit.*, pp. 40-46; Peter Brown, *Augustine of Hippo*, pp. 287-88.

37. Gustave Combès, *La doctrine politique de saint Augustin* (Paris: Librairie Plon, 1927), p. 336. Lamirande (*op. cit.*, p. 32) adds, "He does nowhere suggest the possibility of *converting* pagans by force and he apparently did not urge the application of imperial laws, which is to say that he did not seem to consider the suppression of paganism as a direct concern of the church. Here lies the most significant difference between his attitude towards paganism and his attitude towards Donatism."

compared such pagan activities to those of children playing in the mud who must be corrected by a stern teacher so that they might rub the dirt from their hands and move on to more useful activities. Such restrictions benefited the pagans pulled from their muddy play and were also a protection for the unsophisticated Christian who might be tempted to join them. Indeed, Augustine was less upset by the pagans still indulging in such practices than he was by "Sunday-Christians" who would rush from the church to join their friends at their games and shows. As Van der Meer remarks, too many Christians seemed to embrace the pagan motto: "To hunt, to bathe, to gamble, to laugh . . . that is to live!" — agreeing with the pagan complaint that the worse thing about the high-minded moral life of the Christian was that it was just too *boring!*[38]

Despite his antipathy towards pagan practices and rituals, Augustine insisted that no individual Christian or group of Christians had the right to invade pagan properties and take the law into their own hands by destroying pagan artifacts. This was the business of the state acting as the agent of the one true God and protector of public morals. In fact most of the attacks on pagan shrines were not committed by Catholic Christians but by the radical wing of the Donatists, the Circumcellions, who hoped to be martyred by the enraged pagan crowds. At his daily services Augustine instructed his congregation (who were perhaps already shuffling their feet in anticipation of an early exit to the pagan shows) that they should be more concerned about "breaking the idols in the hearts of pagans" so that they might become good Christians who would thereafter destroy their own pagan shrines.[39]

Augustine's attitude towards the pagan was thus quite different from his approach to the Donatists. He was not satisfied in simply restricting their Donatist practices; he wanted their personal conversion to the Catholic position. While he hoped, of course, that the pagans would become Catholic Christians and be baptized, he did not feel that any force beyond the force of reason should be applied to them. They were not a threat to the unity of the church because they were outside of it. They were not a threat to civil order because they (unlike the Donatists) peacefully accepted the civil laws prohibiting the public practice of their rites. The Donatists, on the other hand, were wandering *Christians,* lost sheep but

38. See *Sermon 62,* 18. Van der Meer, *op. cit.,* p. 47. See Augustine's *On the Harmony of the Gospels,* 1.33.51.

39. *Sermon 62,* 17.

still members of Christ's flock. As a pastor of that flock, Augustine felt a special responsibility to bring the wandering Donatists back to the fold, a responsibility that he did not feel towards the multitude of individuals of other theological species wandering the earth. Because of his conviction of the need for membership in the church to be saved, he hoped and prayed that many of these "alien" herds would join the Christian fold, but he felt no special duty to "compel them to come in." This he could leave in the hands of God. But those who were now members of the sheepfold he felt a special obligation to prevent from wandering away — even if it took the "barking dog" of civil power to keep them in line. By baptism they had already become members of the Body of Christ; it was up to him as shepherd to do all he could to deter them from running away from that Body in a moment of insanity.[40]

Augustine went even further in his toleration of the *Jews*. They were a substantive presence in Hippo and even more in Carthage, prompting Augustine to observe that there were only two kinds of people in Hippo: Christians and Jews.[41] He had great regard for the observant Jew but was disturbed by some of the antics of those who did not take their religion seriously. As he warned his church congregation one day:

> You are told to observe the sabbath spiritually, not like the worldly idleness of the Jews on their sabbath. They use the free time for parties and excess. It would be better for them if they spent the time in useful work, taking care of the land instead of fighting in the stadium shows. And

40. See Lamirande, *op. cit.*, pp. 33-38. See Frend, *op. cit.*, p. 242. See Augustine, *On Baptism against the Donatists*, 1.1.2; *Letter 185*, 6.23. Augustine suggests in his work *Against Gaudentius the Donatist* (1.25.28) that one of the implications of the Scripture story of the banquet is that, although those who were first invited and refused (the Jews) might be left to go their own way, those who were called in afterwards (the heretics and schismatics) could be forced to come in because they already belonged to the church and had a right and duty to participate in the banquet created for them by the Lord.

41. *Sermon 62*, 4. See Van Der Meer *op. cit.*, p. 76. Liguori comments: "The Jews formed no small part of the population of Hippo and Carthage and, though many were true to their religious beliefs and customs, others, with their careless morals and contentious ways, presented a serious difficulty to the zealous bishop in his solicitude for the members of his Christian flock who were only too ready to revert to the practices of their pagan and Jewish ancestry." Sister Marie Liguori, I.H.M., trans., *In Answer to the Jews (Adversus Judaeos)*, in *St. Augustine: Treatises on Marriage and other Subjects*, vol. 27 of the Fathers of the Church series edited by Roy J. Deferrari (New York: Fathers of the Church, Inc., 1955), p. 389.

their women would be more usefully employed in spinning wool on the sabbath than in dancing shamelessly all day long on their balconies.[42]

Augustine believed that the God-fearing Jew was symbolized by the older son in the story of the prodigal son. Like that older son he is forced by his convictions to stand by and watch while others march in to the banquet of the father. It is a sad sight, but the hopeful element in the story is that the father came out to the son who would not join the banquet and said to him: "Son you are with me always. . . . I don't want you to miss our feast. Don't be jealous of your younger brother. You are with me always." It was clear to Augustine that the father in the story (who represents the Divine Father) is bearing witness to those of the Jewish faith who have always worshipped the one God, who have always been near to him. These are the Jews who, while not yet entering the Father's house to share in the banquet, are still able to say to God: "I have not disregarded your commandment" (Luke 15:29).[43] Augustine had a respect tinged with sadness for such Jews who were serious about the practice of their faith, though still blind to the reality of Christ. He was never troubled by their continuing worship according to the Old Law and he never favored civil law against either their person or their practice. The pagan practices were indeed works of the devil, but Jewish worship was a valid but incomplete means of serving the true God.[44]

His tolerant attitude was dictated by a number of factors. First of all, there seemed little temptation among his Christian flock, who were sometimes drawn to imitate the antics of the non-observant Jew, to be con-

---

42. *Sermon 9, 3.* Hill comments: "We get a picture of Jews in Roman Africa forming an active and uninhibited section of society. Augustine is not here being anti-semitic but simply unecumenical. He has no sympathy with, and probably little understanding of, Judaism as a religion, just as he had no sympathy with, but probably more understanding of, heresies like Manichaeanism, Donatism and Arianism" (Edmund Hill, O.P., trans., *Sermons*, part 3, volume 1 of *The Works of Saint Augustine: A Translation for the 21st Century*, ed. John E. Rotelle, O.S.A. [New York: New City Press, 1990-], p. 279).

43. *Sermon 112a, 13.*

44. See Combès, *op. cit.*, pp. 349-50. See Lamirande, *op. cit.*, pp. 349-50. Fredriksen comments: "Augustine's vision of the Jews as a living witness to the Christian truth was both original and, compared with his attitude toward pagans and non-Catholic Christians, uncharacteristically tolerant" (Paula Fredriksen, "*Excaecati Occulta Justitia Dei*: Augustine on Jews and Judaism," *Journal of Early Christian Studies*, vol. 3/3 [1995], pp. 299-324).

verted to the orthodox Judaism of the serious believer. Judaism was, if anything, a more difficult practice than Catholic Christianity.[45] Moreover he saw Judaism as serving the cause of the Christian church in a number of different ways. It provided the church with the heritage of prophecy reaching back even to Adam and was in a sense the *scrinaria,*

> . . . a desk containing the Law and the Prophets for the use of Christians, testifying to the doctrine of the church by disclosing in words what the christians honor in the sacrament.[46]

Even more, through their diaspora the Jews have spread the ancient prophecies of the coming of Christ contained in the pages of their sacred books throughout the known world.[47] They thus prepared the ground for conversion to Christ throughout the world.

It is because of this continuing service to the church in spreading the good news of the Messiah that Augustine believed that, despite their blindness, the Jewish people came under the protection of God's promise to Cain. As he remarks:

> Although they were conquered and oppressed by the Romans, God did not "slay" them, that is, God did not destroy them as Jews. In that case they would have been forgotten and would have been useless as witnesses to what I am speaking of. Consequently, the first part of the prophecy, "Slay them not lest they forget thy law" (Ps. 58:11-12) is of small import without the rest, "Scatter them." For, if the Jews had remained bottled up in their own land with the evidence of their scriptures and if they were not to be found everywhere, as the church is, the church would not then have them as ubiquitous witnesses of the ancient prophecies concerning Christ.[48]

45. Augustine pictures the observant Jew (the older brother of the prodigal) standing at the doors of the banquet hall in a fit of anger seeing the dissolute pass by into the feast. He writes: "And the elder brother is angry when he returns from the fields, and refuses to go in. He is the people of the Jews, whose spirit appeared even in those who had already come to believe in Christ. The Jews couldn't stomach it that the gentiles should come on such easy terms, without the imposition of any of the burdens of the law, without the pain of physical circumcision, that they should receive saving baptism in sin" (*Sermon 112a,* 8).

46. Fredriksen, *op. cit.,* p. 317. See *Against Faustus the Manichean,* 12.23.

47. See *The City of God,* 18.46.

48. *Ibid.*

Augustine interpreted the command "Do not slay them!" as meaning that Jews should not be killed either physically by execution or spiritually by forbidding them to practice their faith and forcing their conversion. Until the end of time they will stand as a warning of what can happen to anyone who pridefully turns his back on Christ the Messiah.[49] Augustine felt no special obligation to convert the Jews or to punish them for their rejection of Christ. Both conversion and punishment could be left in the hands of God, that God who declared through the parable of the prodigal that he still stood close by that elder son who as yet was unable or unwilling to join the banquet.

A final word on Augustine's attitude towards the *Manicheans* deserves brief mention.[50] This was a special case for Augustine because he had himself been a Manichean for over ten years and for part of that time had been a convinced believer and an enthusiastic proselytizer. There is a suggestion that his somewhat abrupt exit from Carthage when he was a young academic was in fact an exile imposed by imperial law. And, when he sought solace in his hometown of Hippo, he was summarily refused entrance into his mother's house because of his fervent Manichean belief. Such was his enthusiasm that soon after, when a dear Manichean friend became seriously ill, Augustine seemed more disturbed by his deathbed conversion to Christianity than by his imminent death.[51] It can be safely said that of all of the great theological debates he would have with Manicheans, Donatists, Pelagians, and Arians, Augustine best understood and was most sympathetic towards the Manichean position. He not only knew what they believed; he knew the sentiments that drew them towards that belief even under the threat of persecution.

The civil suppression of Manicheanism had been in place long before the time of Augustine. The movement was not only seen by imperial officials as a threat to the pagan and thereafter Christian orientation of the society; it also had about it the taint of being an invasion from the East, an

---

49. *Against Faustus the Manichean*, 12.12. See Fredriksen, *op. cit.*, p. 318.

50. For a brief description of Manichean belief and its influence on Augustine, see Donald X. Burt, *Augustine's World: An Introduction to His Speculative Philosophy* (Lanham, MD: University Press of America: 1996), pp. 14-17. For a more generous examination see Gerald Bonner, *op. cit.*, pp. 157-236.

51. See Peter Brown, "The Diffusion of Manichaeism in the Roman Empire," in *Religion and Society in the Age of Augustine* (London: Faber and Faber, 1972), p. 113. See *Confessions*, 3.11; 4.4. See also John J. O'Meara, *The Young Augustine* (New York: Longman, 1980), pp. 83-86.

insidious infiltration of the enemy Persia into the western empire. In its beliefs Manicheanism was far different from Roman Catholicism, but its acceptance of Christ and Paul as prophets and its respect for the New Testament scriptures merited its designation of being a "heresy" prohibited by law. Indeed, the only recorded executions for heresy were those imposed on Manicheans.[52] By the end of the fourth century the civil laws against the Manicheans were enforced with increasing severity and in this implementation many Catholic bishops played an important part, identifying the Manicheans hidden in the midst of the Christians in the towns.[53]

When the bishop Augustine began his serious debate with Manichean opponents, the environment both in the empire and in the church was conducive to calling on civil forces to aid the Catholic cause. But Augustine never demanded such intervention. Instead he maintained that the correction of the Manicheans should be achieved not by inducing anxiety through persecution but rather by quiet discussion, friendly encouragement, and by an understanding sympathy for their plight.[54] Certainly, his reluctance was not based on doubts about the legitimacy of state intervention. He had approved the empire's suppression of pagan practices and shrines. He was even more favorably inclined towards the civil laws that seized Donatist property and made it a crime even to be a Donatist. Why then was he so tolerant of the Manicheans? Perhaps for the following reasons.

First of all, he knew from personal experience what it meant to be a Manichean desperately seeking answers to the mystery of life and death, good and evil. He himself had been mesmerized by the Manichean answers to such ultimate questions. Perhaps it was while remembering his own Manichean daze that he wrote to some who were still captivated by the doctrine:

> Let those be angry with you who have never experienced the work necessary to discover the truth and the caution needed to avoid falling into error. Let those be angry with you who have never discovered how difficult it is to wade through the confusions of the flesh with a pious and clear mind. And, finally, let those treat you angrily who have never themselves strayed as you have strayed. For my part I can't do that. I went through such lengthy confusion before I came at last to recognize

52. See Brown, *Religion and Society, op. cit.,* p. 94. See Lamirande, *op. cit.,* pp. 35-36.

53. See Brown, *Religion and Society, op. cit.,* pp. 110-11.

54. *Against the Fundamental Letter of the Manicheans,* 1.

the simple truth that does not come from exotic legends. I barely succeeded, with God's help, in finally rejecting the empty ideas I had gathered from false theories and doctrines of many kinds. It was only after a long time that I sought a cure for my mental blindness, giving myself finally to the call and persuasions of the Divine Doctor who spoke to me from within. After going through all this how can I be angry with you? I must put up with you as I formerly had to bear with myself. I must be as patient with you now as my friends were patient with me when I was still blindly running madly astray, believing then as you believe now.[55]

Added to this sympathy for the personal confusion of the Manicheans was the fact that the movement did not seem to constitute a particular threat to the church or to the faithful. Though related to Christianity in its acceptance of Christ and Paul as some of its prophets and its reverence for at least part of the Sacred Scripture, the Manicheans were not a divisive force that split the "sheepfold" that was Christ's church. They had not been a part of the Mystical Body of Christ which had cut itself loose and thus were not a visible contradiction of the unity and universality of Christ's church. Furthermore, there was no indication that simple Christians were particularly drawn to Manichean practices (as they were towards the pagan rites), practices which in any case were forbidden by law and indulged in publicly only at great personal risk. In sum, the conversion of the Manichean (as was the case with the Jews) could be left up to God. The only pressure that Christian prelates needed to bring to bear against them was the weight of reasoned argument.[56]

The Manicheans were committed to a rational approach to life and consequently were not reluctant to enter into public debates with Augustine about their teachings. They were better debate opponents than the Donatists (who frequently would not show up) and the Pelagians (whose difference from the Catholic position involved many fine distinctions and rested on differing interpretations of the same Scriptures). Whereas victory in argument with the Donatists had little effect on their continuing

55. *Ibid.*, 2-3.
56. Peter Brown suggests that this attitude of "leave them to heaven" was influenced by Augustine's increasing stress on predestination and grace as the basic causes of conversions and his bad experience with the forced feigned conversions of pagans and Donatists who returned to Catholicism only out of fear (Peter Brown, "St. Augustine's Attitude to Religious Coercion," *Religion and Society, op. cit.,* pp. 268-70). See *Letter 23,* 7 and *Letter 34,* 1.

conviction and energetic imposition of those convictions on others, the debates with the Manicheans were quite effective. There seemed to be no need for civil pressure to "get their attention." They were willing to listen and sometimes even willing to accept defeat in rational argument. Once they had reached that point of an openness to a different point of view, Augustine believed that it could be left to the grace of God to further their final conversion if in his providence this was meant to be.

Indeed, one might say that Augustine's tolerant approach to the Manicheans was always his preferred method of dealing with those of other beliefs. It was only pastoral concern for stubborn sheep who would not listen and concern for their sometimes violent attacks on the sheep that remained that prompted Augustine the shepherd to go beyond plaintive pleading to calling in the power of the state to control the wandering sheep and force them to return.

Bibliography

A. Other Bibliographies

Since this book is aimed at English-speaking students of Augustine, this bibliography emphasizes sources in English. Obviously there are many valuable sources in other languages. The most complete ongoing bibliography of world-wide research on Augustine is found in the annual bibliography published in the *Revue des Études Augustiniennes*. A useful index of articles and bibliography from the 1955-1984 issues of this periodical was prepared by Henri Rochais and Goulven Madec and published through the *Revue* in 1986. The bibliography for each year from 1985 up to the present time appears in the on-going volumes of this periodical.

Other useful bibliographies include the following:

Donnelly, Dorothy, and Sherman, Mark. *Augustine's "De Civitate Dei": An Annotated Bibliography.* New York: Peter Lang, 1991.
Miethe, Terry L. *Augustinian Bibliography 1970-80.* Westport, CT, and London: Greenwood Press, 1982. This work contains a helpful list of previous bibliographies on pp. 3-5.
Van Bavel, T. *Répertoire Bibliographique de saint Augustin: 1950-60.* The Hague: Martinus Nijhoff, 1963.

B. Latin Texts

Patrologia Latina. Edited by J. P. Migne. Vols. 32-47. Paris: 1844-64. (abbreviation: P.L.)

228

Bibliography

Corpus Scriptorum Ecclesiasticorum. Vienna: Tempsky, 1866-. (abbreviation: CSEL)

Corpus Christianorum: Series Latina. The Hague: Nijhoff, 1953-. (abbreviation: CC)

C. English Translations

The Works of Saint Augustine: A Translation for the 21st Century. Edited by J. Rotelle. Hyde Park, NY: New City Press, 1990-.

Ancient Christian Writers. Edited by J. Quasten et al. Westminster, MD: Newman Press: 1946-.

The Fathers of the Church. Edited by R. Deferrari et al. Washington, D.C.: Catholic University of America Press, 1948-.

The Works of Aurelius Augustinus. Edited by Marcus Dods. Edinburgh: T. & T. Clark Co., 1871-1876.

A Select Library of the Nicene and Post-Nicene Fathers. Edited by Philip Schaff. New York: Scribners, 1892.

D. Secondary Sources

Adams, Jeremy D. *The Populus of Augustine and Jerome: A Study in the Patristic Sense of Community.* New Haven: Yale University Press, 1971.

Adler, Mortimer. "War and Peace." In *The Great Ideas* (originally published as volumes 1 and 2 of *The Great Books of the Western World*). New York: Macmillan Publishing, 1992, pp. 901-11.

Armas, P. Gregorio. *La Moral de San Agustin.* Madrid: Difusoria del Libro, 1954.

Babcock, William S., ed. *The Ethics of St. Augustine.* Atlanta: Scholars Press, 1991.

———. "*Cupiditas* and *Caritas:* The Early Augustine on Love and Human Fulfillment." In *ibid.,* pp. 39-66.

Bainton, Roland Herbert. *Christian Attitudes toward War and Peace: A Historical Survey and Critical Re-evaluation.* Nashville: Abingdon Press, 1965.

Barnes, Hazel E., ed. *The Pessimist's Handbook.* Lincoln: University of Nebraska Press, 1964.

Barrow, R. H. *Introduction to St. Augustine: "The City of God."* London: Faber & Faber, 1950.

Beierwaltes, Werner. *Regio Beatitudinis: Augustine's Concept of Happiness.* Villanova, PA: Villanova Press, 1981.

Benn, Stanley I. "Punishment." In *The Encyclopedia of Philosophy*, edited by Paul Edwards. New York: Macmillan, 1967. Vol. 7, pp. 29-36.

Bigham, Thomas J., and Mollegen, Albert T. "The Christian Ethic." In *A Companion to the Study of St. Augustine*, edited by Roy W. Battenhouse. New York: Oxford University Press, 1955, pp. 371-98.

Bonner, Gerald. "*Libido* and *Concupiscentia* in Saint Augustine." *Studia Patristica*, vol. 6, no. 4 (1962), pp. 303-14.

————. "Augustine's Attitude to Women and *Amicitia*." *Homo Spiritalis: Festgabe für Luc Verheijen O.S.A.*, edited by Cornelius Mayer. Würzburg: Augustinus-Verlag, 1987, pp. 259-75.

————. *St. Augustine of Hippo: Life and Controversies*. Philadelphia: Westminster Press, 1963.

Borresen, Kari Elisabeth. "Patristic Feminism: The Case of Augustine." *Augustinian Studies*, vol. 25 (1994), pp. 139-52.

————. "In Defense of Augustine: How *Femina* is *Homo*." *Augustiniana (Mélanges T. J. Van Bavel)*, vol. 40, no. 1, pp. 411-28.

————. *Subordination and Equivalence: The Nature and Role of Woman in Augustine and Thomas Aquinas*, translated by Charles Talbot. Washington, D.C.: University Press of America, 1981.

Bourke, Vernon J. "Voluntarism in Augustine's Ethico-Legal Thought." *Augustinian Studies*, vol. 1 (1970), pp. 3-18

————. *Joy in Augustine's Ethics*. Villanova, PA: Villanova University Press, 1979.

————. "The *City of God* and the Christian View of History." In *Wisdom from St. Augustine*. Houston: The Center for Thomistic Studies, 1984, pp. 188-205.

Brockwell, Charles W., Jr. "Augustine's Ideal of Monastic Community: A Paradigm for His Doctrine of the Church." *Augustinian Studies*, vol. 8 (1977), pp. 91-109.

Brown, Peter. *Authority and the Sacred: Aspect of the Christianization of the Roman World* Cambridge: Cambridge University Press, 1995.

————. *The Body and Society*. New York: Columbia University Press, 1988.

————. *Augustine of Hippo: A Biography*. Berkeley: University of California Press, 1967.

————. "Political Society." In *Augustine: A Collection of Critical Essays*, edited by Robert A. Markus. Garden City, NY: Doubleday, 1972, pp. 311-35.

————. "St. Augustine's Attitude to Religious Coercion." *Journal of Roman Studies*, vol. 55 (1964), pp. 107-16.

————. "The Diffusion of Manichaeism in the Roman Empire." In *Religion and Society in the Age of Augustine*. London: Faber & Faber, 1972, pp. 94-118.

Burleigh, John. *The City of God: A Study of St. Augustine's Philosophy.* London: Nisbet & Co., 1949.

Burnaby, John. *Amor Dei: A Study of the Religion of St. Augustine.* London: Hodder and Stoughton, 1938.

Burt, Donald X. *Augustine's World: An Introduction to His Speculative Philosophy.* Lanham, MD: University Press of America, 1996.

————. "Friendship and Subordination in Earthly Societies." *Augustinian Studies,* vol. 22 (1991), pp. 83-124.

————. "Augustine on the State as a Natural Society." *Augustiniana (Mélanges T. J. Van Bavel),* vol. 40/1 (1990), pp. 155-66.

————. "The Problem of Justifying Moral Obligation." *Proceedings of the American Catholic Philosophical Association,* vol. 49 (1975), pp. 72-81.

————. "To Live or Let Die: Augustine on Killing the Innocent." *Proceedings of the American Catholic Philosophical Association* (1984), pp. 112-19.

————. "Augustine on Divine Voluntarism." *Angelicum,* vol. 64 (1987), pp. 424-36.

————. "Augustine on the Morality of Violence: Theoretical Issues and Applications." *Studia Ephemeridis "Augustinianum,"* no. 26 (1987), vol. 3, pp. 25-54.

————. "Friendship and the State: A Summary of Research." *Collectanea Augustiniana II: Presbyter Factus Sum.* New York: Peter Lang, 1993, pp. 249-62.

————. "Cain's City: Augustine's Reflections on the Origins of the Civil Society (Book XV 1-8)." In *Augustinus: "De civitate dei,"* edited by Christophe Horn. Berlin: Academie Verlag, 1997, pp. 197-212.

————. "Augustine on the Authentic Approach to Death." *Augustinianum,* vol. 28, no. 3 (1988), pp. 527-63.

Camelot, Pierre-Thomas. "St. Augustine, Doctor of Peace." *Cross and Crown,* vol. 6 (1954), pp. 69-80.

Canning, R. "Augustine on the Identity of the Neighbour." *Augustiniana,* vol. 36 (1986), nos. 3-4, pp. 161-239.

Carney, Frederick S. "The Structure of Augustine's Ethic." *The Ethics of St. Augustine,* edited by William S. Babcock. Atlanta: Scholars Press, 1991, pp. 11-38.

Clark, Elizabeth A. "Adam's Only Companion: Augustine and the Early Christian Debate on Marriage." *Recherches Augustiniennes,* vol. 21 (1986), pp. 139-62.

————, editor. *St. Augustine on Marriage and Sexuality.* Washington D.C.: The Catholic University of America Press, 1996.

Cary-Elwes, Columba. "Peace in the City of God." *La Ciudad de Dios,* vol. 167 (1955), 417-30.

Combès, Gustave. *La doctrine politique de saint Augustine.* Paris: Plon, 1927.

Corcoran, Gervase. *St. Augustine on Slavery.* Studia Ephemeridis "Augustinianum," no. 22. Rome: Patristic Institute "Augustinianum," 1985.

Cranz, F. Edward. "*De Civitate Dei* 15.2 and Augustine's Idea of the Christian Society." In Robert A. Markus, editor. *Augustine: A Collection of Critical Essays.* New York: Doubleday, 1972.

Deane, Herbert. *The Political and Social Ideas of St. Augustine.* New York: Columbia University Press, 1963.

Dodaro, Robert. "Eloquent Lies, Just Wars and the Politics of Persuasion: Reading Augustine's City of God in a Postmodern World." *Augustinian Studies,* vol. 25 (1994), pp. 77-138.

Dougherty, James. "The Sacred City and the City of God." *Augustinian Studies,* vol. 10 (1979), pp. 81-90.

Dougherty, Richard. "*Magnum opus et arduum*": *The Structure and Argument of St. Augustine's De Civitate Dei.* PhD Thesis, University of Dallas, 1993. Ann Arbor: UMI, 1996.

————. "Christian and Citizen: The Tension in St. Augustine's *De Civitate Dei*." *Collectanea Augustiniana,* edited by Joseph Schnaubelt and Frederick VanFleteren. New York: Peter Lang, 1990, pp. 205-24.

Dray, W. H. "Philosophy of History." *The Encyclopedia of Philosophy,* edited by Paul Edwards, vol. 6, pp. 247-54. New York: Macmillan, 1967.

Eno, Robert, translator. *Letter 6*, 5. Saint Augustine: Letters, Volume 6.* Vol. 81 of *The Fathers of the Church: A New Translation.* Washington, D.C.: The Catholic University of America Press, 1989.

Evans, G. R. *Augustine on Evil.* Cambridge: Cambridge University Press, 1982.

Figgis, John Neville. *The Political Aspects of St. Augustine's City of God.* London: Longmans, Green, 1921.

Fortin, Ernest L. "Augustine and the Problem of Human Goodness." *University of Dayton Review,* vol. 22, no. 3 (Summer 1994).

————. "The Political Implications of St. Augustine's Theory of Conscience." *Augustinian Studies,* vol. 1 (1970), pp. 133-53.

————. *Political Idealism and Christianity in the Thought of St. Augustine.* Villanova, PA: Villanova University Press, 1972.

Fredriksen, Paula. "*Excaecati Occulta Justitia Dei:* Augustine on Jews and Judaism." *Journal of Early Christian Studies,* vol. 3/3 (1995), pp. 299-324.

Frend, W. H. C. "Augustine's Reactions to the Barbarian Invasions of the West: Some Comparisons with His Western Contemporaries." *Augustinus,* vol. 39 (1994), pp. 241-55.

————. *The Donatist Church.* Oxford: Clarendon Press, 1952.

Gilson, Etienne. *The Christian Philosophy of Saint Augustine.* Translated by L. E. M. Lynch. New York: Random House, 1960.

————. "Foreword to the *City of God.*" *City of God,* translated by Demetrius B. Zema and Gerald G. Walsh. New York: Fathers of the Church, 1950.

————. *Les métamorphoses de la Cité de Dieu.* Paris: Vrin, 1952.

Gustafson, James M. *The Contribution of Theology to Medical Ethics.* Chicago: Marquette University Press, 1975.

Hacker, Andrew. "On Original Sin and Conservatives." In *The New York Times Magazine,* February 25, 1973.

Haggerty, William P. "Augustine, the 'Mixed Life,' and Classical Political Philosophy: Reflection on *Compositio* in Book 19 of the City of God." *Augustinian Studies,* vol. 23 (1992), pp. 149-64.

Harmless, William, S.J. "Christ the Pediatrician: Infant Baptism and Christological Imagery in the Pelagian Controversy." *Augustinian Studies,* vol. 28/2 (1997), pp. 7-35.

Hartigan, Richard S. "Saint Augustine on War and Killing: The Problem of the Innocent." *Journal of the History of Ideas,* vol. 27 (1966), pp. 195-204.

Hawkins, Peter. "Polemical Counterpoint in *De Civitate Dei.*" *Augustinian Studies,* vol. 6 (1975), pp. 97-106.

Helgeland, John, et al. *Christians and the Military.* Philadelphia: Fortress Press, 1985.

Hill, Edmund, translator (and notes). *Sermons.* Part 3 of *The Works of St. Augustine: A Translation for the 21st Century,* edited by John E. Rotelle, O.S.A. New York: New City Press, 1991.

Hunter, David G. "Augustinian Pessimism? A New Look at Augustine's Teaching on Sex, Marriage and Celibacy." *Augustinian Studies,* vol. 25 (1994), pp. 153-78.

————. "The Date and Purpose of Augustine's De Continentia." *Augustinian Studies,* vol. 26, no. 2 (1995), pp. 7-24.

————. *Marriage in the Early Church.* Minneapolis: Augsburg Fortress, 1992.

Innes, Robert. "Integrating the Self through the Desire of God." *Augustinian Studies,* vol. 28, no. 1 (1997), pp. 67-110.

Journet, C. "Les trois cités: celle de Dieu, celle de l'homme, celle du diable." *Nova et Vetera,* vol. 33 (1958), pp. 25-48.

Konstan, David. "Problems in the History of Christian Friendship." *Journal of Early Christian Studies,* vol. 4 (1996), pp. 87-113.

Koterski, Joseph W. "St. Augustine on the Moral Law." *Augustinian Studies,* vol. 11 (1980), pp. 65-77.

Lamirande, Emilien. *Church, State and Toleration: An Intriguing Change of Mind in St. Augustine.* Villanova, PA: Villanova University Press, 1975.

Langan, John. "The Elements of St. Augustine's Just War Theory." *Journal of Religious Ethics,* vol. 12, no. 1 (Spring 1984), pp. 19-38.

Lavere, George J. "The Political Realism of Saint Augustine." *Augustinian Studies,* vol. 11 (1980), pp. 135-44.

————. "The Problem of the Common Good in Saint Augustine's *Civitas Terrena*." *Augustinian Studies,* vol. 14 (1983), pp. 1-10.

Lenihan, David A. "The Just War Theory in the Works of Saint Augustine." *Augustinian Studies,* vol. 19 (1988), pp. 37-70.

————. "The Influence of Augustine's Just War: the Early Middle Ages." *Augustinian Studies,* vol. 27, no. 1 (1996), pp. 55-93.

Liguori, Marie, translator. *In Answer to the Jews.* In *St. Augustine: Treatises on Marriage and other Subjects.* Vol. 27 of the Fathers of the Church series, edited by Roy J. Deferrari. New York: Fathers of the Church, Inc., 1955.

Löwith, Karl. *Meaning in History.* Chicago: University of Chicago Press, 1949.

MacQueen, D. J. "The Origin and Dynamics of Society and the State." *Augustinian Studies,* vol. 4 (1973), pp. 73-102.

Markus, Robert A. *Saeculum: History and Society in the Theology of St. Augustine.* Cambridge: Cambridge University Press, 1970.

————. "Two Conceptions of Political Authority: Augustine *De civitate dei,* xix, 14-15, and Some Thirteenth-Century Interpretations." *Journal of Theological Studies,* vol. 16, no. 1 (April 1965), pp. 68-96.

————. "Saint Augustine's Views on the Just War." *The Church and War,* edited by W. J. Sheils. London: Basil Blackwell, 1983.

————, editor. *Augustine: A Collection of Critical Essays.* New York: Doubleday, 1972.

Marrou, Henri-Irenée. "Civitas Dei, Civitas Terrena: num tertium quid?" *Studia Patristica,* vol. 2 (1957), pp. 342-50.

Martin, Rex. "The Two Cities in Augustine's Political Philosophy." *Journal of the History of Ideas,* vol. 33 (1972), 195-216.

Mausbach, Joseph. *Die Ethik des heiligen Augustinus.* 2 vols. Freiburg im Breisgau: Herder, 1909 (2nd ed. 1929).

McEvoy, J. "*Anima una et cor unum:* Friendship and Spiritual Unity in Augustine." *Recherches de Théologie ancienne et médiévale,* vol. 53 (1986), pp. 40-92.

McGowan, Richard J. "Augustine's Spiritual Equality: The Allegory of Man and Woman with Regard to *Imago Dei*." *Revue des Études Augustiniennes,* vol. 33 (1987), pp. 259-60.

McNamara, Marie. *Friends and Friendship for Saint Augustine.* Staten Island: Alba House, 1964.

Merdinger, Jane E. *Rome and the African Church in the Time of Augustine.* New Haven: Yale University Press, 1997.

Miethe, Terry L. "Natural Law, the Synderesis Rule, and St. Augustine." *Augustinian Studies,* vol. 11 (1980), pp. 91-7.

—————. "Augustine and Concupiscence." *Augustinian Bibliography: 1970-80.* Westport, CT: Greenwood Press, 1982, pp. 195-218.

Mohan, Robert Paul. *Philosophy of History.* New York: Bruce Publishing Co., 1970.

Northedge, F. S. "Peace, War, and Philosophy." In *The Encyclopedia of Philosophy,* edited by Paul Edwards. New York: Macmillan, 1967, pp. 63-67.

O'Donovan, Oliver. *The Problem of Self-Love in Augustine.* New Haven: Yale University Press, 1980.

O'Donnell, James J. "The Inspiration for Augustine's *De Civitate Dei.*" *Augustinian Studies,* vol. 10 (1979), pp. 75-80.

—————. *Augustine.* Boston: G. K. Hall, 1985.

O'Dowd, W. B. "Development of Augustine's Opinions on Religious Toleration." *Irish Theological Quarterly* (1919), 337-48.

O'Meara, John. *Charter of Christendom: The Significance of the "City of God."* New York: Macmillan, 1961.

—————. *The Young Augustine.* New York: Longman, 1980.

Ramsey, Paul. "The Morality of Abortion." In *Moral Problems,* edited by James Rachels. New York: Harper & Row, 1975.

Renna, Thomas. "The Idea of Peace in the Augustinian Tradition 400-1200." *Augustinian Studies,* vol. 10 (1979), pp. 105-12.

Rist, John. *Augustine: Ancient Thought Baptized.* Cambridge: Cambridge University Press, 1994.

Rodet, Henri. *"Pax: tranquillitas ordinis." Ciudad de Dios,* vol. 167/2 (1956), 343-65.

Roland-Gosselin, Bernard. *La Morale de S. Augustin.* Paris: Rivière, 1925.

—————. "St. Augustine's System of Morals." *A Monument to St. Augustine,* edited by M. C. D'Arcy. New York: Sheed and Ward, 1930.

Roten, Johann G. "Mary and Woman in Augustine." *University of Dayton Review,* vol. 22, no. 3 (Summer 1994), pp. 31-51.

Schmitt, Émile. *Le mariage chrétien dans l'oeuvre de Saint Augustin. Une théologie baptismale de la vie conjugale.* Paris: Études Augustiniennes, 1983.

Shinn, Roger. "Augustinian and Cyclical Views of History." *Anglican Theological Review,* vol. 131 (1949), 133-41.

Simon, Yves. *Philosophy of Democratic Government.* Chicago: University of Chicago Press, 1951.

—————. *A General Theory of Authority.* Notre Dame: University of Notre Dame Press, 1980.

————. *The Nature and Functions of Authority.* Milwaukee: Marquette University Press, 1940.

Swift, Louis J. *The Early Fathers on War and Military Service.* Wilmington: Michael Glazier, 1983.

————. "Augustine on War and Killing: Another View." *Harvard Theological Review,* vol. 66 (1973), 369-83.

TeSelle, Eugene. *Augustine the Theologian.* New York: Herder, 1970.

————. "Toward an Augustinian Politics." *Journal of Religious Ethics,* vol. 16 (1988), pp. 87-108.

————. "Civic Vision in Augustine's *City of God.*" *Thought,* vol. 62 (1987), pp. 268-80.

Teske, Roland J. "Love of Neighbor in St. Augustine." *Studia Ephemeridis "Augustinianum,"* no. 26 (1987), vol. 3, pp. 81-102.

————, translator. *Saint Augustine: On Genesis.* Washington, D.C.: The Catholic University of America Press, 1991.

Thonnard, Francois-Joseph. "La notion de concupiscence en philosophie augustinienne." *Recherches Augustiniennes,* vol. 3 (1965), pp. 59-105.

Van Bavel, T. J. "'No one ever hated his own flesh': Eph. 5:29 in Augustine." *Augustiniana,* vol. 45 (1995), pp. 45-93.

————. *The Rule of St. Augustine with Introduction and Commentary,* translated by Raymond Canning. London: Darton, Longman and Todd, 1984.

Van Der Lof, L. J. "The Threefold Meaning of *Servi Dei* in the Writings of Augustine." *Augustinian Studies,* vol. 12 (1981), pp. 43-59.

Van der Meer, F. *Augustine the Bishop,* translated by Brian Battershaw and G. R. Lamb. New York: Sheed & Ward, 1961.

Van Oort, Johannes. *Jerusalem and Babylon: A Study into Augustine's City of God.* Leiden: E. J. Brill, 1991.

White, Carolinne. *Christian Friendship in the Fourth Century.* Cambridge University Press, 1995.

Wilks, Michael J. "Roman Empire and the Christian State in the *De Civitate Dei.*" *Augustinus,* vol. 12 (1967), pp. 489-510.

Willis, Geoffrey G. *St. Augustine and the Donatist Controversy.* London: S.P.C.K., 1950.

Zumkeller, Adolar. *Augustine's Ideal of the Religious Life,* translated by Edmund Colledge. New York: Fordham University Press, 1986.

————. *The Rule of St. Augustine,* translated by Julian C. Resch. De Pere, WI: St. Norbert Abbey, 1961.

Index